'If you have a tendency to be messy and have already broken your New Year resolutions to be neater in future, it will certainly make you feel better about your natural inclinations . . . The authors of this book trawl the furthest reaches of psychology, management studies, biology and physics to show why a bit of disorder is good for you' *Economist*

'The authors conclude that there is an ideal level of messiness that makes any system more robust and productive . . . I would say more on the subject but I seem to have lost my pen somewhere in the detritus towering above me' *Guardian*

'A series of case studies challenging the conventional logic that businesses need good organisation' *Daily Express*

'An entertaining and convincing attack on conventional wisdom. Read it and you need never again feel guilty about your untidy desk or non-existent lesson plan'
Times Educational Supplement magazine

'I hope this book becomes a bestseller. It is time that someone challenged the tautology that order is good, therefore it is good to have order. Mess equals possibility and I look forward to a long and profitable career as a professional disorganiser'
Sunday Times

'There is something seductive in this book on the hidden benefits of disorder . . . a strangely tempting vision'
Daily Telegraph Book of the Week

'It might just be the *Small is Beautiful* of the noughties'
Herald

'A messy desk is a far more efficient filing system than any number of labelled cabinets – it reflects the way people's brains are organised and allows for serendipitous discovery through random connection' *Financial Times*

ERIC ABRAHAMSON is a professor of management at Columbia Business School, Columbia University, and is the author of *Change Without Pain: How Managers Can Overcome Initiative Overload, Organizational Chaos and Employee Burnout*. His groundbreaking work challenging conventional management wisdom has been published in the *Harvard Business Review*, and he speaks frequently to executive audiences around the world.

DAVID H. FREEDMAN is a contributing editor and the technology columnist at *Inc.* magazine and has written for the *New York Times*, *Newsweek*, the *Atlantic Monthly*, *Science*, the *Harvard Business Review* and *Wired*, among other publications. He is the author of *Corps Business: the 30 Management Principles of the US Marines* and *Brainmakers: How Scientists Are Moving Beyond Computers to Create a Rival to the Human Brain*.

A PERFECT MESS

THE HIDDEN BENEFITS OF DISORDER

HOW CRAMMED CLOSETS, CLUTTERED OFFICES, AND
OFF-THE-CUFF PLANNING MAKE THE WORLD A BETTER PLACE

ERIC ABRAHAMSON AND
DAVID H. FREEDMAN

PHOENIX

A PHOENIX PAPERBACK

First published in Great Britain in 2006
by Weidenfeld & Nicolson
This paperback edition published in 2007
by Phoenix,
an imprint of Orion Books Ltd,
Orion House, 5 Upper St Martin's Lane,
London WC2H 9EA
An Hachette Livre UK company

This edition published by arrangement with
Little, Brown and Company (Inc.),
New York, NY, USA. All rights reserved.

1 3 5 7 9 10 8 6 4 2

A CIP catalogue record for this book
is available from the British Library.

ISBN 978-0-7538-2286-9

Printed and bound in Great Britain by
Mackays of Chatham, Chatham, Kent

The Orion Publishing Group's policy is to use papers that
are natural, renewable and recyclable products and
made from wood grown in sustainable forests. The logging
and manufacturing processes are expected to conform to
the environmental regulations of the country of origin.

www.orionbooks.co.uk

For my wife, Valerie, and my children,
Alex and Claire. — EA
and
For messmasters Laurie, Rachel,
Alex, and Jason. — DHF

CONTENTS

A PERFECT MESS

Introduction

There's a spot on Broadway in Manhattan where two magazine stores used to sit across the street from each other. One of the stores featured neat racks of impeccably arranged magazines, any copy of which could be tracked by computer. At the other store, magazines were sometimes scattered about randomly, with *Cosmopolitan* snuggled up against *Fortune*; *Real Simple* alongside *Jet*; and *Smithsonian* elbowing *Psychotronic*. No wonder: Essam, the owner and manager of the messy store, had no computer inventory system to tell him what he sold or which magazines needed restocking. He and his assistant, Zak, operated from memory and straightened up as best they could during quiet periods and at the end of the day.

Not surprisingly, the first store attracted more customers and did a brisker business, selling more magazines than Essam's. Equally unsurprising, only one store remains in business today, the other having been shuttered by losses. But there's a strange punch line: Essam's store is the one still flourishing. He didn't sell as many magazines as his former competitor, but he made more money. The simple reason is that he avoided some of the profit-devouring costs associated with the extra staff his competitor felt it needed to straighten up its racks, as well as the computerized inventory systems it needed to track magazines. Given that profit, not to mention survival, is a reasonable measuring stick of business effectiveness, it's fair to say that any benefits the other store might have accrued by being neater and more organized were outweighed by their associated costs. In other words, one reason Essam's store has been successful is because it's messy.

It's not all that hard to understand how Essam manages to profit, in a sense, from mess. Perhaps it doesn't even seem particularly remarkable once it's pointed out. But suppose that this comparison of the magazine stores isn't merely an interesting curiosity. What if the costs of being neat and well organized *often* outweigh the benefits? What if being somewhat messy, in a broad sense, is a better deal?

It sounds almost ridiculous to suggest that the world has been ignoring the fairly obvious concept that there's a cost to being neat and organized. You'd think that the first question people and organizations would ask themselves before embarking on an effort to straighten up and muster more order would be: will this be worth what it costs me in time and other resources? After all, the idea that organizing doesn't always pay off would have to come as stunning news to offices that have everything filed away neatly, schools with rigidly detailed curricula and standards, professionals who keep their days tightly scheduled, companies that obsessively spell out management and operational procedures, parents who are constantly fighting clutter, militaries that maintain rigid groupings, and city governments that generate volumes of codes.

In fact, neatness and organization can exact a high price, and it's widely unaccounted for. Or to put it another way, there are often significant cost savings to be had by tolerating a certain level of messiness and disorder. But this book is going to show that the disconnect is even more striking. It's not just that the advantages of being neat and organized are typically outweighed by the costs. As it turns out, the very advantages themselves are often illusory. Though it flies in the face of almost universally accepted wisdom, moderately disorganized people, institutions, and systems frequently turn out to be more efficient, more resilient, more creative, and in general more effective than highly organized ones. Just as the cost of neatness has been ignored, so have the potential benefits of achieving the right level and type of mess. While beneficial disorder may not be the rule, it isn't much of an exception, either.

That messiness and disorder can be so useful wouldn't seem such a counterintuitive notion if it weren't for the bias toward neatness programmed into most of us. Specifically, people tend to ignore the cost of neatness, discount the possibility that messiness can't always be excised no matter how hard it's fought, and distrust the idea that mess can work better than neatness. Neatness for most of us has become an end in and of itself. When people are anxious about their messy homes and offices or their disorganized schedules, it's often not because the messiness and disorder are causing problems, but because people simply *assume* they should be neater and more organized and feel bad that they aren't.

This notion that mess and disorder might be harmless or even beneficial shouldn't seem such a strange one. But almost every practical exploration of how we can improve our lives, businesses, and societies suggests ways to be either more ordered or differently ordered. Being disordered — and not just less centrally or hierarchically ordered — rarely comes up for consideration. It's time that we take an open-minded look at messiness in all aspects of our lives and institutions, and consider where it might best be celebrated rather than avoided.

The pages ahead compose a representative tour of the under-appreciated side of the world of mess and disorder. Among the stops: the messiest house ever; a preschool where toy-smashing is welcome; a hardware shop and a bookstore that thrive on making it hard to find goods; the utterly disorganized life of Arnold Schwarzenegger; a hospital where patients throw pizza parties; the Beethoven symphony that is often played out of tune; the desk mess that led to a Nobel Prize; a restaurant that serves courses out of order; and the U.S. city whose messiness makes it kin to historic Paris. The point of the tour isn't to be comprehensive on the subject of mess and disorder. Hardly; any facet of the subject could easily fill volumes. Rather, the goal is simply to explore and highlight some important truths about disorder that have mostly been overlooked.

You may find that the tour takes some unexpected turns. At least we hope you do.

CHAPTER ONE

The Cost of Neatness

If a cluttered desk is a sign of a cluttered mind,
of what then, is an empty desk?
— ALBERT EINSTEIN

K athy Waddill is telling a standing-room-only house of
several hundred rapt professionals, most of whom are
taking notes on broad yellow lined pads sheathed in expensive-
and complex-looking leather binders, about the deep client dis-
comfort they should be prepared to confront when setting up a
first visit over the phone. " 'I'm the worst you've ever seen,' "
Waddill imitates, her voice husky with emotion before it breaks to
a mortified whisper. " 'I'm overwhelmed. I'm so embarrassed.' "

After making the appointment, don't call the client later on
to confirm it, she cautions her audience, her martial voice back,
because he may weaken and cancel. Just show up. Pens flutter in
the audience, and many grunt in recognition of past tactical
errors. When you're with the client, she continues, you'll be
tempted to turn up the lights to get a good look, but resist the
urge. It's often more useful and politic to turn the lights down
or even off, to get a sense of how things really stand by contemplating them in the dark.

To hear of the delicacy with which these clients must be
approached, you might imagine they are cloistered sufferers of
disfigurement, exotic neurological tics, or tawdry, addictive

passions. But actually they're just messy or at least believe themselves so. Waddill is a professional organizer, here in San Diego to address the annual conference of the National Association of Professional Organizers, or NAPO.

An entire industry of sorts has sprung up, quickly picking up steam over the past decade, to nurture the notion that if only we were more organized with our possessions, time, and resources, we could be more content and successful, and our companies and institutions could be more effective. Take into account the hundreds of books, the vast array of home- and office-organizing aids, the classes and seminars, the software, the television shows, the magazines, and the organizational consultants that all purvey some variation on the theme of straightening up, rearranging, acquiring highly effective habits, planning your day/week/life, restructuring organizations, and rigidly standardizing processes, and it's easy to see that neatness and order have become a multibillion-dollar business.

NAPO is the pointy tip of the organizing spear — these are people, after all, who do nothing but organize — and represents a high-growth business in its own right. Founded in 1985 with sixteen members, in 2005 NAPO boasted more than three thousand, up from fifteen hundred just eighteen months before. The conference has attracted 825 members, 275 of them for the first time. These figures and many more are effortlessly ticked off by NAPO president Barry Izsak, a pixieish fellow who blows into rooms at racewalking speeds and is given to dramatic rushes of speech sprinkled with sarcastic asides. Izsak is a studied role model for the highly organized. Eschewing the standard convention uniform of Hawaiian shirt and khakis in favor of a neat brown suit, when interviewed he takes notes on his own responses, offers a document containing precomposed answers to a range of anticipated questions, and, eyeing his interviewer's flimsy, narrow, reporter's notebook with a wince, urges a replacement from an array of more sophisticated writing tools he keeps on hand, including a laptop computer and the sort of handsomely encased broad yellow lined pad that apparently is to the professional organizer what a utility belt is to Batman. But Izsak, a former operator of a pet-sitting service, admits that like many professional organizers he must still constantly fight disorganized tendencies in himself — and almost immediately demonstrates this by discovering, after much shuffling through binders, that he has misplaced his notes for the keynote speech he is about to deliver.

NAPO is not only getting larger, it is also growing in influence and cachet. Professional organizers used to migrate to the field disproportionately from the ranks of teachers, secretaries, and other relatively low-paying careers, notes Izsak. Now, he says, former lawyers and MBA-packing executives are as likely to be jumping in, with incomes for successful organizers climbing into six figures. But even if the average annual income for a NAPO member were only, say, $35,000, then NAPO organizers alone (not all organizers join) would be bringing in a combined $100 million a year. Their clients, of course, are spending much more than that to get organized, since a typical get-organized treatment involves purchasing a number of ancillary organizational products and sometimes requires a complete makeover of a room or section of a home or office, in some cases all the way through heavy construction. The magnitude of these sorts of outlays has not been lost on office- and home-product vendors such as Pendaflex, Smead, Rubbermaid, and Lillian Vernon, all of which are paying sponsors of the NAPO conference. NAPO has also been able to gain significant attention for Get Organized Month (January), a recent upgrade of its successful Get Organized Week.

The NAPO conference is not what an outsider might expect. Most of the lectures, panels, and shoptalk aren't about organizing per se but, rather, about the marketing of organizing skills. The problem, it seems, is not that there aren't enough people in need of organizing. Quite the contrary. As one conference panelist puts it, "Way more people need our help than there are organizers on the planet to help them." Still, there are real challenges, including getting on potential clients' radar screens and convincing them to fork over anywhere from $200 for a bare-bones "assessment" up to thousands of dollars for a thorough organizational working over. But perhaps the biggest obstacle to signing clients — one that comes up prominently in almost all the conference speakers' spiels — is the deep shame that people feel over what they regard as their messy, disorganized homes, offices, and lives. That is, people are too ashamed to even let professional organizers know how big their disorganization problems are.

Fortunately, there's plenty of advice at the conference for getting the messy to suck it up and summon the professional help they desperately need. One panelist advises organizers to point out that not only is the potential client's future happiness and success on the line, but so are those of her children, who after all will take their parents' organizational habits, or lack thereof, as a model. Another warns organizers against turning up their noses at seemingly limited cries for help, such as the ever-popular "I want to reclaim my dining room table." When the organizer gets to the house and surveys the mess on the table, he will easily be able to link it to systemic problems that will require a larger organizing effort, inevitably including the coveted assignment of straightening out the garage.

The names that organizers give to their companies, speeches, and services — "Chaos to Calm," "Oh, So Organized!," "Realizing Dreams through Organization and Productivity," and so forth — suggest the transformative, if not the miraculous. "We change people's lives," says Izsak. "You can write that down." But when it comes to the question of how organizers are actually supposed to go about effecting these changes, the drill tends to be surprisingly simplistic. Successful organizers all seem to operate on catchy variations of what boils down to this very basic advice: Throw out and give away a bunch of stuff. Put the rest on shelves. Set up a tightly scheduled calendar. Repeat. Many organizers freely admit there isn't much more to organizing than that. Waddill, a big draw at the conference with her brash, intimate stage presence, featuring sarcastic mimicry of hapless clients, makes a sort of comedy routine of it. "The client has boxes piled up against the wall," she tells the audience, "and I say, 'A shelving unit gives you the same pile, but you can pull any box out when you need it.' They say, 'Oh, wow!' I say, 'Maybe there's so much paper on the floor because you don't have a wastepaper basket in here.' They think I'm the smartest person in the world. Sometimes it feels like shooting fish in a barrel. But that's why we get the big bucks." The audience laughs and nods enthusiastically, and the last two lines, delivered as a sly, conspiratorial stage whisper, leave Waddill awash in seismic ovation.

Clients seem to eat it up, too — enough to support some forty specialties within professional organizing. There are organizers at the conference who focus on organizing homes, others on offices, and some on organizing relationships. (As one organizer puts it, "People can be clutter, too.") There are Christian organizers here, organizers of the "chronically disorganized" (more on this later, but don't worry — you probably don't qualify), and a few who bill themselves as organizing "all aspects of life." One organizer presents a long talk on the ins and outs of disposing of old documents. (Don't flush them down a toilet where city workers might identify them; don't use them as lining for pet cages; and don't burn them in the sink — though an outdoor bonfire can be cathartic, as long as you poke through the ashes to make sure there are no big pieces left.) Linda Rothschild, an organizer to the rich and famous, is said to be routinely summoned to the estates of the likes of Julia Roberts. Rothschild looks the part, bringing a dash of hipness and glamour to a conference where they are in short supply. She was born to organize, she explains. By the time she was eight, she had cross-indexed her collection of 45 RPM records. "I get more done between 5:30 a.m. and 8:30 a.m. than most people get done in the whole day," she says, conceding that not having children helps in that regard. "We organizers are a group of recovering perfectionists," she adds.

Not easily found at the conference, though, is an answer to the basic question: what's the evidence that being neat and organized is worth the trouble? Not once, in dozens of conversations, speeches, and panel appearances, does an organizer broach the subject of costs versus benefits.

A few scattered comments vaguely address the benefits side. One organizer, for example, shares with her audience the goal she dangles in front of potential clients who are considering reorganizing their kitchen. "You should be able to cook a meal from one spot, without having to move around the kitchen a lot," she says. (Just think of the calories you'll avoid burning.) Several organizers pronounce that the average person spends an hour a day looking for things. But no one seems to know where this figure came from. The claim does, however, appear in many variations in organizers' brochures and Web sites — executives spend an hour a day looking for papers in their office; parents spend an hour a day looking for items in the home; and so on.

One organizer specializing in time management promises to reduce time-wasting problems like perfectionism — all you have to do is take his four-week course on time management.

Something a little more substantive comes from the ebullient Sharon Mann, who is not a professional organizer but rather a sort of spokesperson for Pendaflex, here at the conference to captain the filing-system company's exhibit booth. Sharon has achieved minor celebrity in the world of office organization by fronting the hundred-thousand-member "I Hate Filing Club" on the company's Web site. The site claims that eight minutes of organizing activity per day returns eight hours of time savings per month. Once you get past the somewhat transparent device of mixing per-day and per-month time frames, you end up with the less-impressive-sounding claim that you need to spend three hours per month to get back eight hours per month. Here are some of the ways the Web site advises investing those three hours:

1. Use colored labels on your files, and cut filing time in half.
2. Given that there are thirty-seven hours of unfinished work on the average desk at any one time, buy "filing solution" products and get the work off your desk.
3. Buy a quality label maker like Dymo's LabelWriter 330 Turbo to print your file labels, because 72 percent of people who print file labels end up wasting time wrestling with jammed or stuck labels in printers.

Let's take these in order:

1. Because whatever information a colored label might convey could also be conveyed with a word, the most

time that a colored label could save you is whatever
time you save by glancing at a color rather than reading
a word, perhaps a half second for very slow readers. If
you spend three hours a day filing, then saving a half
second per label examined will save you one and a half
hours, or half your time, only if you examine the labels
of 10,800 files in those three hours — in other words, if
you spend just about all your time examining file labels.
One could imagine unusual situations where a color
scheme might save several minutes at a shot, as, for
example, if there were a need to find the only green-
coded file in a vast sea of red-coded files, or if the entire
population of yellow-coded files had to be pulled. But
since most filing work involves not just looking at
file labels but examining the contents of files, doing
things with the contents of files, walking to and from
filing cabinets, and creating new files, the time saved
with colored labels will be just a tiny portion of the
total filing work. This will come as a relief to the
roughly 8 percent of people who are color blind.
2. This advice seems meant to imply that you have
saved yourself thirty-seven hours of work by clearing
your desk. But if you have thirty-seven hours of
unfinished work, and the work then gets filed, don't
you end up with thirty-seven hours of unfinished
work that is now hidden away in files instead of at
hand on your desk? Plus, you've spent a chunk of
time filing it, not to mention the time spent
purchasing filing-solution products.
3. Other research indicates that 0 percent of people
who don't bother printing labels for their files spend a

single minute wrestling with jammed or stuck file labels.

Izsak says he can prove organizing pays off with a little demonstration he likes to throw into his presentations. In this demonstration he takes two decks of cards, one shuffled and one ordered by suit and rank, and gives each to a different person. He then calls out the names of four cards and has the two deck-holders race to find the cards. Naturally, the person with the ordered deck always wins handily.

But who puts the neat deck in order? A little experimenting with people of modest card dexterity shows that on average it takes 140 seconds to order a deck, plus another 16 seconds to find four cards in the ordered deck for a total of 156 seconds; it takes about 35 seconds to find four cards in an unsorted deck. One could argue that you only have to order the deck once, and then you can find cards more quickly many times. But in that case, you also need to account for the time it takes to replace the four cards in an ordered deck, about 16 seconds — with cards, as with most things in life, it requires repeated effort to maintain order — compared to the fraction of a second it takes to stick four cards anywhere in an unordered deck. Thus, with a preordered deck, it takes 32 seconds to find and replace four cards, versus 36 seconds with a shuffled deck, giving the preordered deck a 4-second advantage. But since it requires 140 seconds to order the deck, taking that trouble wouldn't pay off unless you need to repeat the task at least thirty-five times, and you're meticulous about maintaining the deck's order between each attempt. In real life, decks tend to get shuffled sooner or later, requiring 140 seconds each time to restore order.

Indeed, organizers freely admit that ongoing maintenance

is critical to being organized, and many concede that most clients they organize fail to stick with the program and lapse back into disorder. But that's okay — you just need to have the organizer come back every so often to get back on track. Rothschild tells of one client who had her come to her home twice a month for six years before Rothschild finally suggested that the relationship wasn't working out.

When asked how they determine whether a potential client is likely to get more out of organizing than she puts into it, professional organizers at the conference respond that they don't make that determination; they just provide clients with whatever help they're looking for. Aside from the fact that this answer leaves unexplained the need for all those deft marketing techniques aimed at hesitant clients, it seems surprising that professional organizers have no more rules about when it's appropriate to provide their services than do tattoo artists. Fewer rules, actually, since organizers happily work with children — some even specialize in it.

Perhaps this is why so many panelists and speakers at the conference address the apparently widespread problem of professional organizers harboring doubts about their value. "You yourself have to believe you're worth the price," one organizer says to a crowd, winning loud and grateful applause.

Mess Stress

Considering how little evidence the pros lay out to support the claim that being organized is worth the effort, the world seems to put a lot of energy into fretting about being messy. The determination to get more organized routinely shows up in lists of popular New Year's resolutions — NAPO didn't randomly pick

January as Get Organized Month — suggesting that for many people, being more orderly feels nearly as important as getting healthy, having a satisfying career, being financially sound, and maintaining rewarding relationships.

There's plenty of anecdotal information to suggest that most people worry about neatness and organization. They feel they are too disorganized and messy, or seem so to significant others, or that their workplaces are dysfunctional with excessive messiness or disorderliness. Many of the people interviewed for this book have powerful childhood memories related to neatness or messiness. Among the most common: fear related to a parent's anger at the disturbing of a museum-like living room; contentment in being surrounded by a sea of toys; enchantment at the jammed, disorganized, mysterious trove in an attic or basement. (And that's not even going into the thicket of associations with toilet training and table manners.) You might think there's a clue there as to how to create a child-friendly home, but the holders of these memories, now parents themselves, confess to struggling to keep their homes pristine and their children's toys sorted and shelved, and are frustrated and anxious when they inevitably fall short. Meanwhile, coming home from workplaces closely defined by rules, processes, and hierarchies at which they bristle, they are annoyed at their children's failure to behave predictably.

The unpleasant feeling that each of us should be more organized, better organized, or differently organized seems nearly ubiquitous. And when people brush up against someone else's style of neatness and organization, they become irritated at even small mismatches, casting themselves as Oscar Madisons and Felix Ungers. Or even as Charles Mansons: A man in Neenah, Wisconsin, was so upset over his fourteen-year-old son's failure to keep the house neat that he shot the boy, paralyzing him from the neck down. And a twelve-year-old girl in New York City fatally stabbed her mother during an argument over the girl's messy bedroom.

But this is all anecdotal observation. There isn't much research out there to show whether concerns about mess and disorganization are really running roughshod over our psyches. So a survey of 260 people was conducted for this book. (It wasn't formally randomized but included a fairly broad cross section of Americans.) According to the results, fully two-thirds of the respondents feel guilt or shame about their messiness or disorderliness. And no wonder: 59 percent say they think "somewhat less" or "the worst" of someone who is messy and disorganized, while 70 percent think more of someone who is neat and organized. Seventy-nine percent say they would be more satisfied with their lives outside work if they were neater and more organized, and 60 percent say they feel pressure to keep their space at work neat. Two-thirds believe they would be more successful if they were neater and more organized. Eighty-eight percent think their employers would benefit from being more organized or differently organized. Could their organizations benefit even just a little from being *less* organized? Ninety-three percent didn't see it. Interestingly, though, few appear to be losing the infamous hour a day, at work or at home, locating items. Respondents reported spending an average of just under nine minutes at work and just over nine minutes at home looking for things.

Following is a sampling of comments from the survey and from interviews:

"I have a good friend who is very, very organized and
  neat. . . . Although I generally consider myself fairly neat

and clean, I find that I now compare myself to her. And I do not come out looking so good in the comparison."

"[My boss] suggested to me that I should clean up my desk. When I told him I was able to find what I needed very quickly he responded, 'It doesn't make it right.'"

"I wanted to change from having a life full of stress and unhappiness due to the continual mess in my mind and in my surroundings."

"I used to spend an hour each day planning out my day on an Excel spreadsheet until my boss told me I was spending too much time on it."

"I'm so jealous of a friend of mine. She is incredibly organized, and she has three very young children. When I go over to her house, there is no sign of toys or mess. . . . It kills me!"

Help Me, Oprah

Professional organizers may tap into the thick vein of mess stress, but they don't create it. They don't need to. The message that we're not orderly enough is all around us. It has become a staple of television news, newsmagazines, and talk shows, from Oprah — who has outed unsuspecting people as messy in front of millions of viewers — to *Today*, which has had guests advise viewers on "systematizing your spousal relationship." There are two television series devoted entirely to the restoration of order in the bedrooms, dens, garages, and, consequently, lives of families whose home disorder has become overwhelming. And other shows seek to do much the same for parent-child relationships. Being neat and organized, after all, isn't just about getting rid of physical mess, it's about being systematic and consistent, following a scheme, and imposing the right processes, whether filing papers at the office or dealing with loved ones. There are chains of stores that sell only organizational aids — the Container Store's annual sales have almost doubled over the past four years to nearly a half-billion dollars — and magazines that exist largely to promote an ideal of order in the home. (Sample advice from *Real Simple:* Assign each member of your family a towel color.)

Businesses and other institutions, of course, are supposed to be epicenters of order — it's not a coincidence that we call them *organizations*. But by their own reckoning, a significant percentage of them are never quite organized enough or are misorganized — or so we might assume when trying to make sense of the fact that, according to Stanford University professor Robert Sutton, U.S. businesses spend more than $45 billion each year on management consultants.

Given all the time, energy, money, and more that we spend combating mess and disorder — and the deep, widespread anxieties that motivate the spending — you'd think we'd be pretty clear on the benefits of pursuing neatness. Surely proof that we live better lives and enjoy more successful careers via tighter schedules, tidier homes, more rigid routines, and better filing systems, and that organizations and societies thrive by battling mess or disorder wherever it pops up must be laid out for us somewhere.

The notion is so deeply ingrained that questioning it seems absurd. It's not just the media bombardment or the presence of vast industries ready to "fix" our messiness and disorganization. We've heard it from our parents since infancy, it's echoed by teachers, and it's continually reinforced by our peers, bosses, and spouses. When we see ourselves as failing in some way, we're quick to blame poor organization. Our belief in the benefits of orderliness is as entrenched as the notion of the healthfulness of high-carbohydrate diets once was.

It's just common sense, isn't it? After all, the following statements would surely strike most people as unprovocative:

- Neatness and organization enable us to function more efficiently and in general more effectively.
- Neatness and organization simplify and structure the world in useful ways.
- Neatness and organization reduce mistakes and oversights, and usefully filter out the randomness of the world around us.
- Neatness and organization are aesthetically pleasing and relaxing.

It's not hard to think of scenarios where these statements seem true. But what if we could come up with common situations where they were clearly not true? Can the case be made that, in many situations, chasing after neatness and organization is largely pointless?

What Is Mess?

Let's take a moment to discuss what we mean by *mess*. (In chapter 3 we'll spell out in more detail what we regard as the basic types of mess, but even a vague, simplified definition will do fine until then.) One could have a lengthy technical discussion about the definition and nature of mess, but most people have a pretty good idea of what mess is on an intuitive level. Roughly speaking, a system is messy if its elements are scattered, mixed up, or varied due to some measure of randomness, or if for all practical purposes it appears random from someone's point of view. That's right: mess is often in the eye of the beholder. For example, if a person arranges a CD collection from most favorite to least favorite, a visitor looking over the collection might well have trouble seeing much rhyme or reason to the order and thus could reasonably regard the collection as a mess.

Almost any system can be messy. Mess is not only physical clutter, such as papers or clothes strewn about a room, or superficial disorganization, such as a desk surface covered by teetering piles of papers. A variety of systems can be disordered in many different ways. Thus, a schedule can be messy; traffic can be messy; art can be messy; an organizational chart can be messy; relationships can be messy; a process can be messy; thought can be messy; and so on.

An important distinction: mess, at least in this book, has little to do with chaos theory, complexity theory, networking, emergent behavior, self-organizing systems, distributed management, or any of the anti-centralized-control theories that have been popularized for more than a decade. Chaos and complexity theories focus on finding the hidden order in systems that might appear to be unpredictable or otherwise driven by random forces, or in showing how systems that look quite ordered can eventually evolve into something that looks quite messy. Although there can be some overlap between these theories and the sorts of messy entities considered in these pages, the difference in emphasis is significant. Chaos and complexity theorists are interested in trying to determine how an apparent mess can exhibit deeply hidden order, or how an ordered system can be characterized by deeply hidden mess. We want to examine mess for what it is — a lack of order. Thus, chaos theorists might work hard to show how Pluto's very neat-looking orbit is in fact chaotic and will eventually change dramatically, but to us it's simply a neat orbit. Complexity theorists might study how a swarm of ants running off in all different directions is in fact driven by a set of precise rules, but to us it's a messy swarm of ants. We're basically only interested in accepting mess as plain old mess and then taking a look at what the significance of the mess might be to people and organizations. (We'll also take a look at the science of mess, where mess can simply be defined as more or less pure randomness, which again clearly distinguishes it from the domains of chaos and complexity theory, where pure randomness is generally unwelcome.)

Unfortunately, the technical term *chaos*, as used by scientists, is now, thanks to a legion of chaos-science popularizers, routinely confused with the everyday word *chaos*, which can otherwise be a reasonable synonym for *plain old mess*. It's a little irksome that chaos theorists misnamed their work on hidden order with a word that means an absence of order. But it is done, and so we'll avoid the word *chaos* in this book.

Flattening organizational structures or distributing control or replacing hierarchies with networks isn't getting at what we mean by *mess*, either. (If you're not familiar with any of these concepts, that's fine, because we won't deal with them in any important way in this book, and you can safely skip this paragraph.) Again, there's a bit of overlap, but the fact is that flattening, distributing, or networking doesn't necessarily make a system messier, disordered, or less organized. In fact, any of these can lead to a nightmare of overorganization, as many companies discovered in the 1990s. As a simple example, consider an office where there are eight levels of management but where every manager tends to give his subordinates a huge amount of freedom to do almost whatever they want, and then compare it to an office where everyone is on the same single level of management, but before someone can undertake a task she must gain approval from the group. The former may be more hierarchical, but in most meaningful ways it's likely to be more disorganized. A gaggle of geese can remain in a formation without any centralized command, but the gaggle still isn't a mess, because each goose follows a rigid set of rules that keep the gaggle neatly ordered. The business management consultant and author Tom Peters has often exhorted managers to thrive on chaos, liberation, and disorganization but couches his advice in terms of highly specified networked "structures" that in the end are another form of order, even if it's one that's more mess friendly. For us, the question isn't so much one of how control is distributed but, rather, of how much order is in the system in any form.

Being messy and disordered and disorganized, as we mean it, is just what you probably think it is: scattering things, mixing things around, letting things pile up, doing things out of order, being inconsistent, winging it. You get the idea.

Finally, a word on entropy. Entropy is a fundamental concept in physics, roughly corresponding to a measure of a system's disorder. When people refer to entropy, it is usually in the context of the law of nature that states, in short, and again speaking roughly, that any system left to itself will probably, over time, become more disordered rather than more ordered. Or to put it another way, it takes extra effort to neaten up a system; things generally don't neaten themselves. This concept is actually important to us — it's another way of expressing the concept of the cost of neatness — but we feel no need to put that or anything else we have to say in this book in the more technical language of entropy. In fact, we'd really like to avoid it, because the various efforts to popularize the concept of entropy and apply it nonscientifically to the world around us have done so in the context of assuming that an increase in entropy — that is, mess — is a bad thing. And as you've probably noticed, we have a slightly different take on the matter.

Chapter Two

A Mess Sampler

Desks

Industrial psychologist Andrew DuBrin at the Rochester Institute of Technology has noted, "Whenever you see a photo of a powerful person, the person always has a clean work area." He's right, of course. A Fortune 500 CEO or a U.S. senator posing in front of a desk surface obliterated by heaps of paper would risk being judged ineffective and undisciplined. If nothing else, the failure to keep a neat desk suggests vague, non-leadership-compatible issues of character, in much the same way that divorce did until about the 1970s.

To be sure, CEOs and senators usually have assistants to help them keep their desks clear. But in the worlds of business and government, at least, it's not just people at the top who might feel pressured to maintain tidy desks. Organizational policy, written or unwritten, tends to be unfriendly to the cluttered desk. General Motors and United Parcel Service are among the many U.S. companies with formal "clean desk" policies; the *New York Times* is among those without one, but that wasn't much comfort to staffers said to have been frostily instructed by former executive editor Howell Raines on the proper technique for stacking books on their desks. (Horizontally, in his opinion.) Some organizations go ahead and proudly spell out policies on their Web sites in black-and-white so the public can appreciate the pride employees take in being told what to do with their desktops. The following is excerpted from the "code of business conduct," posted on the Web by Iowa-based bank First Federal Bankshares:

> Work areas should be kept neat and orderly. The Company must always look its best. Just as we are judged by our personal appearance, so is the Company. Good housekeeping makes it easier to organize your work, prevents loss of items, and provides a professional appearance. Excessive display of personal items is unprofessional. Supervisors and managers are expected to maintain a professional appearance in their departments and areas, and they may request that you remove items if they detract from a professional appearance. In addition, they may require you to clean or straighten your work area.

And these sorts of policies, whether formal or not, aren't always just gentle suggestions. There's no way of knowing how many times messy desks have played a role in hampering careers. But some institutions are explicit about the price of messiness. Bradford, Pennsylvania, fired its police chief for not having a neat desk. Australia's postal service demoted an employee and fined her US$2,300 for refusing to remove from her desk a photograph of herself with friends — her fourth personal item, one more than the agency allows.

Fortunately for the world, Albert Einstein did not work for UPS or the city of Bradford. Einstein's desk at the Institute for

Advanced Study in Princeton, New Jersey, was maintained, by all personal and photographic accounts, in stupendous disarray. (Einstein makes a good role model here not simply because he is so widely accepted as having been highly effective at his job, but also because, as we'll soon see, Einstein might be regarded as a sort of godfather of the science of useful mess.)

In general, if one looks at organizations where people tend not to have neat-freak managers breathing down their necks — in other words, where they have a choice in the matter — people tend to have messy desks. Our survey backs this up, as do professional organizers. In particular, academia is an unrestrained haven of the messy work space, so much so that faculty at colleges and universities often behave as if they've been told their reputation will grow in direct proportion to the height of the piles on and around their desks. One Columbia University professor's office has gradually become so densely packed with towers of papers and books that the school finally assigned him a second office so that students could meet with him in relative comfort and safety. When Nobel laureate and University of Chicago economics professor Robert Fogel found his desk becoming massively piled, he simply installed a second desk behind him that now competes in towering clutter with the first. His colleague at the school, chemist Stephen Berry, a recipient of a MacArthur "genius grant" award, works among a landscape of eighteen-inch-high piles that have harbored individual documents for as long as two decades.

Well, perhaps messy desks are the stuff of cranky genius. Maybe these folks would have been even more productive if they had followed conventional get-organized wisdom and sought out the promised time-saving efficiency and functionality of neat desks. Except when people study working efficiency — as did, for example, husband-and-wife Microsoft senior researchers Abigail Sellen and Richard Harper, authors of *The Myth of the Paperless Office* — they tend to find that messy desks can offer extremely functional environments. Academic types defending the practices of academic types? Actually, it doesn't take a genius to figure out why it makes perfect sense to keep a messy desk.

First, there's the cost of maintaining a neat desk. To keep a desk surface free of papers, except perhaps for small "in" and "out" piles, you have to get most incoming documents either filed away, thrown out, or handed off to someone else. (Let's assume you're not just shuffling them off into other piles on your floor or in your closet, since that would hardly be getting organized.) You can stick them into files in a filing cabinet, which would look pretty neat. But it takes time to read through and appropriately file each document if you want to be able to access it when you need it and if you want to be able to keep track of which documents are associated with what incomplete tasks and what sorts of deadlines.

In addition, you'll spend time each day searching through files, struggling in some cases to figure out where you filed a document and which documents need immediate attention. (We'll be talking later on about the difficulties that filing systems can cause in retrieving documents, but here's a quick example: if you have a higher-priority item and a lower-priority item relating to, say, the same client, should you file them together in a single client folder or separately in more-urgent and less-urgent folders?) If and when you find the right documents, you'll pull them out and shuffle them back onto your desk so you can work with them and then later will refile them. How much time you spend on your filing and retrieving each day will vary wildly with work complexity and the volume and types of documents you receive, but whatever it amounts to, it's time you'll be taking away from your real work.

Or you could follow the advice of many professional organizers and adhere to a "one-touch" policy for documents: whatever task is associated with the document, do it right away, so you can file it and forget it, chuck it, or pass it along. It certainly sounds like a good idea to go ahead and get the work done as it comes in, since you have to get it done sooner or later anyway. Except, of course, that you really don't have to get all the work that comes to your desk done; a lot of it will eventually prove safely ignorable. What's more, some of it will be of much higher priority than the rest. But under a strict one-touch system, you'll find yourself spending time dealing with office-supply forms and seminar flyers, even when that career-making-or-breaking report to the managers is due in three days. Of course, you don't necessarily have to be rigid about the one-touch system. Surely it's no problem if you take some of the less-important documents and place them at a corner of your desk until the report is done. And even though that other document is pretty important, you don't have to deal with it right this second and interrupt your thoughts, so you just slide it over there and . . . uh-oh.

A messy desk can be a highly effective prioritizing and accessing system. People with messy desks enlist any number of different strategies, often unconsciously, for keeping the work they need at hand. In general, on a messy desk, the more important, more urgent work tends to stay close by and near the top of the clutter, while the safely ignorable stuff tends to get buried at the bottom or near the back, which makes perfect sense. And yes, you'll spend a certain amount of time rooting through the piles to find documents. This is where professional organizers claim you'll lose anywhere from an hour a week to an hour a day. But, in fact, as long as the mess is kept to a reasonable level, you'll probably do better time-wise than you would with a neat desk. First of all, the documents you most need will tend to be at hand anyway. According to our survey, people who said they keep a "very neat" desk spend an average of 36 percent *more* time looking for things at work than people who said they keep a "fairly messy" desk. And that figure doesn't take into account how much additional time those with neat desks spend sorting and filing, or processing low-priority documents, in order to keep their desks so neat.

The various piles on a messy desk can represent a surprisingly sophisticated informal filing system that offers far more efficiency and flexibility than a filing cabinet could possibly provide. Messy desk owners typically, for example, have separate piles for urgent, less-urgent, and nonurgent documents. Within any one of those piles, you could keep together documents relating to, say, the same client. If you want to draw special attention to a document within the pile, you can displace it or turn it so it sticks out. If a document could reasonably go into either of two piles, you can place it so it straddles both piles. If you have to find a document, you can track it down not only by urgency and client but also by how long it's been since you last saw the document and by what other documents came in around the same time, since the older, less-handled stuff is likely to be together closer to the bottom. If you keep a messy desk, some of these strategies probably sound familiar, though you may never have thought about the method to your clutter. And, as Sellen and Harper have pointed out, that's one of the great characteristics of a messy desk: it will tend to naturally reflect the way you think and work.

Thought and work are unpredictable, varying, and ambiguous. They're messy. Why shouldn't your desk be messy, too?

And a few more advantages. How many times have you waded through a pile of papers on your desk to look for a particular document only to stumble on a different one, which inspires you to accomplish an even more important task than the one you had originally intended — a task you would never have gotten to if you had filed that document safely away in a drawer? Even more satisfying can be the experience of coming across something in a pile that rings a bell with regard to something else you saw on your desk a few minutes ago, or in the previous day's rummaging, facilitating a useful connection.

That's what happened to Leon Heppel, a biomolecular researcher at the National Institutes of Health in the 1950s. Heppel was notorious among his fellow researchers for the clutter on his desk, which he would occasionally cover with a sheet of brown butcher paper so he would have a clean surface on which to deposit a new layer of clutter. One day, he came across a letter sent to him by researcher Earl Sutherland, describing Sutherland's recent work with an unusual biomolecule and its effect on cells. Later, digging through wrapper levels, Heppel came across a letter that had been sent to him earlier on by the researcher David Lipkin, in which Lipkin described the action of a different biomolecule. Regarding the two letters side by side, Heppel realized his two colleagues were very likely describing different ends of the same cellular process. He forwarded Sutherland's letter to Lipkin and Lipkin's to Sutherland, setting off a chain reaction of insights that ended with Sutherland's Nobel Prize–winning discovery of how hormones regulate cells.

Perhaps all of this helps to explain why, according to a survey conducted by professional staffing firm Ajilon Office, office messiness tends to increase sharply with increasing education, increasing salary, and increasing experience.

More than one professional organizer commented at the NAPO conference that the right attitudes about organization ought to be taught in elementary school. Good idea. An excellent example emerged from a recent visit to a fifth-grade public school class boasting rows of pristine desks and a spotless floor space, all unmarred by even a hint of clutter, except for one desk near the back of the room that had a teetering pile of clutter on the floor beside it. When asked about the pile, the teacher laughed and explained that she has a rule: the students can keep anything they want at their desks, as long as it all fits inside their desks at the end of the day. But every day one student seemed to fall short of the goal by about a seven-inch stack — he always had a few extra books, a pile of art in progress, several puzzles, and more. A daily struggle between teacher and student ensued, until after a few weeks the teacher had an epiphany. "I realized this wasn't about discipline," she said. "It was about curiosity. He just found all this stuff really interesting. And why are these kids here? To be neat? Or to be stimulated? I told him he could keep the extra things in a pile by his desk, and we haven't had a problem since."

Lawn Order

Kathleen Manton-Jones and her then-four-year-old daughter Grace moved to Winterhaven, a subdivision of Tucson, in 1997. A community of about 235 small homes comfortably spaced along broad, flat streets, Winterhaven is best known in Greater Tucson for placing itself on display to throngs of touring onlookers for two weeks every year around Christmas, during which time about four out of five Winterhaven homeowners take the trouble to deck out their houses in vast arrays of holiday lights. While not quite so self-consciously festive the rest of the year, Winterhaven is a community where most residents can walk for several blocks and expect to be hailed by friendly neighbors at every turn.

But for the past few years Manton-Jones has been gathering fewer neighborly waves and more than a few glares when she's out for a stroll. Some of her fellow Winterhavenites have gone out of their way to confront her. One day her daughter, nine years old at the time, ran to answer the doorbell, and Manton-Jones heard a man speaking loudly and angrily. She came to the door and found a large, red-faced man in a suit trying to force a document into the hands of the terrified girl. Later, another man told Manton-Jones, at the end of a pointed finger, "Maybe you just don't belong in Winterhaven." Another accused her of single-handedly driving down property values in the community. Several simply wouldn't speak to her. Then Winterhaven's board of directors — technically, the community is a corporation — started heaping fines on her. The board went on to threaten to place a lien on her home.

It's hard to picture Manton-Jones raising this sort of ire in any community, let alone one as seemingly as innocuous Winterhaven. She is slightly shy but quickly becomes relaxed and unleashes an easy laugh. A former marathoner with a neat veil of dark hair, she is an artist who makes ends meet by holding down a clerical job at a local community college. Her daughter is like any eleven-year-old, and her husband is a trim, quiet fellow with a steady grin. For the past decade her passion has been landscaping, having first fallen in love with lush, free-flowing gardens she saw in Europe and South America during her former husband's tours of duty in the military, and then even more so with the staggering variety of hardy, colorful desert grasses, flowers, and shrubs she encountered in Texas.

As it happens, it was Manton-Jones's landscaping interests that landed her in trouble in Winterhaven. Specifically, her affront to the community is having replaced most of her neat, plain green lawn — a form of plant life ecologically and historically alien to the region — with a more natural, varied, and water-thrifty landscape of indigenous flowers, grasses, and shrubs. She quickly found out that the residents of Winterhaven are, by and large, emotionally, politically, and, to hear them tell it, legally committed to having neatly trimmed green grass and little else surrounding the homes in their community.

If any one thing could epitomize our obsession with the neat and orderly, it might be the close-cropped grass lawn. An early-twentieth-century invention initially made popular by wealthy homeowners eager to bask in the hip gentility then associated with badminton, lawn tennis, and croquet, lawns require a staggering amount of care to achieve the ideal look of a flat, monotone tarp. Americans lavish $8 billion a year in products and services on them and pour fifty million pounds of pesticides and manufactured fertilizers over them, making the flying of tiny yellow "hazardous to children and pets" flags a familiar sight, and leading many experts to refer to them as "chemical lawns." Suburbs are often not the havens of peace and quiet they are made out to be, if for no other reason than that they are literally abuzz with the growling and whining of the lawn mowers, weed whackers, edgers, and leaf blowers required to keep lawns tidy.

Aside from all the maintenance they require, lawns are ecological disasters. Closely trimmed grass has short roots and doesn't hold moisture well. That means, for one thing, that grass tends to croak when not regularly watered; the watering costs for a fifty-foot-by-fifty-foot lawn can add nearly $100 per month to a Boston-area water and sewer bill, for example. It also means that heavy rain doesn't readily soak into the soil, leading to runoff and attendant problems with flooding, erosion, and the distribution of the pesticides, fertilizers, and other chemicals needed to avoid the dreaded sparse lawn or green-brown patches. Grass offers almost nothing of use to birds and other normally welcome wildlife.

The problem isn't simply that the vast majority of us have become conditioned to embrace the neatness and order of tidy lawns or even that we ignore the significant drawbacks to them. It's that so many people react in horror when a neighbor explores a less ordered, if more sensible, alternative. Since 1990, the U.S. Congress has required that a quarter of landscaping budgets for federal highways go to plant native wildflowers, yet a homeowner who would be tempted to pull the car over to admire just such a magnificent, messy, untrimmed wildflower meadow might spit out his morning coffee if he looked out the kitchen window to see the same meadow sprouting up across the street where neatly mowed grass used to be. Natural landscapes may be beautiful, unique, nearly maintenance-free, and environmentally friendly, but their patchy, brushy, multi-heighted, multicolored, and altogether disorderly look drives some communities nuts.

You'd expect natural landscaping to be an easier sell in the Tucson area, which is in the Sonoran Desert and receives an annual rainfall of twelve inches, often leaving only recycled wastewater running in its aquifers. Sure enough, local government has little interest in seeing large quantities of water diverted to lawn sprinklers and has actively promoted natural landscaping with considerable success — one of the few large communities in the United States to do so. To a visitor, the absence of grass is initially jarring, but the astounding multihued variety of flowering cacti, shrubs, and wildflowers displayed in its place quickly becomes enchanting. At times, the impression isn't so much of landscaped lots as of a sprawling desert garden onto which low-cast, earth-toned homes have been discreetly placed as an afterthought.

But even here there are plenty of fanatical holdouts. Some two hundred of them live in Winterhaven. Though Tucson's water rates can climb to five times those in wetter parts of the country, discouraging lawn watering, for historical reasons Winterhaven's water sources aren't subject to the city's control, and Winterhaven provides its residents with all the water they want for a flat rate of $48.50 a month. In other words, they grow lawns largely because they can.

On a stroll through the surrounding neighborhoods, Manton-Jones points out some of the alternatives that the community finds more palatable than natural landscaping. A few yards are mostly baked dirt. Another consists of a large bed of pebbles, and one is entirely bricked in. None of these yards has offended the community enough to inspire fines or threats; after all, they may not be pretty or alive, but they are neat and orderly. Continuing along occasionally requires detouring around filthy puddles taking up half the street, formed by runoff from sprinklers, and in some spots the asphalt is rippled and torn from being frequently submerged — a strange problem in a desert city. We also pass a house with natural landscaping. The owner of this home had quietly paid his fines, later expressing his feelings in the form of a large metal sculpture in his front yard on top of which sits a lawn mower, extending upward like a middle finger.

Bret Rappaport smiles ruefully when he's told of Kathleen Manton-Jones's plight. He has heard this sort of story all too many times. Rappaport's day job is lawyering at a classy twenty-seventh-floor office in a downtown Chicago law firm, where he represents the interests of well-heeled business clients. He doesn't quite look or act the part; he is lumbering, loose-limbed, and broad-featured, and manages to come off as a little scruffy even in a nice suit. An inveterate camper and hiker, Rappaport in the early 1990s ended up representing, pro bono, five Chicago residents with natural landscaping who were being threatened with prosecution under the city's "weed laws." Intended to keep homeowners from letting grass lawns go to pot, weed laws are often wielded against natural landscapers by communities offended by the unlawnlike, untrimmed disorder. An extreme example is that of a former resident of the Buffalo, New York, suburb of Kenmore, who in 1984 was hit with fines of $30,000 for refusing to raze a twenty-foot-by-twenty-foot patch planted with a dozen different species of wildflowers. "It just didn't have that manicured look of the neighbors' yards," he reportedly said at the time. On appeal to a state court, the fine was eventually reduced to $100, but death threats and gunfire from irate townspeople ensued, and one day, while the owner was away, the plot was mowed down by a neighbor, against whom charges were quickly dismissed.

Prosecutions continue today, as for example in the case of a woman in the St. Louis suburb of Florissant, who lost her 2005 jury trial in county court to keep her natural landscaping. But Rappaport rarely gets involved in legal battles now. He sees himself as more of a botanical diplomat, trying to help natural landscapers avoid controversy by greasing their communities' transitions to floral tolerance. Surrounding his own home in the town of Deerfield, forty-five minutes north of Chicago, is a varied, colorful prairie landscape in miniature, composed of native grasses and flowers such as little bluestem, Solomon's seal, and trillium, as well as rye and sideoats grama. The landscaping encompasses a tiny pond, and a small, sparse stand of trees crosshatched by a few trees that have fallen, left as shelter for animals, and now bearing small signs DO NOT DISTURB — WILDLIFE TREE. It's lovely. And it requires no watering, chemicals, trimming, or reseeding. (Rappaport burns small patches of it each year in imitation of nature's technique for managing growth and renewing the soil.)

There is also some conventional grass around the landscaping. It's a key component, along with a lot of explaining, to heading off neighborhood objections, Rappaport says. If a natural landscape — even a dense, free-form one jammed with a dozen or more species that range and soar in random-looking patches — is surrounded by a thin, neat strip of lawn, then it's usually better tolerated by the lawn-happy. That's because the landscaping then tends to be seen, almost like an optical illusion, as a specialized garden within a lawn, even though the lawn's square footage is dwarfed by that of the natural landscape. "If you throw paint on a wall it's vandalism," says Rappaport. "If you put a frame around the splotch, it's art. People just need to see that sense of order and intent."

Almost all of his neighbors continue to keep neat lawns. He points out the consequences: heavy erosion and silt deposits by the street's several culverts, through which rain runoff from the lawns rushes as if from a cannon. The runoff, he says, joined with that of other heavily lawned Midwestern communities, carries silt and toxins and occasionally causes flooding downstream all the way to the Gulf of Mexico. "Today the Gulf is dead, dead, dead," he says. But his neighbors have been fairly tolerant, at least, of Rappaport's lawn alternative. And down the street, Patty Glicksberg and her family have followed Rappaport's example and replaced much of their own lawn with prairie landscape. "I started off with a computer diagram of how the different wildflowers would be arranged in a nice, neat mosaic, so that I'd get the perfect combination of colors every season," Glicksberg explains. "Then [Bret's wife] Jina told me one of the flowers I was planting only came up every other year, throwing my whole scheme off. I freaked out. But finally I relaxed and decided you just need to let this stuff do what it's going to do, and that's what's most beautiful about it."

Back at his Chicago office, Rappaport concedes that he and other proponents of natural landscaping haven't made great inroads into the nation's obsession with fastidious lawns — replacing lawns with Astroturf and the like is a faster-growing trend. But he savors the small victories. Walking to the large office window, he indicates city hall, where administrators once plotted the prosecution of natural landscapers, and points out a variegated patch alongside the building. "It's a prairie landscape," he says. "It's the best thing about my office."

Corporations' Big Plans

Each year, the top graduates of prestigious business schools are snatched up by management consulting firms such as McKinsey, Bain, and the Boston Consulting Group, which specialize most prominently in helping companies strategize. It might seem surprising that business school superstars, as a rule, don't end up running companies, but they don't; they're more likely to end up giving advice to those who run companies, particularly advice on what new high-level strategies the companies should adopt. Well over twice as many 2005 Harvard Business School graduates went into consulting as into general management. (In fact, running companies tends to be a distant third choice of top business school graduates, behind consulting and financial services.) Not only is the pay typically better at top consulting firms than in industry, but there is, in theory, an opportunity to have far more impact. A management consultant can have a shot at setting the directions of many companies, instead of just one, and all without necessarily having to sweat the less intoxicating details involved in implementing the strategies or sticking around to see if they work and paying the price if they don't.

Bill Starbuck — no relation to the coffee shop — could fairly be considered part of the management consulting industry, although in a more meta sort of way, in that he doesn't simply perform strategic planning so much as analyze the process and impact of strategic planning. Like many in the strategic planning field, he entered this rarefied world through the academic side, as one of the many business school professors who consult to companies. And so it was that the strategic planning unit of France Telecom hired Starbuck to come and share his thinking. The executives in the unit could have reasonably imagined they'd be getting an active, highly competent mind: Starbuck is a storied New York University professor with an endowed chair, a former president of the Academy of Management, and an editor at one time or another of seventeen different professional journals. And if the France Telecom managers didn't know it ahead of time, it was clear at the first sight of Starbuck's solid bulk, shaved head, and laser gaze that they would be getting a no-punches-pulled take on things as well.

Even so, they did not expect Starbuck to tell them, along

with all the senior executives of the company, that they were deadwood. In fact, minutes into the presentation the entire audience was, as the French like to say, *bouche bée* — that is, open-mouthed in unpleasant surprise. It was nothing personal. Starbuck didn't mean to suggest that the France Telecom strategic planners in particular were useless. This highly respected expert on corporate strategic planning was simply insisting that corporate strategic planning in general, along with other forms of long-range, formal planning, is a waste of time.

Was "Indiana" Starbuck, as he sometimes refers to himself, simply struggling to live up to his hard-earned reputation for iconoclasm? This seventy-something former cat breeder, software developer, and free-spirit polymath, who has been active in the fields of sociology, psychology, and mathematics, among others, and with the current official title "professor of creative management," openly boasts of occasionally making statements he knows to be untrue just to "confound" the people around him.

If Starbuck can't resist slinging it once in a while, his charge that formal planning is useless is surely among his most suspect pronouncements. Formal strategic planning, once the domain of the military, became a big deal at corporations in the 1950s and has remained so continuously, except for a period in the 1980s when it fell out of favor as a reaction to an overobsession with it in the 1970s. Today, senior executives at most major organizations consider strategic planning to be not only part of their job description but also one of their highest callings. Former General Electric chairman Jack Welch, for example, held annual retreats with each of his unit heads for strategic planning sessions. Simple common sense alone might dictate that high-level, long-term, formal planning is essential for an organization's survival, not to mention its ability to flourish. Strategic planning is how companies figure out what they're going to be when they grow up — that is, which goods and services they're going to offer in the coming years, and how they're going to organize themselves so as to do it more effectively than their competitors. A company that didn't engage in formal, high-level planning would be improvising, reacting, guessing — zigging here, then zagging there, instead of forging ahead along a carefully laid-out path. It would end up behaving in a very messy fashion.

It's not as if no one had ever examined the value of formal planning. Numerous studies have demonstrated that strategic planning works. Except that when Starbuck reviewed them, he found the studies typically involved interviewing senior managers to ascertain how useful they thought their strategic planning was. And what do you know? Strategic planners tended to find their strategic planning *very* useful. For a more objective assessment, Starbuck reviewed data on how a corporation's profits fared as compared to the amount of strategic planning the company had engaged in. The results: companies that did a lot of strategic planning performed, on average, no better than companies that did less strategic planning.

Not only does Starbuck see no surprise in that finding, he argues that it would be a miracle if it were otherwise. The main reason, in a nutshell, is that managers import a raft of poor assumptions into the planning process. For starters, says Starbuck, senior managers tend to badly misperceive their markets, their industries, and even their own organizations. Studies back him up. When senior managers were asked even the most basic questions relating to their areas of responsibility, they tended to fumble embarrassingly. In one study, corporate heads of finance were asked to estimate their companies' sales volumes over the past five years; 60 percent of them couldn't come close. Managers did about as poorly estimating most other facets of their corporation's performance and capabilities, as well as the salient characteristics of their competitors and of potential customers. The one question managers consistently aced was that of whether the companies they worked for were large or small — anything more complicated was hit or miss. "The perceptions of executives are usually terribly wrong," says Starbuck. "Sometimes it's truly ludicrous." Even managers at the scale of global politics seem clueless when it comes to characterizing their own domains, notes Starbuck, recalling that U.S. secretary of defense Robert McNamara repeatedly declared the Vietnam war to be going well in the mid-1960s, and that Joseph Stalin once named "gaiety" as the Soviet Union's outstanding quality. More recently, the phrase "mission accomplished" returned to haunt the White House with regard to Iraq.

The misperceptions tend to emerge from the very structure of organizations, says Starbuck. Because assessments have to be communicated up and down an organization, and because managers' standings can rise with positive assessments and fall with negative ones, the process tends to produce oversimplified assessments that are spun to emphasize the positive. Managers tempted to speak out against these distortions fear they'll be seen as pessimistic troublemakers. What's more, managers tend to hew to the outlooks espoused by their bosses, so that when senior managers — who are typically too far removed from the front lines to observe directly what's happening at their own organizations, never mind the world outside — ask for input from their subordinates, they end up hearing "echoes of their own voices," as Starbuck puts it. The distortion becomes even worse in strategic planning, where the need to come up with and justify specific plans leads managers to further massage data to fit a scheme, and later observations are likewise massaged to make the plans appear to have worked. The result is a vicious cycle of bad perceptions engendering bad plans that lead to worse perceptions, and so on.

Even if managers had terrific information about their companies, industries, and markets, long-range formal planning would still be doomed, argues Starbuck. That's because business-world predictions going out more than a few months might as well be coin flips. Customers and competitors behave in unforeseen ways, new trends emerge, politics take strange turns, nature lashes out — from the point of view of a team of managers sitting in a conference trying to read the future, the world behaves essentially randomly. IBM chairman Thomas Watson reportedly predicted in 1943 that the world market for computers would peak at the number five, and managers at corporations everywhere haven't done all that much better since. In particular, people tend to downplay the likelihood of oncoming significant change in their universes. In one study, three-quarters of managers ended up underestimating the level of change that ultimately took place in their industries by two-thirds or more — that is, things changed three times as fast as managers had assumed they would. Only in a few staid, insulated industries, like casket manufacturing, do forecasters perform reasonably well with any consistency.

Managers needn't feel embarrassed at their failure to read the future correctly. The U.S. government's ultrasophisticated computer models for forecasting the economy hardly do much better. One study found that a technique of simply guessing that the gross national product will remain whatever it is right now for the next three months did better on average than three out of four of the government's leading models. A technique of guessing that the GNP will change over the next three months exactly as much as it changed over the past three months did better than all four. Businesses, of course, rely heavily on the government's models for their own strategic planning.

No one should be surprised that long-range plans based on a shaky grasp of the past and present and a wild stab at the future turn out not to be very helpful. But even if companies strategized with good information and predictions, says Starbuck, they'd still be wasting their time. That's because while it takes months or years to implement strategies and get them rolling, competitors can pick up on a company's strategic shifts almost immediately, and, if the strategies look promising, quickly imitate them. Even the obsessively secretive Apple CEO Steve Jobs, who has unhesitatingly wielded lawsuits against employees and Apple-friendly bloggers alike in an effort to suppress advance information of new products, has consistently failed to keep a lid on strategic moves, as, for example, when word of an embryonic iPod cell phone leaked out some six months before the phone was introduced. And if competitors were slow to respond, it still wouldn't matter, says Starbuck. The notion that a company will benefit by implementing new strategies well before its competitors do — the so-called first-mover advantage — has long since been discredited. Historically, companies that are slower to move into new types of products and services are more likely to do well than the companies that pave the way, as long as there aren't billion-dollar infrastructure costs involved. (Monopolistic strategies are the exception, Starbuck notes, but, unfortunately for strategic planners, are illegal.) Google was inspired by the more senior, groundbreaking, and now obscure Alta Vista search engine, and the Oreo cookie was a bald-faced rip-off of the Sunshine Hydrox. "At best you just end up in a Red Queen's race," says Starbuck — that is, just running in place. Companies that instead rely on informal, shorter-term planning, says Starbuck, are in a good position to react profitably to unexpected shifts in the business environment, whether or not in imitation of a rival.

In fact, says Starbuck, long-range planning probably has an *adverse* effect. That's because formal planning can end up locking companies into faulty strategies, focusing everyone's energies on opportunities that never materialize, and causing companies to ignore real opportunities that spring up in their place. If you're an automaker and your planning has led you to embark on long-term efforts to provide the world with more and bigger SUVs, you'll be slower to pick up on the sudden interest in hybrid vehicles, and it will take you longer to do anything about it. According to the data, though, companies that are heavily committed to formal strategic planning don't, on average, do worse than less-planful companies. No better, but no worse. One likely reason is that many companies tend to be quick to ignore their own planning — they make the plans, print them up as impressive documents in shiny binders, stick them on shelves, and then leave them there, because even imperfectly informed managers can recognize when plans aren't likely to work out as, well, planned. In addition, it's the biggest, most successful companies that are likely to have the extra resources to waste on greater levels of formal planning; they may indeed end up suffering from planning-induced profit shrinkage, but since they were better off to begin with, the effects may not be obvious when compared to other companies. In other words, when a company does well, it may have the confidence and extra money to engage in more formal planning, after which it does a little less well.

Despite the evidence that formal planning is at best useless, companies still rely on it. You might think the word would have gotten out on strategic planning. Of course, one way that shifts in management thinking propagate through the business world is via management consultants — like the ones who get hired to help with strategic planning. Maybe that's why Starbuck doesn't often get asked to speak to strategic planning groups anymore. Just ask the France Telecom strategic planning unit. Though you'd have to do some digging, because the group was disbanded not long after Starbuck spoke there.

Noisy Calls

If you've noticed that cell-phone conversations seem a great deal less garbled than they used to, you might want to know that part of the credit belongs to International Telecommunications Union recommendation G.711.II, which specifies a mathematical technique for dealing with cell-phone noise. Specifically, this technical standard applies to the essentially random background sounds picked up by a cell phone's microphone — traffic hubbub, the conversations of passersby, the hiss of wind gusts, the tinkle and clatter of silverware in a restaurant, the drone of an air conditioner. Many engineers throughout the cell-phone-speaking world are well versed in employing G.711.II and similar techniques, and some companies even specialize in it.

Why worry about cell-phone noise? That may seem a silly question. As your average cell-phone-equipped nine-year-old might explain, background sounds can interfere with the conversation. Engineers might hasten to add that transmitting background sounds takes energy, which drains cell-phone batteries more quickly and hogs part of the limited and costly communication channel that could otherwise be applied to callers' voices. In the world of communications, and in fact in all forms of information transmission, there is *signal* — that is, what we hope to distinguish and derive information from, generally a speaking voice in the case of a cell phone — and there is *noise*, which is most everything else, including background sounds. Noise is a form of mess. It would seem obvious that it is advantageous to neaten what ultimately comes through our phones by getting rid of as much background noise as possible.

Yet none of this would explain why recommendation G.711.II describes a means for *adding* background noise to cell-phone conversations. But it does. And the companies that operate cell-phone networks pay good money to have the noise put in.

Some of that money goes to a Montreal company called Octasic, for which the technique of adding background noise into cell-phone conversations is a core competence. Frédéric Bourget, a senior product manager at Octasic and something of an expert in background noise, explains that there's a bit of a history to the relationship between phone networks and noise. Back before the 1990s and the rise of all-computerized phone networks, engineers working with both landlines and cell-phone networks had to wrestle with all sorts of noise, including the sizzle of electronic circuitry, the buzz of home wiring, the crackle of stray radio signals and sunspots, and the disconcertingly out-of-sync echo of the speaker's own voice bouncing back and forth through the lines like an aural yo-yo. Remember when a call across the United States entailed having to speak up to be heard? That loss of volume over distance was a characteristic deliberately added to the long-distance network by AT&T engineers, because as much as it squelched the speaker's voice, it even further reduced the echo of the voice, allowing the shouting speaker to be heard clearly over the echo. But even with this and other tricks, cell-phone conversations of the 1970s and 1980s were often nightmares of electronic groans, pops, and whooshes.

As the phone networks went digital in the 1990s, transmitting voices as strings of 0s and 1s, all this electronic noise became relatively easy to clean up — a computer has little trouble differentiating between the 0s and 1s of a voice and those of a sunspot or between a voice and its echo. That left background sounds as the one remaining form of phone noise, and that was really only an issue with cell-phone conversations, which after all routinely take place on busy streets, in cafeterias, and at airports. Seeing an opportunity not only to eliminate this final distraction but also to conserve precious cell-phone battery life and channel capacity, engineers finally developed sophisticated computer techniques for stripping out the background cacophony and sending only the speaker's voice. And during the pauses between speech, the network wouldn't have to transmit *anything*, no matter what was going on in the background. Why take the trouble to pipe through the roar of a nearby lawn mower? The only thing the person on the other end needed to hear was the speaker's voice, punctuated by glorious near-silence. What could be more agreeable? What could be more efficient? What could be neater?

Just one little problem: callers hated it. Specifically, the absence of background noise leads to three difficulties. First of all, the engineers hadn't completely gotten rid of the voice echoes; they had merely suppressed them to the point where they couldn't be noticed over the background noise. When the background noise is removed, the faint echoes can be made out again, and that turns out to be a big problem. Unlike background noise, which is random and messy, an echo is a type of *correlated noise* — its pattern follows that of the speaker's voice, but is shifted in time. Our brains are good at ignoring a stream of random noise, but neater, correlated noise is highly distracting.

Second, background noise creates a sense of "presence." It lets you know that the call is still connected, even if the person at the other end isn't speaking at the moment. "We've been trained to hear small background noises in phone conversations," Bourget explains. "Perfect silence sounds like a hang up. The background noise isn't really just noise. It's a form of information, providing feedback that someone is still there." People who hear complete silence at any point during a phone conversation tend to interrupt the conversation with "Hello?" and "Are you still there?"

Finally, we don't live in sealed containers. We live in a world where things that make noises are constantly near us, where in a sense even the space around us has a faint murmur to it. This noise feels right to us; at an unconscious level, it is reassuring. The technical term for this type of background noise, in fact, is *comfort noise* — engineers like Bourget call it *CN* — and trying to talk to someone in the absence of it is a bit disorienting and even a little creepy. Our brains rebel at the unnatural neatness.

The background noise had to come back. But engineers were loath to give up the battery life and channel capacity they had saved by eliminating its transmission. So they came up with a compromise. The background noise would still be stripped out, but it wouldn't be entirely discarded. Instead it would be "sampled" — that is, a computer in the network would analyze it and pull out key characteristics, such as how often its pitch varied and by how much. These characteristics would then be transmitted to the other end of the network, where a computer would use a mathematical technique — G.711.II, for example — to reconstruct a simulation of the background noise and add it back in with the voice.

This tortuous-sounding trick fools listeners of cell-phone

talkers everywhere just fine, even if it would never occur to them to appreciate it or even notice. It's not a perfect solution, of course. Once in a while, background noise can be so excessive that a little creepy silence might be welcome. And there's one type of background noise that trips up the technique: music on hold. When someone tries to speak over music on hold, the network assumes the music is noise, strips it out, and substitutes a simulated version, which, depending on the music, often comes out sounding something like a raspy wheeze. It would be a lot easier for companies like Octasic if doctors' offices played random traffic and air-conditioner sounds to its cell-phone callers on hold.

On the other hand, maybe it's only fair that music sometimes ends up as noise. After all, noise sometimes ends up as music. But that's for another chapter.

The Bias Toward Neatness

Perhaps it's not surprising that in a large world where countless trillions of events and situations unfold, we were able to find a few exceptional examples where neatness is pointless or even problematic, and mess plays a benign or even beneficial role. But trust us — we're just getting warmed up.

That there is a heavy and somewhat blind bias toward neatness and organization is a little strange, considering all the negative associations so many of us have with highly ordered systems. Order reached a zenith of sorts, at least in Western civilization, with Nazi Germany. (What, in contrast, could be messier than the Garden of Eden?) Obsessive-compulsive disorder and some forms of autism are to an extent diseases of overorganization. The question, then, isn't whether or not too much neatness and organization can be a problem. We all know it can. The question, rather, is where to draw the line. But oddly enough, it's a question that hardly anyone asks. Most people simply assume they're on the overly messy and disorganized side of the line and believe they would do well to drag themselves in the direction of neatness and order.

Let's be clear on a few important points. First, it's obvious that at a certain level mess becomes dysfunctional. We're not saying that messier is always better. We're not anarchists calling for the dissolution of national government, social order, and organizations. Burying oneself in extraneous clutter and operating without rhyme or reason quickly becomes paralyzing — those are examples of what we call *pathological mess*, about which we'll have something to say later on. Some situations leave little room for mess; for example, nobody would want to go to a messy eye surgeon. Rather, we argue that there is an optimal level of mess for every aspect of every system. That is, in any situation there is a type and level of mess at which effectiveness is maximized, and our assertion is that people and organizations frequently err on the side of overorganization. In many cases, they can improve by increasing mess, if it's done in the right way. At a minimum, recognizing the benefits of mess can be a major stress reducer — many of us are already operating at a more-or-less appropriate level of mess but labor under the mistaken belief that we're failing in some way because of it.

Also, we are in no way saying that people should be slobs; a certain amount of cosmetic neatening — as with Bret Rappaport's framework of neatly trimmed lawn — can go a long way. Indeed, as you'll see, we encourage it in many situations.

At the NAPO conference, Barry Izsak offered the observation that "disorganization is a human condition." He meant it by way of reinforcing the notion that everyone needs help getting more organized. For us, it raises this question: if disorganization is a human condition, why do so many people rush to squash it wherever it pops up?

Now let's take a look at how society got itself into this . . . situation.

CHAPTER THREE

The History of Mess

Order is Heaven's first law.
— ALEXANDER POPE

Most of this book was written on a laptop computer that occasionally refused to do anything but display the message, "Operating system not found." The first time it happened, the computer was sent, under warranty, to the manufacturer, which replaced the internal disk drive, the power supply, and the keyboard. The second time, the manufacturer replaced the disk drive again, along with the display screen and an unidentified checkbook-sized plastic board crammed with electronics. (All replaced parts were returned in a plastic bag with the computer.) The third time, a sharp, open-handed blow was delivered to the side of the computer near the base of the screen, at which point the computer resumed its normal operation. From then on, the recurring glitch was handled on-site without intervention from the manufacturer.

Everyone knows that whacking an electronic or mechanical device sometimes fixes it. And for a simple reason: malfunctions are often a matter of a loose or corroded electrical connection between two components, or a moving part that's out of alignment, and a good bump that gets the innards randomly lurching may well restore the connection or alignment. It isn't neat, but it can be perfectly effective. Even one scientist whose benchtop apparatus won him and a colleague a Nobel Prize in physics wasn't too proud to occasionally give the equipment a gentle, therapeutic rap. Then again, scientists have good reason to appreciate the messy art of apparatus whacking. Disorder has been comfortably assimilated into, and in some cases made a central figure in, many branches of science.

There was once a time when the world embraced mess and disorder. Then mankind came along. Prehistoric man wouldn't at first have been significantly less messy than most other animals. But over time, a preference for certain types of order must have conferred certain advantages in his fight for survival: a knack for categorizing mushrooms into poisonous and nonpoisonous varieties, for keeping hunting grounds free of human signs that would tip off prey, for storing precious tools and hides in one corner of the cave to enable fast packing and swift flight in case of emergency, to schedule shifts for guard duty. Archaeological sites dating as far back as 1.5 million years suggest that early hominids established caches of tools, and that by 20,000 BC some hunter-gatherers had separate areas for eating, cooking, tossing garbage, and even for leisure activities such as carving stones. Many anthropologists have argued that the Neanderthals, a species of man that branched off from *Homo sapiens* — us — a half million years ago and thrived in Europe for a hundred thousand years, died off because they seemed to show less of a proclivity for order than our own primitive ancestors, to judge by the unearthed remains of the messier Neanderthal sites.

The big jump in organization for the human species came with the transition from hunting and gathering to farming, given the latter's requirements for long hours of hard work scheduled by day and by season, the arrangement of space to maximize production, the fencing in of animals, and the gathering and sorting of seeds and harvests. University of California at Los Angeles professor and well-known author Jared Diamond, for one, has questioned whether the whole agriculture thing was a smart move, pointing out that hunter-gatherers might have had it pretty good; today in Africa's Kalahari Desert hunter-gatherers work fifteen hours a week, give or take, and spend most of the rest of the time sleeping and in leisure activities. Today in the United States, by contrast, many farmers sometimes work fifteen-hour days. On top of the work differential, farming societies throughout history have suffered the recurrence of famine, sometimes triggered in part by rigid farming routines that deplete soil and other resources. But for better or worse, mankind was off and running, from a neatness-and-order point of view.

With farming eventually came the rise of civilizations, all of them dependent on various forms of order — if considerably looser and in some cases far more brutal ones than those we know today — for getting things built, for containing crime, for mediating social affairs, for trade, and more. And with civilization came a societal elite who could demand more opulent and decidedly neater digs for themselves and their courts, even while the vast majority of the population continued to live in, as well as work in, the dirt. But privilege was also often associated with extremes of mess, as for example in the gorging, orgies, and blood sports of ancient Rome.

Great organized religions arose to impose order on an otherwise vague conception of the world, and to mitigate, at least in perception, the sometimes cruel randomness of life's events. The very first thing we learn in the Bible, for example, is that God is the ultimate professional organizer:

In the beginning God created the heaven and the earth.

And the earth was without form, and void . . . and God divided the light from the darkness. . . . And God made the firmament, and divided the waters which were under the firmament from the waters which were above the firmament. . . . And God said, Let the waters under the heaven be gathered together unto one place, and let the dry land appear. . . . And God said, Let there be lights in the firmament of the heaven to divide the day from the night; and let them be for signs, and for seasons, and for days, and years. . . . And God said, Let us make man in our image . . . male and female created he them. And . . . God said unto them . . . have dominion over the fish of the sea, and over the fowl of the air, and over every living thing that moveth upon the earth.

After the Jews are brought into the desert in Exodus, Leviticus details an exhaustive list of rules, followed by Numbers, which is essentially a thorough audit of the Israelites. Much of the Old Testament is, in fact, taken up with the sort of listy, prescriptive and proscriptive material that might have found its way into an ancient version of *Organizing for Dummies*.

Disorder's reputation took a big hit with Christianity, much of it related to the fact that early church leaders were not keen on diversity of thought in their flocks. Around AD 100, the bishop Ignatius warned the community this way:

It is therefore befitting that you should in every way glorify Jesus Christ, who hath glorified you, that by a unanimous obedience "ye may be perfectly joined together in the same mind, and in the same judgment, and may all

speak the same thing concerning the same thing. . . ."
[Corinthians] Thus . . . do ye, man by man, become but
one choir. . . .

This sentiment is the forerunner of the claim, advanced today
by many a religious, government, and business institution, that
to do or say anything other than exactly what the institution
specifies is to be sacrilegious, unpatriotic, or other than a team
player, respectively. (As a bonus, Ignatius also took the trouble
to specify that Satan suffered from a "stench" problem, which
must have suggested to many an association between evil and
garbage.) The church went on to invest much energy in categorizing offenses, especially sexual ones, by their seriousness, enabling a uniform code of punishment for them that became
widely accepted in Ireland, England, Germany, and France in
the latter half of the first millennium. Oral sex between males
required up to twenty-two years' penance, for example — triple
the sentence assigned an impoverished woman who murdered
her infant. (Of course, the Kama Sutra also categorized sexual
acts, though its authors saw no need for the punishment part.)
Alexander Pope would later state the church's attitude toward
disorder more succinctly, "Order is Heaven's first law," as quoted
at the start of the chapter. A spine so badly twisted that it left
him standing four foot six was apparently not enough to inspire
Pope to wonder whether God is really all that big a stickler for
neatness.

Aversion to mess eventually began to wend its way into the
components of daily life. In the thirteenth century, the German
knight and minstrel Tannhäuser, who may be the first neat freak
of record, spelled out in verse what fertile territory lay before
order-minded reformers of the day:

A man of refinement should not slurp from the same spoon with somebody else. . . .

A number of people gnaw a bone and then put it back in the dish — this is a serious offense.

A man who clears his throat when he eats and one who blows his nose in the tablecloth are both ill-bred, I assure you.

If a man wipes his nose on his hand at table because he knows no better, then he is a fool, believe me.

It is not decent to poke your fingers into your ears or eyes, as some people do, or to pick your nose while eating. These three habits are bad.

Refrain from eating with both hands.

In the 1523 tract *Diversoria*, the Dutch theologian Desiderius Erasmus named several more table-side outrages, describing a German inn this way:

Some eighty or ninety people are sitting together, and it is stressed that they are not only common people but also rich men and nobles, men, women and children, all mixed together. And each is doing what he or she considers necessary. One washes his clothes and hangs the soaking articles on the stove. . . . Garlic smells and other bad odors rise. People spit everywhere. Someone is cleaning his boots on the table. . . . Everyone dips their bread into the general dish, bites the bread and dips it in again. The place is dirty, the wine bad. . . . Everyone is sweating and steaming and wiping themselves. . . . There are doubtless many among them who have some hidden disease.

Thus did Erasmus beat out *Seinfeld* by nearly five centuries in his condemnation of double dipping.

The fact that Tannhäuser and later Erasmus felt a need to rail about such habits suggests that they were prevalent and that meals were often occasion for happy and innocent nose-picking, soup-spoon sharing, and bone replacing. Perhaps if it weren't for those two visionaries of neatness, and of course for many others after them who gave voice to similar admonishments, meals would still be so today.

While religion was continually clamping down on messy thinking, science had a few things to say about order in the world as well. In Greece in the second century, Ptolemy put forth his model of the universe, with the Earth at its center, surrounded by nested, perfectly spherical shells in which were embedded the sun, moon, stars, and planets — the latter mounted on minispheres that added yet more motion to the contraption, needed to square it with observation. It was excruciatingly elaborate, highly ordered, and brooked no variation, making it just the sort of thing that a divine universe-builder would construct. Never mind that no amount of tweaking enabled the model to exactly match observation. What mattered was that the model was satisfying in its intelligent-designer feel, its uncompromising symmetry, and its seemingly biblical Earth-centricity. The church, not surprisingly, was distressed when, in the early seventeenth century, Galileo and others became too prominent in their support of the almost deplorably simple sun-centered model published by Copernicus in 1543, and modified in 1609 by the German astronomer Johannes Kepler.

But the church, as it turned out, had relatively little to fear, at least in terms of messiness, from the suddenly burgeoning scientific insights of the Renaissance. The new model of the solar system, when considered more carefully, seemed to hint not at a less carefully ordered universe but, rather, one that was even *more* ingenious in its construction. The world, it appeared, adhered to a series of immutable laws that, while subtle, could yet be cracked to show how all was divinely planned and organized. Instead of writing Latin tracts on the number of angels that could dance on the head of a pin, learned men could enlist a new tongue to tease out the heartbreakingly neat gear work of the universe. Or as Kepler put it, "The chief aim of all investigations of the external world should be to discover the rational order and harmony which has been imposed on it by God and which He revealed to us in the language of mathematics."

Isaac Newton unveiled in the late seventeenth century what seemed to be the bulk of these laws, revealing a perfectly regulated clockwork universe whose components were fashioned from matter, gravity, and light. Europe soon became obsessed with actual clockwork, as precision engineering made possible timepieces with second-per-week accuracy. Now mortals, whether dandified socializers, captains of commerce, or dour Puritans scornful of wasted time, could reliably enjoy the same sort of unfailing organization that characterized the doings of the divinely efficient cosmos itself. The sentiment even took hold across the ocean in some quarters of the nascent United States. "Lose no time; be always employed in something useful; cut off all unnecessary actions," advised Benjamin Franklin, an early advocate for the highly effective. Franklin practiced what he preached, assiduously avoiding, for example, the time-wasting habit of interacting with his wife and son for much of his life.

Taylor Made

Franklin aside, the United States in its early years held promise as a proud bastion of disorder. To some extent, it owed its independence to the sheer messiness of its ragtag, highly improvisational military efforts, which were nearly guerilla in comparison to the rigid formation fighting of the snazzily dressed British units. The fractious structure of the nation, as hacked out by a turbulent Continental Congress, seemed to invite mess, setting up as it did an endless tension between the three branches of the federal government and between the federal government and the states. The United States started off with a highly ordered, tightly regulated financial system architected by Alexander Hamilton, but Thomas Jefferson soon razed it, preferring to leave monetary control to the whims of the market rather than to the designs of large banks and regulators. As the industrial revolution took hold in Britain and then spread through Europe at the end of the eighteenth century, the United States, whose farms employed three out of four Americans, became determined to catch up. By the middle of the nineteenth century, the United States was leading the world in the invention of new machines. The rapidly increasing mechanization of labor and the rise of factories created pervasive new forms of mess. One was pollution, as factories proved well suited to spewing filth of every sort wherever it was convenient to do so. Another was traffic, caused by the pull of cities on what had been a primarily rurally situated population, and by the dense flow of raw materials and goods between companies. But in some ways, it was a third, more subtle form of factory-related mess that would ultimately prove the most frustrating and anxiety-producing, especially to Americans. The thriving, machine-driven economy made so many goods affordable that for the first time in history a significant percentage of the population could afford to have enough stuff to make finding a place for it all a challenge. Technology's growing sophistication would only continue to exacerbate the situation. According to a study conducted by the Gartner Group, Americans place 133,000 PCs in the trash every day.

As companies became more specialized and complex, they started striving to be more organized, and toward the end of the nineteenth century some people became expert in helping them do it. Library-book-categorization inventor Melvil Dewey — who had changed the spelling of his first name from the letter-wasting "Melville" with which his parents had saddled him — was a tireless promoter of efficiency tools ranging from shorthand to preprinted business forms. Edwin Seibels invented what we now know as the filing cabinet, complete with tabbed file folders to replace the awkward practice of organizing and storing documents by rolling them up and sticking them in pigeonholes in a desk or cabinet. Henry Gantt created a chart-based system for precisely scheduling a number of overlapping tasks. And Europe was not without its contributors to the growing order-mania in industry: Frenchman Henri Fayol codified the responsibilities of the manager, namely to plan, organize, command, coordinate, and control. But even these bold innovators were utterly eclipsed by the far more formidable figure of Frederick Taylor who, in the opening years of the twentieth century, conducted exhaustive studies of the way laborers went about their work at the Bethlehem Steel Company in Pittsburgh. The resulting 1911 book, *The Principles of Scientific Management*, would not only incite the business world once and for all to declare mess and disorder mortal enemies but would also indirectly do much the same for all of society.

Taylor, who at the age of twelve had started strapping himself into a harnesslike device of his own design at night in an effort to tame the nightmares that would plague him throughout his life, argued in his book that while industry had done a fair job of maximizing the efficiency of its machinery, it had neglected a weak link: the human worker, or as he put it, the "awkward, inefficient, or ill-directed movements of men." Just as Newton's laws of motion had seemingly provided a means to predict and thus in theory control the exact behavior of any physical system in any situation, so Taylor believed the seemingly messy process of human effort could be deconstructed and made orderly. By studying, measuring, and recording every element of every manual task with a stopwatch and a notebook, managers could calculate standardized procedures for every step that every worker must follow every time for maximum output. "The best management is a true science," Taylor wrote, "resting upon clearly defined laws, rules, and principles as a foundation. . . . It is only through enforced standardization of methods, enforced adoption of the best implements and working conditions, and enforced cooperation that this faster work can be assured." Presented with a straightforward and low-cost means for boosting productivity — that Taylor's methods quickly increased output were indisputable — U.S. industry and soon European companies as well threw themselves into "scientific management" practices that sought to stamp out variation and happenstance. In 1914, just three years after the publication of Taylor's book, sixty-nine thousand people showed up for a Taylorism-inspired "efficiency exposition" in New York's Grand Central Palace. Needless to say, Henry Ford's pioneering development of the assembly line, which enabled the cheap production of millions of identical items, owed much to Taylor.

The suggestion that Taylor's methods might find a place in child rearing was absurd enough to delight readers of the best-selling 1948 novel *Cheaper by the Dozen* — made into a hit movie in 1950 (and to which the more recent Steve Martin vehicle bears almost no resemblance) — in which the goofily rigid father of twelve children applies Taylor-style efficiencies to household tasks to comic effect. But many fans of the book and movie might be surprised to learn that it's not a fictional tale. The book was written by two of the children who were brought up in exactly this fashion, and there was little funny about it at the time. The father was Frank Gilbreth, a professional Taylor disciple who really did believe that forcing a detailed, pervasive, unbending standardization of behavior was as appropriate for his kids as it was for the laborers under his influence. Taylor trained the family via whistle and stopwatch to assemble within six seconds. The children were required to track their weight, homework, and chores via chart — only prayer was exempt — and had to bathe with a few quick strokes of soap while listening to French or German gramophone recordings. Conversation involving subjects other than math or current events was banned at the dinner table, and family meetings were governed by *Robert's Rules of Order.* The shorter girls dusted the lower half of the furniture, the taller girls the upper half. Eleven of the children were subjected to a mass tonsillectomy, which Gilbreth tried to film as a tool for speeding up surgeons. Gilbreth himself tried shaving with two razors at once but wounded himself so badly he reluctantly abandoned the effort. One of his sons would later recall that what bothered his father about the incident was not slashing his throat, but having to waste two minutes of his day stanching the bleeding.

Though Frank Gilbreth is the only person to become well

known for it, part of a generation of parents became caught up in the Taylorian efficiency craze — even though Sigmund Freud and others studying the new science of the unconscious were warning about the sorts of pathological compulsions that could stem from the overly rigid treatment of young children. And parents weren't the only ones outside the business world swept up by Taylorism. A group of Protestant churches in New York established a "church efficiency committee." *Engineering Magazine* reported on complaints of insufficiently rapid witness questioning at a criminal trial relating to an incident in which twenty people had been killed. Politicians sung efficiency's praises. Japan sent teams of experts to the United States and Europe to study modern, efficient practices and enthusiastically imported them; they later spread through much of Asia.

Strict Taylorism was ultimately discredited in the eyes of most experts in the late 1920s by a series of studies conducted at the Hawthorne plant of the Western Electric Company. These studies clearly demonstrated that worker output improved when *any* change was introduced to the work environment or processes. This sort of improvement, now known as the *Hawthorne effect*, is simply due to the fact that people tend to try harder when they know they're being observed. Worker output improved no more under a Taylor-style regimen than it did under clearly meaningless changes, such as lowering the lights or turning them up, so long as management was standing there to record the results. But while the wild enthusiasm for strict Taylorism faded, what never quite disappeared was a now-ingrained inclination to organize, schedule, arrange, and standardize at work, home, and everywhere else, as a means of squelching variation, improvisation, unpredictability, and anything that smacked of extraneousness.

Einstein's Theory of Mess

In 1905, a twenty-six-year-old Swiss patent clerk unknown to the science community submitted five papers to scientific journals for publication. One of them spelled out a so-called theory of relativity, setting our concept of space and time on its ear. A second introduced the equation $E = mc^2$, which would lead to the development of the atomic bomb and nuclear power. A third explained how light could behave more like a billiard ball than a wave, which paved the way for quantum mechanics, now the central theory of all of physics, and which, along with relativity, supplanted Newton's far less messy laws. Can you name the subject addressed by either of the other two papers? If not, don't feel bad. The editors of the *New York Times* apparently couldn't do any better, judging by the fact that they omitted them from a time line of Albert Einstein's contributions published to commemorate the hundredth anniversary of his "miracle year." Perhaps they and many others would be surprised to learn that according to a recent study, one of these two often-overlooked papers has actually proved more influential to science than the other, more famous, three. In fact, the study, which, per science-community convention, counted the number of times papers were cited by other scientists in their own published papers, reckoned this work to be the most influential paper in all of modern science.

The paper addressed the phenomenon known as *Brownian motion.* In 1827, the scientist Robert Brown peered at a drop of water through a microscope and saw that tiny grains of pollen in the drop seemed to be jerking around as if they were alive. For more than seventy-five years, this widely observed motion remained an utter mystery to science, and a conspicuous one. Einstein solved it. In the paper, he reasoned that if matter was made of molecules — bear in mind that as of 1905 there had never been any clear evidence that this was true — and if the molecules were randomly bouncing around as would be expected in a liquid, then once in a while, just by chance, more of these molecules would bounce into one side of a grain of pollen in the liquid than would bounce into the opposite side, causing the grain to lurch. Thus, over time the grain would be expected to jerk here and there, as excesses of molecules randomly hit the grain, first on one side and then on another. Einstein whipped up some tricky math to calculate what sorts of arrangements of molecules might provide the random hits needed to produce the observed pollen jerking and, in this way, gave the world its first look, if an indirect one, at the molecular structure of matter. (The fifth paper Einstein published in 1905 used a different approach to deduce the size of molecules.)

An explanation of dancing pollen probably doesn't strike you as the sort of thing that would climb to the top of the all-time science hit parade. The understanding of matter's structure was a revelation, but that by itself isn't what ended up making the paper so important. It has more to do with Einstein's insight that purely random activity on the part of many little things could produce striking and important behavior on the part of bigger ones. As it turns out, this sort of interesting randomness-fed behavior shows up almost everywhere scientists look. And the mathematical technique Einstein cobbled together to analyze the behavior, a technique now called *Brownian motion theory*, has proved so effective that a number of universities worldwide have entire departments whose members do little else but study new ways to apply Brownian motion theory and its offshoots to the world around us. This research, and still other approaches centered on randomness — which is often referred to by scientists as *fluctuations*, *noise*, and *stochastics* — has become critical to understanding how financial markets work, how the galaxies formed, how electronic devices function, how ecosystems thrive, and how genes work. More than a dozen Nobel Prizes have been awarded for randomness-related research. (*Friendly reminder*: None of this has anything to do with chaos theory. Chaotic systems aren't about randomness — they actually tend to be highly ordered.) In fact, randomness is thoroughly inescapable in nature, if for no other reason than the fact that quantum mechanics holds that every elementary particle in the universe is subject to deeply random behavior at every instant in time. The very birth of the universe itself is thought by physicists to have been a *quantum fluctuation*, a sort of random hiccup in reality.

Over the past decade, the respect accorded randomness by scientists has climbed to an entirely new level, thanks to a once-obscure phenomenon known as *stochastic resonance*. In a nutshell, stochastic resonance applies to a paradoxical-sounding situation in which adding some sort of randomness to a system makes it more effective — as if the more static you picked up on a radio station, the more clearly you heard the music. (Which isn't far from the truth.) Though the phenomenon was first proposed in the early 1980s, it wasn't until the early 1990s that scientists began to recognize how frequently it turns up in nature, in everything from climate changes to evolution. Now there are tens of thousands of papers published every year on stochastic resonance and its applications. A number of them focus on a particular system that many believe to be especially reliant on the phenomenon as a critical element of its functioning: the brain.

In other words, as managers, homemakers, and just about everyone else were becoming increasingly determined throughout much of the twentieth century to bring more order to every facet of their lives and environments, an enormous body of evidence was accumulating in the scientific community to support the claim that not only is disorder integral to the fabric of nature, but adding more of it can sometimes *improve* things.

What Is Mess? (Redux)

Chapter 1 laid out a simple, intuitive notion of what mess is. Now it's time to spell out a few things.

Mess Isn't Necessarily an Absence of Order Often a system is messy to some extent because of the lack of one specific type of order, even though other forms of order are present in abundance. Thus, a room might be uncluttered but noisy, with people running in and out of it. What's more, mess often arises from a *failed* order rather than from an absence of order. You could fill a room with all sorts of neat bins and cabinets for storing things, but if the bins and cabinets overflow, you've got a mess. Most messes encountered in daily life are failed orders — someone had an organizing scheme in mind, but for one reason or another it didn't work.

The Types of Mess

Clutter: Elements scatter out, often prolifically, from normally accepted positions.

Mixture: Elements are randomly ordered or otherwise atypically combined within normally accepted positions.

Time sprawl: Tasks and events are scheduled loosely or not at all or are left somewhat unprioritized; or intended priorities are ignored, as in the case of procrastination.

Improvisation: Processes, tasks, and events aren't predetermined.

Inconsistency: Processes and procedures change frequently. If the changes are arbitrary, they tend to lead to greater levels of mess, but reasoned changes can still be quite messy.

Blur: Categorization schemes are kept loose, are often ignored, or both. Any degree of vagueness might contribute to blur, though vagueness could just as well fit into the category of *convolution* (below).

Noise: Processes and information are exposed to a possibly disruptive, but not necessarily random, outside influence.

Distraction: Focus wanders between different elements.

Bounce: Activity levels are higher than is strictly necessary and customary and tend to be unpredictable.

Convolution: Organizational schemes are eccentric and opaque, as when they are dependent on intuition or are in some way illogical.

Inclusion: Relatively few filters are in effect to restrict the number and type of entities in the system; or a particular filter is absent, allowing in an entity normally excluded.

Distortion: An entity is misaligned, bent, stretched, broken, decayed, displaced, marred, or otherwise presents in other-than-standard condition.

These descriptions also imply corresponding descriptions of types of neatness and order. Specifically:

Arrangement	Categorization
Homogeneity	Insulation
Scheduling	Focus
Planfulness	Stillness
Consistency	Clarification
Purging	Preservation

The Width, Depth, and Intensity of Mess A mess is *wide* if it involves multiple groups or layers, as for example several rooms in a house or different departments in a company. A mess is *deep* if many entities in a single group or layer are involved in the mess, as for example a month's worth of laundry scattered across a single room. A mess is *intense* if, for a given number of entities, the level of disorder is especially high or potentially painful, as for example if a driver in Las Vegas takes a few wrong turns and ends up lost thirty miles out in the middle of the desert.

The Scale of Mess The type, width, depth, and intensity of mess can all vary in a single system at a given time, depending on the scale at which you consider the system. Thus, a neighborhood of filth-caked, misaligned buildings and cars parked helter-skelter might appear messy, but the apartments inside each building might be pristine.

Having a little historical context and a broader understanding of the nature of mess will come in handy as we explore some of the surprising roles that mess can play in our lives and in the workings of the world — and why disorder is not always the villain it's been made out to be. In fact, sometimes a *lack* of disorder can be dysfunctional. Remember the two decks of cards from chapter 1? As it turned out, you could find four random cards much more quickly in a shuffled deck once you properly accounted for the time it took to order the other deck. But here's another point to consider about an ordered deck of cards: What's it good for? Of all the things in all the world that are done with decks of cards, few require an ordered deck of cards. The first thing you do with an ordered deck of cards is *shuffle* them. It's not just that disordered decks require less work to maintain; they're much more useful. The usefulness of mess isn't so rare a thing as you might think, as we're about to see.

CHAPTER FOUR

The Benefits of Mess

When Arnold Schwarzenegger started posturing about running for governor of California, his office was besieged by calls from a range of politicians, activists, and power brokers who wanted to get on his schedule. All were told something they had trouble believing: Schwarzenegger didn't have a schedule. He refused to make appointments except in unusual circumstances and always had. He lives what he calls "an improvisational lifestyle." It didn't mean you couldn't get to see him; it meant that you called him up, and he was either free to meet with you just then or you called back another time. If he did meet with you, it might be for five minutes or five hours — he'd see how it went.

The public tends to see Schwarzenegger as a nattily dressed, highly disciplined, controlling man who appears to have carefully planned every moment in his increasingly influential life — and he encourages that view. But Schwarzenegger is a master at looking neat while keeping major aspects of his life steeped in mess. Planfulness and consistency have attained the status of commandments among most of those who aspire to professional success, and yet Schwarzenegger has overachieved through improvisation and inconsistency. Not everyone admires him, but it's hard to argue that he's not highly effective.

Schwarzenegger's predilection for winging it goes back to his early bodybuilding career. When other weight lifters were focusing on set regimens of exercises that often left them plateauing short of their seam-splitting goals, Schwarzenegger pioneered an approach that called for constantly shaking up routines with random variation. The same philosophy that successfully swelled his pecs and lats has also helped swell his box-office draw, wallet, and political prospects. Schwarzenegger is a study in unpredictable, contradictory behavior. He's a movie star/politician/entrepreneur/athlete; a sometimes brutish right-winger who married a Kennedy; a professed admirer of Hitler's speeches and close friend of alleged Nazi war criminal Kurt Waldheim who has won two awards from the Simon Wiesenthal Center for support of its Holocaust studies; a blood-and-guts film star who has embraced comic roles; a self-confessed extreme party animal who has donated countless hours establishing fitness programs at inner-city schools; and now a populist governor who plays to the cameras and crowds while boasting of cutting back-room deals in his cigar-smoke-filled office-tent. Hardly the résumé of a man sticking to a plan. Schwarzenegger has certainly maintained long-term goals of attaining celebrity and power, but these goals are far too vague to be considered an organizational scheme.

Schwarzenegger's messy formula for success has been highlighted by his short but spectacular political career. He went back and forth on deciding to run for governor, finally announcing his candidacy at the last minute. He held off until well into the race before formulating a platform, then came up with one that was a messy hodgepodge of incompatible-seeming principles and allegiances, leaving him a fiscally conservative Republican who offers qualified support for gay unions, abortion rights, gun control, and offshore oil-drilling bans. As governor, he has signed bills to protect animal rights and vetoed bills to raise the minimum wage. There has been considerable talk of a constitutional amendment that would let the foreign-born Schwarzenegger run for president, but even the possibility of a shot at the presidency doesn't seem to have focused Schwarzenegger's ambitions. Since becoming governor, he has already appeared in one film and has entered negotiations to appear in *Terminator 4*.

By blending several types of mess — the time sprawl of not keeping a schedule, the improvisation in his commitments, the blurring of political and social boundaries, the inconsistency in his stances, the distraction in jumping between careers — Schwarzenegger has essentially fashioned himself as an easily customizable and recustomizable figure. He has managed to maintain a malleable public persona and a nimble agenda that's easily adjusted to take advantage of unexpected opportunities and fast-changing, unpredictable situations. His refusal to lock himself into a worldview or set of easily categorized allegiances enables him to tailor each new stance to suit his needs. Almost anyone can find a way to feel in step with at least some aspect of Schwarzenegger's eclectic, action-hero-garnished mix of views. In short, Schwarzenegger's disordered approach to his professional life provides an excellent example of a major benefit of mess: flexibility.

Flexibility: Messy systems adapt and change more quickly, more dramatically, in a wider variety of ways, and with less effort. Neat systems tend to be more rigid and slower to respond to changing demands, unexpected events, and new information.

Flexibility can emerge from any of the twelve different types of mess we discussed in the last chapter: clutter, mixture, time sprawl, improvisation, inconsistency, blur, noise, distraction, bounce, convolution, inclusion, and distortion. A few more examples:

- Improvisation enables a group of jazz musicians to shift at any moment to address an audience's response to the music, while a symphony orchestra is tied to the music as written. (Though not always as tightly as you might think, as we'll see in chapter 13.)
- The blur of an organizational chart that doesn't pin down employees into tightly defined specialties and responsibilities makes it easier to reconfigure resources around new challenges.
- Good boxers keep bouncing around randomly between blows, not only making themselves harder to hit but also enabling them to create openings in their opponents' defenses.

Messy people and organizations behave differently than neat ones — a difference that can provide advantages. A system that's neat and orderly has to keep struggling to fight off randomness, and when randomness inevitably leaks in, the system is thrown off. Being open to a certain level of randomness, on the other hand, allows it to work in your favor. Specifically, messiness can confer six key benefits: flexibility, completeness, resonance, invention, efficiency, and robustness. We've considered flexibility; let's look at some case studies that illustrate how the other five benefits of mess can emerge in practice.

Completeness: Awash in Useful Mess

People and organizations often embrace a bevy of filters and neatening schemes that they think renders a random, dense, cluttered world easier to deal with. But sometimes these schemes do more harm than good. It's an idea that seems to have occurred, if at a purely intuitive level, to Harvey Katz in 1953, a few months after he returned from the Korean War. Katz is a big man, blunt and boisterous, and unafraid of competition. Good thing, because he had just opened up a hardware store in the small Boston suburb of Needham, and from his front window he could see seven other hardware stores in and around the town square. Hunting for an edge, Harvey noticed how many customers came by seeking odd items that none of the hardware stores in town, including his own, ever bothered to carry. Replacement handles for adzes, size 0-5 screws, eighteen-volt flashlight bulbs — no one could justify carrying items that might ring up a couple of sales a year. But on those rare occasions when Harvey did happen to have an item that the other stores in town didn't, customers seemed especially grateful. More important, Harvey, who has a flawless memory when it comes to who buys what, noticed that those customers usually came back. A new strategy was forged: stock it all. It was an idea that flies in the face not just of fundamental economic theory but also of lemonade-stand-level business know-how. Who in their right mind would set out to clog a business with a glut of slow-moving inventory?

Harvey's Hardware today looks quite neat on the outside.

It's adorned with a large wooden sign with gilded, hand-carved-looking letters — a sign that would be at home on a three-star restaurant or an artisan's shop. But step inside, and you might think you've stumbled into a basement stockroom. Every square inch of shelf and wall space and the vast majority of floor space — even the ceiling — is crammed with a riotous mélange of wares, all of it jammed together, some of it so old the packaging is discolored. The aisles are narrow and asymmetrical and indistinguishably lined with tall, dense, unbroken shelving. What little space there is to walk through is made into an obstacle course by various wares stacked in unlabeled piles. The lighting is on the dim side. There are no aisle placards or any other store navigational aids, nor does any logical scheme of organization suggest itself. There is a prominent staircase leading to a lower floor but no hint of what might be down there, nor in an additional room that branches off on one side.

For all this mess, Harvey's, which is no larger than a typical small-town hardware store, sells more than $2.5 million worth of hardware each year, compared with a little more than $900,000 for the average U.S. hardware store, according to the National Retail Hardware Association. People drive an hour or more to shop there, passing Home Depots and a dozen conventional hardware stores along the way. And Harvey's doesn't discount anything.

Harvey's still adheres to the everything-under-the-sun philosophy. People with stubborn hard-water stains in their washing machines can always count on Harvey's for a tube of Rover rust remover. Among the dense clutter can be found odd-size halogen bulbs and jumbo S hooks that clerks at other stores will swear don't even exist. Manufacturers' reps sometimes show up at the store armed with "planograms" that map out the most efficient and effective way to display their merchandise, but they end up walking away, shaking their heads, when they see that Harvey's allots approximately half the minimum space per item that they need to work with. According to Harvey, the jammed-up feeling communicates the scope of the inventory and creates an ambience compatible with a hardware-buying frenzy. It must: Harvey's packs in $113 worth of inventory per square foot, more than three times the average for hardware stores. Sales per square foot are $503, close to four times the average. In other words, not only does Harvey benefit from needing less space than others to offer an enormous selection of goods, but the goods apparently fly off the shelves faster because of it. The average customer purchase is nearly 50 percent larger than at other hardware stores, probably in part because when you shop for something at Harvey's, you can't help running across several novel items you didn't know you needed.

A lot of inventory sits around for years unsold, but Harvey's has turned the willingness to let quantities of merchandise gather dust into an advantage. For example, the store keeps part of its warehouse space filled with items needed for weather emergencies: pumps and hoses for rainstorms, shovels and ice melt for snow, and so forth. Those reserve inventories are never used to fill floor stock; they're left untouched and ready for mobilization should a crisis arise. When heavy rains bring flooding once every few years, cleaning sump pumps off the shelves of every other store in eastern Massachusetts, the line of people waiting for pumps at Harvey's snakes through every aisle in the store. Every customer gets one.

How do customers deal with the disorder they confront in the store? The fact is, you weren't intended to make your own way through Harvey's. Staff members are trained to greet customers who walk through the door, or any customer who pauses in an aisle, with an offer to help them find what they're looking

for and to provide home-repair advice. Other hardware stores —
indeed, retailers in general — have become as neatly organized
as Web sites, clearly annotating themselves throughout with
aisle signs and shelf labels and brightly signed displays that
allow customers to self-serve efficiently, and enabling businesses to keep a minimum of staff on hand, mostly to make sure
everything stays neat and organized. But neat stores can't be
densely packed with inventory, so selection is limited, and good
luck to customers who need assistance. Though labor costs at
Harvey's are higher than average, the store's outsized revenues
drown out those costs. Annual sales per full-time employee at
the average U.S. hardware store are $102,000. At Harvey's, they
come out to $228,000. Of course, messiness can also lead to
lower-than-usual labor costs, as with the Manhattan magazine
store that profited simply by doing less organizing than its competitor. But Harvey's is more concerned with the *space* cost of
neatness than the *labor* cost of neatness — and additionally benefits from the appeal of its mess.

The staff at Harvey's is so adept at keeping the mess under
control that when the store finally computerized seven years
ago with a system designed for hardware shops, Harvey and his
employees found they couldn't use three-quarters of the features built into the software. Why have a computer tell you
when to reorder duct tape when an employee will tell you when
you're down to your last few rolls after grabbing one for a
customer? Some inventory and ordering information is still
scattered throughout the store in various paper files whose locations are known only to Harvey, but the store is never out of
stock of anything. (Though things can get a little sticky when
Harvey is on vacation.) By casting aside the typical filtering and
neatening schemes and tolerating a high level of mess, Harvey's

has provided generations of grateful customers a form of completeness, in inventory and service, they can't find elsewhere.

And what of those seven other, neater stores? Harvey's drove them out of business, one by one.

Completeness: Messy systems can comfortably tolerate an exhaustive array of diverse entities. Neat systems tend to whittle away at the quantity and diversity of elements, eliminating some that would have proved useful or even critical.

Completeness is usually a direct benefit of messiness in the form of inclusiveness — a resistance to the conventional process of paring down things for efficiency's sake. Two other examples of how inclusiveness can pay off:

• Restaurants and food distributors around the world know that when it comes to seafood, almost any chef's or consumer's need can be addressed at Tokyo's Tsukiji fish market, a vast, sprawling conglomeration of small booths, tanks, and buckets from which three thousand tons of more than 450 different types of marine life are sold every day.

• It's common knowledge that Thomas Edison experimented exhaustively before hitting on a form of tungsten as an ideal filament for the lightbulb. But few realize how indiscriminate Edison was in trying out other materials. In fact, he spent years of his life trying to get a long-lasting glow out of almost every substance he could get his hands on, without worrying much about why some substances might be more likely to work than others. The list included not only every type of metal he could wrestle into filament form but also tar, hair, soot, lime, paper, and some six thousand forms of flora, including cotton, coconut shell, cork, and bamboo. If it sounds as if Edison may have cast his net ridiculously wide, bear in mind that Edison's initial success came not with tungsten bulbs but with commercial bulbs containing filaments of cotton, bamboo, and paper.

Resonance: In Tune with the External

The world around us is messy. Inevitably, then, when we set up ourselves and our systems to be neat and orderly, we're creating a sort of barrier, with high randomness on the outside and low randomness on the inside. But while the barrier may succeed in keeping out mess, it can also cut us off from the very aspects of the outside world that are critical to our success. A good example lies a block northeast of London's bustling Paddington Station, where squats the sooty, sprawling complex of aged, halfheartedly ornate but not entirely graceless buildings that make up St. Mary's Hospital. Tucked just inside the hospital's courtyard, far from the main entrance, is a small doorway that leads to a narrow spiral staircase carrying a thin stream of harried hospital staff and resigned patients. Few make it as far as the fourth floor, where a translucent-windowed door leads to a small room that in turn leads into a cramped office overlooking the havoc on Praed Street below. What light makes it through the window grime reveals that the crowded office appears to function as a laboratory. A sort of desk-cum-lab-bench running along the wall under the windows offers a variety of surfaces and bins, all of it occupied haphazardly by teetering piles of petri dishes, test tubes lying helter-skelter on their sides, cigarettes, open books, pages of notes, newspapers, and a variety of odd implements and containers.

You might guess the lab's occupant has just stepped out, but in fact he did so three-quarters of a century ago. This is Alexander Fleming's bacteriological lab — reconstructed from photographs and preserved as a sort of museum — just as he left it when he went on vacation in late August 1928. When he returned on September 3, he was sorting through the clutter when he noticed that a small, ragged circle of mold had invaded one of the petri dish bacterial cultures. The staphylococci in the culture seemed to steer clear of the mold, describing a sort of bacteria-free moat. Intrigued, Fleming dragged the dish under a microscope and discovered penicillin.

Fleming probably routinely benefited from the messiness of his lab simply by virtue of the fact that not being neat saved time that he was able to put to better use. But far more important is that if Fleming hadn't been messy, he probably wouldn't have discovered penicillin. Disorder created connections — that is, *resonance* — between the lab and the world around it, as well as between the lab work and Fleming himself. If Fleming hadn't left open petri dishes scattered by an open window before going on vacation, the mold that drifted in — possibly from an allergy lab downstairs — most likely wouldn't have. What's more, mess preserved and highlighted the unexpected development. Even if exposed to mold, a petri dish that had been neatly stored in a rack with many others might not have been noticed before it was cleaned. On the disordered desk, the contaminated dish with its antibacterial circular swath ended up sitting under Fleming's nose. (And speaking of useful mess under Fleming's nose, his only previous major contribution to science was the discovery of *lysozyme*, a mildly antibiotic substance found in various bodily fluids, which Fleming had found after sneezing on a bacterial sample.) Of the role that mess played in his discovery, Fleming himself had little doubt. Years later, as a group of scientists took Fleming on a tour of their spotless and well-organized lab, one of them wondered out loud what sort of amazing discoveries Fleming might have made in this sort of facility. "Not penicillin," replied Fleming.

> *Resonance:* Mess tends to help a system fall into harmony with its environment and with otherwise elusive sources of information and change, deriving useful influence from them. Neatness tends to insulate a system from and remain at odds with such influences.

Other forms of mess that can produce resonance:

• Noise, in the general sense of external random disturbances, is the type of mess most closely associated with resonance. Few people, for example, appreciated the fact that engine noise is a safety feature in cars until drivers of ultraquiet electric cars realized that pedestrians and bicyclists were sometimes slow to get out of the way because they didn't hear the cars coming, a problem exacerbated by antilock brakes, which have nearly eliminated the warning sound of skidding tires.

• Improvisation can lead to resonance, too, as can be verified by any out-of-town visitor who has learned that the best way to connect with a city's character and charms is to wander around, rather than hitting the standard tourist traps.

• Resonance can even come from time sprawl: enemy troops can time movements to fall between the easily predicted passes of overhead reconnaissance satellites, so the Pentagon knows to occasionally task distant satellites to provide random peeks at the action for a more reliable sense of what's going on.

Invention: Creative Disorder

Anyone who has ever sat down in front of a blank sheet of paper and tried to force creativity knows that inspiration doesn't usually happen that way. Rather, it tends to spring unexpected from novel connections, and novel connections, in turn, often go hand-in-hand with mess. That proved true when the Case Western Reserve University business school wanted a new marquee building for 2002. School decision makers found themselves drawn to architect Frank Gehry's controversial but widely acclaimed style.

Designs such as the titanium-clad Guggenheim Museum in Bilbao, Spain, and the Dr.-Seussish Ray and Maria Stata Center at the Massachusetts Institute of Technology blend swooping and jutting fun-house-mirror elements into imposing forms that imbue interior spaces with complex personalities and rarely fail to elicit emotional responses from observers. Case Western hoped for its own attention-grabbing design, and Gehry and his associates didn't disappoint, ultimately unveiling a scale model of a building of wildly askew components seemingly caught in midexplosion, all of it wrapped and pierced by a river of writhing metal ribbon.

The school approved the design and brought in a small army of contractors to build it. The contractors duly admired, in a shocked and fretful way, the model of the God-awfully complex structure they were about to undertake, and then asked for the blueprints, to which Gehry's team replied that there weren't any. The contractors thought the group was joking, but Gehry and his associates assured the contractors they were serious. But constructing a building without blueprints, the stunned contractors might well have sputtered, would be like trying to put together a television set from scratch without a wiring diagram. Gehry's group maintained that the contractors could derive the measurements they needed by studying the model of the building. The contractors rejoined that doing so wouldn't result in a precisely scaled-up copy of the model — they'd have to work as much with impression as measurement. Exactly, said Gehry.

As it turns out, Gehry is concerned not with the precise angles or dimensions of a building, but with the emotional impression it instills in observers and inhabitants. The ability to convey this impression is elusive and fragile, he maintains, and can easily be lost in the neat, unambiguous precision of a two-dimensional drawing. Gehry partner Jim Glymph puts it this way: "When you break it into two-dimensional sections, everything can seem so close to the model. But when you put it all back together, you might lose a subtle curvature that you would think would make no difference — and without it the building is completely dead."

To capture the building's intended emotional content, Gehry maintains, everyone working on the building should keep creating throughout the construction process. Withholding blueprints is a way of making sure that happens. Forgoing a detailed plan is disruptive — it creates convolution, making a neat and well-defined process messy. It subverts the contractors' familiar methods and procedures, forcing them to work with the Gehry team in the task of translating the look and feel of the model into a full-scale structure. Sure enough, the shocked Case

Western contractors, fearing a disaster, staked out Gehry's offices to try to determine how to proceed. "I had never, ever, spent more than an hour in an architect's office prior to this job," says Ed Sellers, chief operating officer at Cleveland-based GQ Contracting. "I made twenty-two trips on this job, spending four and five days at a time in their office. Because we didn't have documents that completed the design, we found ourselves completing the design."

Freed from the constraints of a blueprint's rigid specifications and standard operating procedures, the contractors and architects were able to collaboratively rethink the design and construction techniques in any way necessary to achieve the project's goals. That led to an eruption of innovation. GQ ultimately developed a new technique for framing curving interior walls with unconventional materials, a breakthrough that met the challenges of the Case Western building and later led to a highly profitable new line of business. Hunt Construction in Indianapolis created a new approach to surveying construction sites; Columbia Wire and Iron Works in Portland, Oregon, came up with a machine to double-bend steel beams; New York–based DeSimon Structural Engineers developed two new framing methods for structural steel; A. Zahner Company in Kansas City, Missouri, invented a new way to assemble metal panels. Not only was the finished building a stunning hit, completed on time and within budget, but most of the contractors were so pleased with the invention into which they had been pushed that they ended up changing the way they do business. Even in the highly conservative construction industry, not all surprises have to be nasty ones.

Invention: Mess randomly juxtaposes and alters a system's elements and rotates them to the fore where they're more easily noticed, leading to new solutions. Neatness tends to limit novelty and the unexpected and sweeps them aside when they do occur.

Other examples of mess-driven invention:

- Many celebrated chefs prefer to work amid a dense spread of ingredients and tools to facilitate their experimenting with new food combinations and techniques.
- Distraction can help, too. Most of us have experienced the surprise thrill of coming up with a solution to a conundrum only after taking our minds off the problem.

Efficiency: A Messy Route to the Target

In the finger-pointing over U.S. setbacks and frustrations in the war on terror — be it the failure to prevent the 9/11 attacks, the inability to round up al-Qaeda's chiefs, or the difficulties in reestablishing order in Iraq — most of the criticism has centered around a lack of sufficient organization on the part of U.S. government agencies and the military. There weren't enough security procedures at airports; intelligence and law-enforcement agencies weren't tightly coordinated; the military didn't undertake enough planning for postwar Iraq; and so forth. But another way to look at the problem is to recognize that the terrorist enemies of the United States have been difficult to contend with because they are a mess. By leveraging their disorder, a relatively small number of terrorists, with few resources to draw on, have consistently confounded the most heavily equipped and highly ordered military and intelligence forces in history. Mess, in other words, has provided terrorists with efficiency.

Consider al-Qaeda. Its membership is scattered about the world, often mixed into the population. Its actions are unpredictable and inconsistent. Unlike traditional terrorist organizations, al-Qaeda isn't neatly organized into cells or set groups of people who work together and coordinate with other cells. In fact, it may not even be appropriate to call al-Qaeda an organization at all; it has at times been referred to by experts as more of a movement or even a philosophy. It springs up here and disappears there, constantly pulling in new members. Because its adherents don't bother to emplace hierarchy, standards, or even much communication, it tends to do governments little good to capture a few of them. Al-Qaeda members typically lack knowledge about the existence of other members, let alone what they're up to, and have no means to contact them. Al-Qaeda has no single enemy or set of targets and no single plan of attack, so no country can be sure if it is likely to be hit, or if so, when or how. All this has made al-Qaeda a nightmare for experts who simply wish to know what they're up against. "Since so little about al-Qaeda's organization is fixed, counterterrorism analysts and strategists have to be ready to adapt their views to shifting realities and prospects," notes David Ronfeldt, a senior social scientist at national-security think tank Rand Corporation. Much the same is true of the insurgency in Iraq.

As effective as disorder has been for terrorists, the highly ordered approach to defense by the United States has often proved unproductive or worse. The military can dispatch tightly coordinated battalions of soldiers equipped with state-of-the-art weapons, and patrol the skies with missile-equipped drones, but whom do they fire at? Tens of thousands of analysts pore over wiretap transcripts, airline passenger lists, and financial records, but few trails materialize. Meanwhile, a convoy of army trucks is a sitting duck for so-called improvised explosive devices, and even the Pentagon — the very building that houses many of those analysts — becomes a reachable target. A report from the National Consortium for the Study of Terrorism and Responses to Terrorism, funded by the U.S. Department of Homeland Security, found that existing counterterrorism efforts "show no evidence of reducing terrorism and may even increase the likelihood of terrorism and terrorism-related harm." *The 9/11 Commission Report* echoes that sentiment in sections, suggesting that U.S. interventions in Iraq and Afghanistan may well ultimately have the effect of turning those countries into "breeding grounds for attacks against Americans at home." And yet the focus of new U.S. antiterrorism efforts tends to be on establishing ever-higher levels of order. The Federal Bureau of Investigation, the Central Intelligence Agency, and the National Security Agency are undergoing near-constant reorganization, and the U.S. military is spending some $100 billion on the Future Combat Systems project, focused on setting up sensor networks and communication links for better command and control.

It's true, the United States itself isn't in a position to become highly messy in its battle against terrorism. The nation can't disperse its military to hide among the population or dismantle the ordered infrastructure of civilian life that presents so many vulnerable targets. Nor can it drop the commitment to democracy and humane behavior that prevents running roughshod over vast numbers of innocent civilians in order to get at a small number of terrorists. But merely recognizing that the enemy's disorder is its greatest strength — rather than obsessing over an imagined lack of order on the part of the United States — might go a long way to suggesting some new strategies.

For example, some experts have recommended trying to pass on bewildering amounts of false information to known terrorists rather than capturing and interrogating them; because the terrorist networks are so loose, there would be no good way for the terrorists to stop it or even monitor its flow. Others have advocated focusing on midlevel terrorists rather than terrorist leaders, because studies show that in a disordered network it is often the nodes in the middle that carry the greatest workload and whose sudden absence is most disruptive. Instead of concentrating on efforts to painstakingly filter and analyze the millions of pieces of near-random information that intelligence agencies gather about everything from air travel to bank deposits — the FBI alone has already scrapped three different computer systems that have failed to prove useful in its antiterrorism efforts — the intelligence and law enforcement communities could turn to computer programs designed to continually pore over vast, unrelated streams of data to pull out possible connections. And rather than trying to prevent every possible attack, the United States could do a better job of preparing its troops and civilians to survive attacks. Thicker armor on vehicles and torsos can sometimes do a lot more good than networks of sensors. Likewise, high-tech security expert Bruce Schneier has pointed out that the only effective antiterrorism security features that have emerged for air travel have been stronger cockpit doors and passengers more prepared to fight back. Mess isn't an invincible weapon, but it's one that needs to be appreciated to be countered.

Efficiency: Messy systems often accomplish goals with a modest consumption of resources and can sometimes shift some of the burden of work to the outside world. Being neat requires a constant expenditure of resources and tends to leave the burden of work trapped in the system.

Other examples of how mess can produce efficiency:

• The leader of a search-and-rescue operation must sometimes consider whether it will be more effective to organize a careful, methodical search or to simply scatter whatever people are at hand to begin searching immediately and even frantically. The latter approach can be especially appropriate when seconds count, as in the abduction of a child or when someone is missing in the water by a beach.

• Inconsistency often pays off for competitive runners, many of whom achieve maximum aerobic efficiency by adopting a highly varied conditioning regimen, continually altering the speed, length, difficulty, and frequency of their running routines.

Robustness: Well-Rounded Strength

Messiness is often taken as a sign of weakness. In a person, it's regarded as a character flaw. And most companies would be quick to assume that the less tightly organized a competitor is, the more vulnerable it is. But in fact, disorder can confer certain kinds of strength — a phenomenon that a private early-childhood school called the Little Red Wagon has used to its advantage. Not that you'd see any disorder if you walked into the school on opening day. What you'd be likely to notice is that the walls of the two large classrooms are almost entirely bare. It's a strangely disconcerting sight, one that might lead a visiting parent to infer a poverty of imagination or energy on the teachers' parts and fear for the level of stimulation and good cheer in the classrooms. But Gail Leftin, the founder and director of the school, is used to addressing such anxieties. "When you put up a poster with the alphabet, you're telling the children several things," she says. "That they're supposed to learn the letters. That they're supposed to learn them in this order. That the apple in 'A is for Apple' is a *red* apple, so that I guess apples are supposed to be red. But what you're not telling them is *'why.'* Why do they have to learn the ABCs? Why should they color apples red?"

It's not that children shouldn't learn and do these things, she explains. Leftin questions whether they should learn it just because a piece of paper on a wall or even a teacher says so. "When children learn from a poster, or from a teacher's lesson, then what they're really learning is how to follow directions and remember facts that are handed to them," she says. The overriding operating principle of the Little Red Wagon, as it turns out, is to provide as little prepackaged learning to the children as possible. There is no set curriculum. There are no carefully planned-out projects. There is no prewritten play that they will put on for parents. The children will develop it all themselves as they go along in a sort of festival of creative mess.

The basic idea at the Little Red Wagon is that groups of children are provided with a variety of simple materials — Leftin keeps basketfuls of corks, clay, colored sand, and feathers on hand, as well as conventional toys like dolls, cars, and blocks — and little direction in terms of what to do with them. Sometimes a teacher will read the group a story to suggest a particular theme, such as the jungle, space travel, or dinosaurs, though no effort is made to get the children to adhere to the theme when the story is over. When they start playing, the teacher sits with them and observes, sometimes asking a child to explain what she is doing, answering questions, providing crafts-related technical help (such as suggesting a way to fix a piece of yarn to a cork), taking notes about what the children are doing and saying, and occasionally taking a snapshot with a digital camera.

The teachers are usually surprised by what the children do. Still, as each child sees what the others are up to, the projects usually end up converging on a loose theme. A group that was gluing circles on paper, for example, started to focus on eyeglasses, which led to an exploration of seeing, and finally centered on how the body works. One boy started pounding on a doll with a block; instead of admonishing him, a teacher expressed interest, and the boy explained he needed an injured patient on which to practice medicine. Soon half the class was involved in running a hospital.

Although the Little Red Wagon teachers don't "teach" in a conventional sense, neither are they passive observers. They're trained to look for opportunities to interject questions that might naturally lead to learning of numbers and phonics and other standard concepts. When a teacher points out that a child has three squares in her picture, she is prompting the group to think about counting. When two children finish building a tower together, a teacher might suggest they help her write a "Please don't touch" label to preserve it. Because this sort of learning is attached to material that the children have gravitated to on their own, they tend to be more interested in it and understand it in a useful context. They're more likely to remember lessons imparted this way, too; it's like the difference between trying to memorize the driving directions someone dictates to you and having a route burned into your brain by finding it on your own.

Leftin notes that in conventional schools teachers have to waste much of their time and energy on getting students to focus on the rigidly structured activity or lesson. She tells the story of being invited to speak about her program to teachers and administrators at a larger school. When one teacher asked how Little Red Wagon's teachers deal with discipline problems, Leftin told the stunned group that she couldn't answer the question, because her school had never had one. Discipline problems typically arise when children become bored or frustrated, as often happens with preplanned lessons or activities. At Leftin's school, every child is always interested in what he is doing, because he chooses to do it. That leaves the teachers free to help the children get the most out of their activities, instead of having to keep them in line.

As for the blank walls, they quickly become filled with the children's work and with snapshots of individual children in midproject, captioned with quotes from the teachers' notes. "The walls become a way of documenting the learning journey for kids and parents," says Leftin. "The walls are our curriculum. We just don't know what it is until they're filled."

The Little Red Wagon's disordered, curriculumless approach seems especially risky at a time when states have rushed into standardized testing for elementary school students, leading to more sharply defined, rigid curricula as early as kindergarten. But Leftin has tracked Little Red Wagon graduates and found they generally score well above average on standardized testing in early grade school. Still, the real advantage to the Little Red Wagon approach, she says, is the creativity, confidence, and boldness that it imparts — the school's messy approach to education instills an intellectual robustness that holds up in any classroom or testing situation. Children who are exposed to more focused curricula specifically geared toward testing, in contrast, often have difficulties with creative exercises and even with any new curriculum. "The children here feel very rewarded for experimenting and creating," she says. "That stays with them and helps them when they encounter rigid curricula later on."

Parents seem to agree. While most private early-childhood schools in the area have had to market aggressively, Leftin now fills her school to its capacity almost entirely through word of mouth and ends up having to turn away students. As the Little Red Wagon's reputation has grown, more schools have approached Leftin with requests to explain her techniques. Everyone seems to agree that our schools need improving, but not many people would have thought that mess was a missing ingredient.

Robustness: Because mess tends to loosely weave together disparate elements, messy systems are more resistant to destruction, failure, and imitation. Neat systems tend to have more sharply defined strong and weak points, and thus are often brittle, easily foiled or disrupted, and easily copied.

A few more examples:

- Mixture can lead to robustness — as for example with mutts, who tend to be hardier than purebred dogs thanks to the random interweaving of less-similar genes from unlike parents.
- Noise can produce robustness, too. Conventional computer chips generate errors when faced with noise in the form of high levels of random electron motion in their circuits, but new quantum computers now in the works won't just tolerate noise at the atomic level, they'll directly employ it to solve problems millions of times faster.

- Navy SEALs rely on improvisation rather than orders to achieve the sort of mission robustness that can keep them out of enemy hands during dangerous infiltrations, leaving them ready to adapt to unpredictable, complex, and fast-changing situations.

Now that we've seen a few examples of how mess and disorder can work in a person's or organization's favor, we're ready to zoom in for a closer look at the different ways people relate to mess.

CHAPTER FIVE

Messy People

There are many ways to be messy. But other than a few terms like *slob* and *pack rat*, we don't have much terminology to describe personal messiness. Let's fix that. After all, if we're going to accuse someone of being messy, we ought to be at least a little organized about it.

Types of Messy and Neat People

The mess terrorist: Inflicts dysfunctional mess on others to achieve advantage or personal satisfaction. Examples:

- An employee who completes a task in a deeply disordered fashion to avoid being assigned that task in the future. A proactive variation is to demonstrate such a muddled understanding of a task's instructions that the task is withdrawn.
- The nineteenth-century French farmworkers who tried to prevent the encroachment of mechanized harvesters and other new farm machinery on their

livelihoods by jamming the equipment with their wooden clogs, or sabots — thus leaving us with the term *sabotage*.

- The lawyer who responds to a subpoena for a client's records by turning over hundreds of unlabeled crates of documents in no discernible order.

The order terrorist: Inflicts dysfunctional order on others to achieve advantage or personal satisfaction. Examples:

- The health-insurance claims processor who rejects any claim that diverges in even the most trivial way from perfect compliance with complex, confusing paperwork rules.
- The police officer who tickets a motorist for not signaling a lane change on an empty road.
- The department manager who chastises subordinates for tackling tasks helpful to the company because the tasks are outside the department's formal responsibilities.
- The parent who always makes a child put away all toys before leaving her room.

The entrenched messmaker: Creates a mess impenetrable to others to maintain influence. Examples:

- The administrative assistant who sets up a filing system or appointment book so idiosyncratic that no one else can find or schedule anything.
- The consultant who wrote New York City's impenetrable tangle of codes regulating the shadows that proposed buildings will cast on other buildings, necessitating his hiring to determine compliance.

The order phony: Creates an appearance of order while hiding a mess. Examples:

- The designer who maintains a sparsely decorated, neat-as-a-pin apartment used only for entertaining, while living in a messy apartment next door.
- The couple who remove all clutter from most of their rooms, throwing it into stupendous, disorganized heaps in a few rooms closed off for that purpose.
- The professional who fastidiously enters appointments in an electronic organizer but ignores what's in it.
- The suit-jacket-and-tied television news anchorman whose jeans and boots are hidden by the desk.

The mess phony: Creates an appearance of mess while hiding order. Examples:

- The teenager who spends twenty minutes in the mirror fashioning a look of casual disarray.
- The senior manager who kills time so he can harriedly show up late to meetings.
- The store manager who takes sorted goods off neat racks and piles them mixed together in bins to create a bargain feel.

The mess pervert: Derives pleasure from mess for its own sake. Examples:

- The student who leaves her dorm room deeply littered with dirty clothes, spoiled food, and worse, in part because it feels more comfortable than a neat room.

- The manager who believes that the massive clutter in his office, which is disrupting the flow of work through the company, confirms how busy and important he is.
- The boss who constantly and unapologetically forgets or ignores meetings at which she's needed.

The order pervert: Derives pleasure from order for its own sake. Examples:

- The handyman who replaces each tool in its bin the moment he stops using it, even if he may need it again any moment.
- The parent who insists on serving dinner at precisely the same time each night, regardless of the fluctuations in everyone's schedules.
- The manager who demands that requests for vacation be submitted three months ahead of time.

The orderly procrastinator: Avoids real accomplishment by endlessly reneatening and reordering. Examples:

- The professor who spends entire days reorganizing her computer files.
- The homemaker who maintains a large alphabetized collection of spices that is restraightened and replenished with each spice usage.
- The middle manager who keeps massaging his task list without actually achieving any of the tasks on it.
- The mother who spends more time gathering and sorting toys than playing with her children.

The mess savant: Finds surprising ways of extracting new functionality from messes. Examples:

- The researcher who matches graduate students to projects by letting them scan through the mess on his desk to see what catches their interest.
- The manager who schedules conflicting meetings that sometimes result in overlapping attendees usefully swapping ideas and teaming up.
- The chef who leaves an array of random ingredients splayed out around her, leading to her trying out novel combinations.

The order prig: Takes satisfaction from demonstrating a higher level of order than yours. Examples:

- The neighbor who, unsolicited, offers the name of his landscapers.
- The colleague at a meeting who, when the boss starts discussing deadlines, pulls out his electronic organizer with a flourish and starts loudly tapping away.
- Martha Stewart (though perhaps a bit less so, postincarceration).

The order hero: Misattributes positive but largely random outcomes to his order schemes. Examples:

- The mayor who claims a local drop in crime is due to her anticrime programs, even though it mirrors a national fluctuation.

- The hedge-fund manager who touts the fund's good results over the past few months, when markets have been rising.
- The CEO who attributes a modest rise in recent sales to his new long-term strategy.
- The racehorse trainer who credits a new workout regimen and race strategy for the big win.

The mess distractor: Misattributes the failure of her order schemes to the messiness of external events. Examples:

- The mayor who claims a two-year rise in the local crime rate exceeding the national average is due to a dip in the national economy.
- The hedge-fund manager who insists the fund's collapse was rooted in a change in tax laws, rather than to his disastrous investments based on misreadings of long-term markets.
- The CEO who attributes a drop in yearly sales to adverse weather.
- The racehorse trainer who blames sloppy track conditions for three consecutive losses.

The order bigot: Declares her scheme of order is better than yours. Examples:

- The Apple Macintosh user who insists Windows is harder to use.
- The high school teacher who makes students buy a particular dictionary.

- The management consultant who recommends removing or adding a layer of management to improve corporate performance.

The mess-iah: Offers to sell you the secrets to achieving order utopia. Example:

- Anyone who proposes to help you get organized, establish highly effective habits, do more in less time without worry, declutter, simplify your life, continually improve your processes, reorganize your organization, or plan for success.

Ways People Can Be Messy

Collectively Messy Sometimes a set of individual messes ends up being pooled to cause a large-scale mess, as with, for example, car pollution or murmuring in a courtroom or a cluttered family room. More subtly, a collective mess can emerge even when there are no discernible individual messes, as when, for example, a company's information about its clients is dispersed among individual employees. Each employee may very neatly track information about several clients, but the company may still have no good way of getting an overview of its entire client list or even of figuring out which employees have the needed information on a particular client.

Appropriately Messy It's hard to argue that nuclear power plants, tax records, and parking lots shouldn't be well organized. But there are also many elements of our lives that, although often kept neat and highly ordered, are probably better off left at least a little messy, as for example vacations, friendship, art, naps, memories, pets, divorce, sports, desserts, dating, playing, getting fired, reading, sex, combat, raising children, and death.

Cosmetically Neat Messy Some people simply don't care how messy and disorganized they seem to others. But those who do care can take just a little time to look neat and organized, even if they really aren't. An infrequent bather with well-combed hair can look neater than an ultrahygienic colleague with unkempt hair. Likewise, heaps of paper can be gathered into piles and stuffed in a drawer unsorted; clothes can be heaved into closets; meetings can be scheduled to take place in your own office so you don't have to remember to be on time for them; a car over-due for a safety inspection and an oil change can be run through a car wash; and an employee can adopt a precise-sounding title like "assistant manager of internal customer relations," even though she does whatever she feels like doing on a given day.

Weak-Link Messy People can go through great trouble to set up a carefully organized system, only to have the system crumble into utter dysfunction because the order is highly dependent on a single element that's vulnerable to disruption. Some exam-ples: the dropped electronic organizer, the shopping list left at home, the administrative assistant out with the flu, the emergency-response command center with no working phone connection.

Sloppily versus Structurally Messy When you're sloppily messy, you don't stick to an established scheme of order. When you're structurally messy, you don't *have* an established scheme of order or you have a poor one. Some sloppy messes: strewing clothes around the bedroom, showing up late to a 9:00 a.m. meeting, allowing your car to wander into another car's lane. Some structural messes: leaving CDs in piles on the floor because you don't have bins or shelves for them; not being able to find everyone you need for an impromptu meeting; colliding with another car in an unlaned parking lot.

Transiently Messy Even people who are normally well organized can wisely recognize that there are times when organizing needs to take a backseat to higher-priority tasks for a while, allowing mess to reign for a limited time. Thus, there is the office that becomes densely cluttered during the two weeks it takes to finish the big report; the football team that skips the huddle as the clock is running out; the supply sergeant who relaxes the tight controls on ammunition when his unit is facing a sudden enemy offensive.

Provocatively Messy Sometimes people generate or tolerate mess out of curiosity, playfulness, or experimentation. That's the case with a professor at the U.S. Naval Academy who sometimes left perishable food out for as long as years to observe its evolution; a school administrator who lets students plaster certain walls, sidewalks, and monuments with graffiti; and a manager at a button-downed firm who occasionally shows up at the office in island-casual dress.

Contextually Messy In some situations we expect people to be messy, and in others we expect neatness. We wouldn't blink, for example, at a cluttered artist's studio, but might be appalled to see the same degree of clutter in the office of a large-company CEO — as if discipline has no place in art, nor creativity in business. Some people manage to bend these unwritten rules of contextual mess, though, as for example the artist who generates his works via mathematical equations, or the charmingly eccentric average-Joe CEO who looks comfortable in an apron slinging hash alongside employees on the front line.

Constitutionally Messy Inspired by large companies and government agencies that want a more ordered way to assess job candidates, experts have come up with personality tests that, among other things, endeavor to judge how organized or disorganized a test taker is by nature. The venerable Myers-Briggs test, for example, rates people as either "judgers" who are "planned" and "orderly," or "perceivers," who are "flexible" and "spontaneous." There's good reason to be skeptical, though. Aside from the question of whether orderly people can be encouraged to loosen up, there's the fact that the test itself isn't as neat an evaluation as some would like to believe. People who take the test twice have a better than 50 percent chance of ending up with a different assessment the second time.

Existentially Messy Some people seem bound to weave mess into the very course of their lives. These might include those who jump from job to job, move from town to town, or try on spouses and significant others in a serial fashion. Career criminals probably fill the bill, too. And most of us know people who always seems to stumble from one minor crisis to another, with never an end in sight. They may simply be remarkably unlucky, or it may also be that some people thrive on instability.

Genetically Messy In the last U.S. census, more than seven million people listed themselves as multiracial. What's more, compared to the general population, a disproportionate number of them — some 40 percent — were under age eighteen, suggesting that there's an upward trend. Aside from the fitness-for-survival advantages to genetic mixing well established in the plant and animal kingdoms, the blurring of human genetic lines might go a long way toward easing the societal tensions and conflicts that often go hand in hand with divisions in race and culture. Progress along these lines will no doubt be slower in many other countries, some of which have much neater ideas about appropriate lineage. In Iraq, for example, about half of all marriages are between first or second cousins.

Some Common Mess Strategies

Many people say they never have time to get organized, when, in fact, they constantly engage in useful organization strategies that keep things sufficiently under control. Here are some of the effective mess-management techniques that people frequently enlist without appreciating their efficiency and effectiveness:

The Mini-mess Tolerating a constrained, clearly delineated pocket of mess within a larger area can make it much easier to maintain a higher level of order in the area. Some people set aside one section of kitchen counter, one bedroom closet, a few shelves in a den, or a desk in an office as a sort of mess sink, which removes the pressure of straightening out an entire room. In the same way, messy bulletin boards and refrigerator surfaces can keep the rest of a kitchen free of mail, children's drawings, and other paper mess.

The Full Moon Mess can have natural cycles in which it builds up for a while before being at least partially organized at predictable periods. It may be a matter of tolerating disorder for most of the week until free time comes up on the weekend, or of putting up with it through the school year and paring it back over the summer, or of ignoring it and then massaging it in sync with the ebb and flow of work pressures, parenting duties, and even mood.

The Tower of Power Almost anything looks pretty neat if it's in a pile. You don't necessarily have to get the items in the pile in any particular order or even keep like things together. Gravity can be an amazingly effective glue: the magazines, CDs, books, photographs, playing cards, receipts, and bag of pistachios spread across a coffee table can all be made to pose in a neat, stable, not terribly obtrusive stack. The neatness level can always be kicked up a notch by adding a bin where a pile forms — a way of building around mess instead of fighting mess.

The Archaeologist A large heap of items crammed helter-skelter into a drawer, filing cabinet, closet, or attic, or under a bed or desk, or even behind a couch, needn't be dysfunctional, as long as the more important items tend to remain accessible at the top or outermost layer. That tends to happen naturally, as the oft-retrieved items don't sit around long enough to get buried deeply, while the rarely needed items become entombed in levels that can be fun to excavate years later. Mess can also be secreted away in spots not normally considered storage areas, including behind or under furniture, or behind or between washing machines and dryers and other heavy appliances.

The Maintenance Plan Some people confronted with the piles and heaps and scatterings that have formed over time treat them like nuclear waste — something that requires a massive, costly cleanup and until then must not be trifled with. But others, more reasonably, are quick to make small adjustments to the mess to keep it under control and functional, such as scanning through a pile to make sure nothing important has been buried; getting rid of a layer or two of deeply buried, useless heaped mess to make room for a new layer; or corraling enough of the excess clutter in one part of a room to reclaim a usable area.

The Code Blue A potential mess crisis can be safely navigated via a brief, intense burst of organizing activity focused on the most critical elements. Word of an unexpected and imminent visitor might trigger a frenzy of highly efficient straightening out that transports the loose clothes from the floor and into the closet, sends a week's worth of scattered newspapers into a bin, and gets the dishes into the sink, leaving a home perfectly presentable even after weeks of relative neglect. It works for offices, too.

The Satellite Mess There are 1.5 billion square feet worth of self-storage units available to rent in the United States. The money saved by not hiring a professional organizer could pay for years' worth of storage.

Mess Mismatches

Nearly everyone has a story about dealing with a significant other's mess-related quirks or vice versa. (The same can be true of business partners.) Mess in itself never seems to be a problem; it's the difference in how the two people view the state of order in their home that rankles. The tensions aren't always associated with a highly ordered person paired with a highly messy person; even small differences in overall mess tolerance, or merely in tolerance for different types of messes, can and apparently often do lead to stress and resentment. From the survey conducted for this book and from interviews:

> "I am so intent on getting rid of piles that my husband leaves about that I once threw out a very large check. We were living in an apartment building and had to go through a very large outside Dumpster with many garbage bags to find our trash and then to locate the trash bag with the check."

> "I once overheard [a colleague] on the phone scolding his wife for assembling his sandwich with the items in the wrong order."

> "I asked my wife to get rid of the piles, figuring she'd just throw it all out, but when I got home I found she had spent the entire day going through just half a pile."

> "He is so methodical and meticulous when he finally cleans a room, it could be used as an operating theater! Meanwhile, the rest of the house looks like a bomb exploded."

> "I used to yell at her for leaving crumbs after she made toast, but now I'm the one who makes toast and she yells at me for leaving crumbs."

> "I rearrange the dishes after he loads the dishwasher."

> "My husband can't stand it when the bed isn't made, but I can't stand it when the dishes aren't done right away."

> "I have to constantly straighten up, because if I don't my husband trips over the clutter and gets injured."

How large a toll does mess stress take on relationships? The conventional divorce and relationship literature tends to bury mess and disorder within the broader category of "arguments over household chores" or the like. But in our survey, nearly 80 percent of respondents who are currently living with someone said that differences over mess and disorganization were a source of tension, and one out of twelve named mess tension as a factor in a divorce, separation, or breakup. The survey also turned up some interesting differences in how men and women who live together perceive their own and each other's messiness and disorganization. In a nutshell, men see themselves and the women they live with as being about equally neat and organized, while women tend to see themselves as being somewhat neater and more organized than the men they live with. Women, interestingly, give harsher marks to both themselves and their partners than men do.

Mess can impact the balance of power in a relationship. If one person maintains a home or office in the sort of messy state in which she knows where everything is, the other is at her mercy when it comes to finding things. A mess-friendly person paired with someone who guards a low tolerance for mess is in an excellent position to effortlessly wreak havoc on the other's peace of mind. (People who readily and injuriously trip over clutter might be particularly wise to stay on the good side of their partners.) Nor are mess haters always easy to appease. One husband surprised his germaphobic wife with a thorough bathroom cleaning that included bringing a shine to the toiletry-littered top of the toilet tank. The wife was horrified to see the clean surface — she instantly and correctly calculated that getting at it must have required putting the toiletries into temporary but sickening contact with the contaminant-ridden bathroom floor.

Compromise is clearly the way to go for pairs of people inclined to work out mess-related issues. That can simply involve a mess-friendly person taking a little care to be neater, and a mess-hostile person taking a deep breath when a bit of clutter pops up. But here are two other strategies that can come into play:

• *Complementary mess* takes the general form of "I'll struggle to keep one sort of mess under control, and you struggle to keep a different sort of mess under control" and is most applicable when each person tends to be especially sensitive to a different form of mess. Some typical examples: one person can't stand having dust or any sort of grime around the home, and the other can't tolerate clutter; one hates having a messy kitchen, the other a messy bedroom; one person hates messy desks, the other disorganized files; one needs to have the house straightened out before leaving in the morning, the other before going to bed at night. Usually implicit in this compromise is a willingness to tolerate, to some extent, the other person's insensitivity to your own neatness needs. Thus, the grime-sensitive person accepts that the other person will obliviously, not disrespectfully, track footprints onto clean floors.

• *The mess demilitarized zone* defines boundaries between areas that will be subject to the mess preferences of one person, areas subject to the preferences of the other, and areas over which neither holds mess-related sway. It's most useful when one or both people need to have some space where they brook no compromise to their preferences. Thus, one person might be free to be gloriously messy in the den, the other zero-tolerance-ordered in the living room, while both grit their teeth a bit in the kitchen.

Finally, a few words on fighting over mess with children. We've already noted that parent-child mess arguments have on occasion led to violent death — and who knows how many times such clashes have merely led to injury, let alone emotional trauma? In a poll of parents with children ages six to twelve, just under 90 percent of the parents reported that "the condition of their children's rooms was a source of 'mess distress,'" and 34 percent said that their kids' "slovenly habits" were a "frequent source of arguments between parents and offspring." Some suggestions from get-organized gurus: set a timer every night to let your children know how long they have to spend straightening up their rooms; confiscate toys left on the floor at bedtime, and make your child do chores to earn them back; force children who won't spend time cleaning up to spend time in the "penalty box" instead. Just remember, when teenagers go off to college, many end up reveling in spectacularly messy dorm rooms during what may be one of the most productive periods of their lives.

The Seven Highly Overrated Habits of Time Management

1. *Being focused.* By zeroing in on specific goals and maintaining consistent habits designed to achieve them, time management orthodoxy tells us, we will avoid the distractions and less useful encounters that delay our progress. A few questions present themselves. What happens if after years of focus and consistency, you discover you've picked the wrong goals? Why have a growing number of high-competence institutions, like the University of Chicago and the U.S. military's special operations forces, placed such a strong emphasis on cross-training and cross-functional interactions? How do you know that the things you are excluding from your life as time wasters are really time wasters if you're excluding

them from your life? And why do so many interesting and successful people have backgrounds that are brimming with inconsistency, false starts, and career twists?

One such person is Ben Fletcher, an Oxford-trained experimental psychologist who went on to become a business-school dean, and who now heads the School of Psychology at the University of Hertfordshire in the United Kingdom. Fletcher has more recently founded a business consultancy called FIT that specializes in helping companies reduce workplace stress. The most common cause of stress at organizations, Fletcher explains, is mistreatment at the hands of managers, who often tend to be overly assertive, rigid, and intolerant. In working with managers to help them improve their behavior, he found that while managers could usually understand and accept the fact that they had been acting inappropriately, they were rarely able to make and maintain long-term changes in their behavior with subordinates. People are simply too conditioned to acting the same way every day, he says, which often means being locked into harmful habits. Focus and consistency, in other words, become barriers to solving problems. So Fletcher asked the managers to alter other, easier-to-change behaviors in their lives, like the route they took to work or what they ate for lunch or where they sat at meetings — anything at all, as long as it introduced some variation in behavior. The results were surprising: over the course of as little as a few weeks, managers who threw monkey wrenches into their routines in this way found that they were also able to change the way they treated subordinates. The reason, says Fletcher, is that people tend to get trapped in what he calls "habit webs." When they try to effect an important, useful change, they find they're stuck tight. But if they snip away at individual, thin, supporting strands of the web, the web can eventually be loosened enough to permit more important change. "New behaviors lead to new experiences, and eventually that helps people change the way they think," he says. Fletcher has gone on to show that randomly varying easy-to-change habits not only helps people become better managers but also helps them lose weight and repair relationships with spouses and children.

2. *Packing more in.* The unstated assumption when people enlist all sorts of strategies intended to help them get more done in a day is that getting more done in a day is necessarily a good thing. Yet, some of the most ineffective people are masters at flinging themselves from task to task in a take-no-prisoners fashion, leaving each person they encounter feeling strangely untouched. On the other hand, those of us who are perpetually looking back at the end of the day, wondering how we got so little done, usually find that the important things are still getting accomplished and the people who are important to us are getting our full attention for as long as they need it.

3. *Keeping a list.* All get-organized experts treat list keeping as a fundamental tenet of their religions, but the fans of personal productivity guru David Allen are especially fanatical about it. According to Allen and his legions of supporters, getting tasks and obligations down on paper — or on computer, since Allen also touts task management software — will immediately ease anxiety and increase concentration. What's a little hard to understand is how someone who can be so strikingly uplifted by the creation of a to-do list never came to think of starting one before Allen suggested it. In any case, it's hard to argue that writing task lists is a bad thing. The problems arise with the faith people put in their lists. Even putting aside the possibility that you'll lose or leave behind the

list, if you're only going to worry about accomplishing what's on the list or, more realistically, the items that happen to be at the top of the list, then tasks left off or allowed to slip down the list simply aren't going to get done. How do you make sure the right things are always on the list and in the right sequence? That would depend on which productivity guru you want to pledge your allegiance to. Allen wants you to arrange items on the list according to convenience — that is, tasks that you can accomplish together should be listed together. Stephen "Highly Effective Habits" Covey, on the other hand, emphasizes placing the items that are most important to your goals at the top of the list. Thus, you can choose between writing the report that's critical to your job and neglecting to get the front porch light replaced, or remembering to buy duct tape when you pick up the new front porch light and neglecting to get the car registration renewed.

Allen's and Covey's vaguely New Agey books are hugely popular, but what if the satisfaction people claim to get from adhering to their techniques isn't a function of the joy of getting more done but, rather, is a testament to these gurus' skill in convincing people that following their advice will make them better people? It's the one skill that all successful personal productivity and get-organized gurus appear to have in spades. Interestingly, both Allen's and Covey's more recent books suggest that the real point of all the lists and files and habits is to enable you to take time to contemplate the meaning of life and your unique place in the universe. Perhaps you really do need to follow a rigid set of one-size-fits-all time-management rules, such as those pertaining to keeping to-do lists, to get at what's special about you. Or maybe even productivity gurus eventually come to wonder about their own place in the universe.

4. *Sticking to a schedule.* A strict schedule is a great idea, assuming you can precisely anticipate every turn of events that will take place over the course of the schedule and correctly guess what you and those who influence you will think and feel about everything that goes on moment to moment. Otherwise, building in some flexibility may be a good idea. Tight schedules are brittle: if one item on the schedule is thrown off, the entire remainder of the schedule may be out of whack. Assuming that deciding what you do over the course of a day or week is important, you will want to take your time and think very carefully about how you set up a schedule from which you don't intend to deviate. Some people, in fact, will need to exert more effort setting up a schedule than they could possibly make up by having a carefully crafted schedule. A simple example would be spending 1.5 hours on Travelocity finding the most convenient flights possible for a trip and in the end saving an hour in travel time over the very first flights you looked at. Things can really get out of hand when you try to combine packing as much into your day as possible with rigid scheduling. This may work to some extent for dentists and hairstylists, but others may want to take a step back and reassess some basic assumptions about their lives — for example, those people who spend hours carefully mapping out a visit to Disney World on a minute-by-minute basis so as to maximize the number of attractions they can visit.

5. *Making kids get with the program.* There are parents who find themselves constantly fighting with their young children over routine tasks like getting dressed, washing up, and sitting down to breakfast. But some child therapists suggest that the underlying problem often is not the child's intransigence but, rather, the parents' inflexibility over the order in which tasks

are performed. Many children, it turns out, like to have the sequence mixed up from day to day so that it seems less like a burdensome ritual. Adults might also benefit from mixing up the order in which they do things, but somewhere along the way most of us were trained to strive for consistency and routine and now feel obligated to pass on that bias to the next generation. One way to indoctrinate children into the culture of time management is to purchase the Time Tracker from Learning Resources, a $34.95 device that combines an electronic timer with bright red, yellow, and green lights intended to visually condition a child to adhere to a strict schedule. Thousands have been sold, according to the company. (Presumably, adding some sort of mild-electric-shock-delivering feature to the device would be crossing the line, at least in some U.S. states.)

6. *Longer-term planning.* We've discussed what comes of businesses taking the trouble to map out their intended actions and strategies over the coming years. Why shouldn't that work about as well for individuals? In fact, it probably does. With the U.S. divorce rate hovering around 50 percent, and the career-changing bible *What Color Is Your Parachute?* now well into its fourth decade of bestseller-hood, it's not hard to conclude that people are often kidding themselves when they think they're capable of making decisions that will seem wise five years from now.

7. *Getting it done now.* Procrastination isn't always a bad thing. For starters, it can keep you from working on tasks that ultimately turn out to be less important than you thought. Or as Calvin Coolidge put it: "If you see ten troubles coming down the road, you can be sure that nine will run into the ditch before they reach you." (Not that Coolidge was much good at

identifying the tenth trouble. Or at anything else.) The U.S. Marines have a saying, too: Plan early, plan twice. By which they mean, put off planning for an event as long as possible, because if you do it well ahead of time circumstances will probably change and require replanning. In fact, putting off undertaking almost any form of neatening or organizing will likely have some advantage, because it's much more efficient to organize a large set of things at one shot than it is to try to organize them in pieces as they come along. If you want to organize your e-mail into categories, for example, you'll do a much better job of it when you have a few hundred messages to consider rather than trying to set up categories based on a few dozen messages.

Stanford University philosophy professor John Perry has noted that habitual procrastinators who follow conventional advice and try to focus in on a few important tasks will usually find the approach self-defeating, since the very nature of procrastination involves putting off the important tasks at the top of the list. Better, he says, to take advantage of the fact that procrastinators put off work by throwing themselves into less important tasks and find a way to thrive on accomplishing those less important tasks — at which point you might well discover you're in great shape after all. On his Web site, Perry writes this of his own procrastination:

Take for example the item right at the top of my list right now. This is finishing an essay for a volume in the philosophy of language. It was supposed to be done eleven months ago. I have accomplished an enormous number of important things as a way of not working on it. A couple of months ago, bothered by guilt, I wrote a letter to the editor saying how sorry I was to be so late and expressing my good intentions to get to work. Writing the letter was, of course, a way of not working on the article. It turned out that I really wasn't much further behind schedule than anyone else. And how important is this article anyway? Not so important that at some point something that seems more important won't come along. Then I'll get to work on it.

CHAPTER SIX

Messy Homes

A Home Neatening

Melissa, Ben, and their three-year-old son, Monty, live on the twentieth floor of an apartment building in a moderately posh East Side neighborhood in Manhattan, where units like theirs go for around $1.5 million. Most non–New Yorkers would be surprised at how little that kind of money buys at this sort of address; in this case, a two-bedroom, two-bathroom apartment with a tiny kitchen and no dining room. Melissa takes us on a tour of the apartment, which turns up nothing untoward. Yes, it's a cluttered apartment, except for the relatively spacious and nearly empty foyer, but the overall sense is that of a slightly cramped, very lived-in space — nothing that a few hours of routine straightening up couldn't handle.

To Melissa, though, the disorder is nothing short of shameful. She is a warm, talkative, Ivy League–educated, successful songwriter who cowrote a Broadway musical and is the mother of a happy three-year-old. But all this is as nothing when she confronts her failure to keep the apartment neat. She can't have people over. There are intimations of clutter-related tension in the marriage. Her mother was messy — to this day, her mother keeps multiple pairs of reading glasses around the house because she can't keep track of any one pair, can you *imagine?* — and now Melissa has turned out to be messy. What if she passes this curse on to Monty?

Brian Saipe, professional organizer, listens with obvious sympathy. An animated, compact man with boyish good looks, Saipe has been called in by Melissa at $100 per hour to nip this multigenerational tragedy in the bud. He responds to Melissa's confession with a matter-of-fact stream of smooth chatter — he is, in his own words, after all, a "domestic therapist." Disorganization is nothing to be ashamed of, he tells Melissa. It's not a sign of moral failure. It's more like a sort of virus — a virus that invades all parts of your life, killing everything. She nods wanly, having suspected as much.

Reluctantly, Melissa reveals that there is another level to her living hell that she has yet to show Saipe. She refers to it as her "garage," with heavy oral quotation marks. She leads the way back to one of the bathrooms, where a previous peek had revealed nothing more sinister than a stray rubber duck and a few dried toothpaste stains. This time she indicates the opaque, closed shower door, then looks away and waits. She has never shared this with an outsider, she mumbles. For a brief moment, the horror of what lurks behind that door hangs heavy in the air.

Saipe, undaunted, squares his shoulders and flings open the door in the practiced fashion of a mechanic popping a car hood from which oily smoke is seeping. Confronting us is a seven-foot-tall wall of . . . well, nothing stands out as immediately identifiable. This dense shower-space heap might contain body parts, plutonium, sacred scrolls, or the components of a time machine. What's more, after hesitating for a moment, as if surprised by the light, the pile has started to shift and teeter, and commences to topple over. But Saipe actually seems to have expected this — the lurching forth of compacted clutter from behind sprung doors is the stuff of routine in his world — and he deftly deploys most of his body to restrain it, while somehow maneuvering the door back into place. "Let's begin here," he says, with no hint of discombobulation or irony.

The "garage," as it turns out, represents the apex of Melissa's shame. Yes, she and her husband, Ben, have managed to pack several closets to the gills as well, but that's par for the course. Filling up a shower is, in her mind, beyond the pale and a sure sign of the deep toll that the mess virus has taken in her family's life. Once fully excavated — it takes about a half hour — the contents of the shower-garage are revealed to be mundane. There are toys, electronic gear, kitchen utensils, and many types of bags. But the single biggest category of stuff in the pile turns out to be organizing implements, including shelves, hook assemblies, wastebaskets (three of them), and bins and boxes. Similar implements later show up strewn elsewhere in the apartment, and Melissa confesses to having spent $500 on organizing tools in just one trip to Bed Bath & Beyond. There are several getting-organized-related tomes mixed into the home library. This is all typical, Saipe assures Melissa, explaining that do-it-yourself organizing is usually a lost cause.

Now it's time to pare down the apartment's eclectic inventory to a manageable size. The Colonel, as Melissa now only half-teasingly calls Saipe, adheres to the "SPACE" technique, one of a small zoo of acronym-based verbal aids that organizers enlist to organize the organizing process. SPACE, which is one of the more popular ones in the industry, stands for *s*ort, *p*urge, *a*ssign a home, *c*ontainerize, and *e*qualize. *Sorting* involves pulling everything out of drawers, closets, and other hiding places, heaping it on the floors, and then moving it around until things are grouped logically. (Clothes with clothes, toys with toys, and so on.) *Purging* means shipping as much as possible out of the home, whether via trash, family and friend giveaways, or charity donations. (Some people also consider the options of eBay or garage sales or, as a last resort, remote storage.) *Assigning a home* means finding a place for the stuff that's retained. (Socks in a sock drawer, for example.) *Containerize* is simply a matter of getting loose collections of like items into boxes or bins or onto shelves. *Equalize* — some organizers use *evaluate* — means fine-tuning the system as necessary until it is running like clockwork.

Purging proves the hard part, and it is where the Colonel, who has changed into a T-shirt and shorts for the job, shows his tough side. Not sure? he asks rhetorically, when Melissa pauses over a battery-powered corkscrew. Then chuck it. As a rule, he says, people use only 20 percent of their possessions and won't ever miss the other 80 percent.

Melissa hesitates again and again, though. The plethora of stuffed animals throughout the apartment were gifts to Monty. (The Colonel pointedly opines that once a gift is given, it's the recipient's to throw out.) The furry handcuffs were a souvenir of the Broadway musical. (The Colonel is silent.) The Tony Robbins section of the library? The seashell collection tucked in a drawer? Be strong, the Colonel advises.

Husband Ben isn't around for the organizing — also typical, says the Colonel, nonjudgmentally — so Melissa has to render some decisions on his behalf, during which process a certain ire leaks out. "He hasn't done yoga since we moved here," she grumbles, tossing a mat into the reject pile. "He hasn't played guitar since we moved here, either," she adds, but is able to restrain herself from tossing out his guitars. Melissa seems to resent

Ben for managing to hang on to a raft of unneeded items without, as she sees it, sinking to her level of shameful disorganization — though in fact Ben's two closets are only marginally neater than hers.

Containerizing requires a trip to the Container Store, where Melissa, perhaps drained from the effort of purging, becomes oddly infantilized. She picks out childish organizing implements like pencil holders with animal faces (which the Colonel patiently directs her to put back), declares that she is hungry, and clings anxiously to a proffered arm. The Colonel is ready with a pep talk: Did she know that the average American spends one hour a day searching for things? That's twelve hours per week, he adds for emphasis. If Melissa questions the math, she shows no sign of it. She does point out, though, that not long ago she misplaced a contract and had to interrupt her husband at work to have him fax her a copy of it.

Over the course of four visits from the Colonel, Melissa's apartment is rendered utterly, perfectly neat and ordered. There isn't much stuff left, and what's left is all tucked away in an appropriate place. The furniture has been rearranged. Not surprisingly, the lived-in look is gone. As an unexpected side effect, the apartment seems dingier — with nothing else to look at, one becomes aware that the furniture is a little worn and mismatched, the rugs are a bit threadbare, the walls sport a range of flaws. In any case, Melissa seems happy, if a little weary of the whole process, and says she's determined to hew faithfully to the new program.

Professional organizers have certain impressive skills — motivational vigor, patience, a flair for the logical arrangement of time and space — and offer a large bag of tricks. Hiring one will likely get your home straightened up, if at a cost of at least a few thousand dollars. Perhaps reading one of their books will help you do it on your own. Maybe having gadgets to keep empty bags sorted and shoes lined up will come in handy, too.

But professional organizers and their tools may ultimately do more harm than good, even ignoring their cost. The biggest problem is that the marketing of the home-organization industry perpetrates and amplifies — even if it doesn't originate — the notion that most of us have a lot of neatening up to do. On top of that, the litany of organizing advice communicates that straightening up is a job that requires a big commitment, expertise, a large block of time, and an array of paraphernalia.

One of the main points of this book is that there's already too much emphasis on and advice about how to get organized. We'd prefer that people consider less-ordered alternatives in many situations, including the home. However, it's not entirely irrational or in any way wrong to want to straighten up your home, and some of the help and advice in that arena is worth engaging. In fact, professional organizers clearly accomplish something that's useful to many of their clients. But the important part of straightening up is actually quite simple, and you can do it for free, easily, with no expertise. You may not even have to do any more than you're doing now.

Let's boil everything down to what's really involved in straightening up. We'll present it in the form of our own catchy acronym, ACE:

*A*w, relax
*C*arve out time
*E*ject some stuff

Aw, Relax

People tend to worry about home mess too much and often for no good reason. Many of us are busier than ever with work or parenting or both, and letting your home get a little, or even more than a little, messy probably isn't going to hurt anyone. But there's a great deal of external pressure to keep a reasonably neat home, and not just from the constant stream of "be neat" messages we get from the media. It also comes from friends, colleagues, neighbors, and relatives. The fact is, many people will think less of you for keeping a messy home. And occasionally, they'll even let you know about it.

In one unpretentious neighborhood in Florida, a young professional couple with two children sometimes left toys and tricycles and the like sitting in the yard. A group of their neighbors, some of whom are full-time homemakers or retirees with a little more time on their hands, decided they were tired of looking at the modest clutter and came over one morning when no one was at home to clean up the yard. One can imagine how mortified the couple was to learn about the secret tidying party. Neighbors aren't likely to come inside your home to do the same, but relatives and more outspoken friends won't always resist the urge to make comments about your clutter. And while people meeting you for the first time probably won't say anything about the messiness of your home, they may well be busy forming a vivid first impression based on it. According to a study at the University of Texas at Austin, people walking into the room of a stranger when he isn't present form surprisingly strong and detailed opinions about that person — including the conviction that a cluttered room is a sign of a person who isn't "conscientious."

And just hope your messy home doesn't one day get introduced to a jury of your peers. When Michael Jackson was facing charges of molesting a thirteen-year-old boy, the courtroom was presented a video tour of the pop star's home taken by the local sheriff's office during a raid. Of central interest, according to several news accounts of the video tour, was the lack of conventional order in Jackson's home. As CNN put it, "The video showed the house cluttered with shoe boxes, books, and a variety of objects stacked on the floors." Agence France-Presse noted, "The overall image was a peculiar mix of ostentatious opulence and cluttered confusion." Mentioned almost parenthetically in some of the accounts, and omitted altogether from others, was the fact that the raid had turned up pornographic magazines that contained both Jackson's and his accuser's fingerprints. Apparently, the real damning evidence was those scattered shoe boxes.

If you're a parent, aren't you failing your children by keeping a messy home? Aside from the fact that you're passing on the curse of messiness, you're also making your children stupid, according to a study at the Pennsylvania State University. Researchers there looked at historical British databases of information on twins to determine that "disorganized" homes tend to produce children with lower cognitive skills. Oh, by the way — home order, as characterized in the study, also correlated with parental socioeconomic status and the level of parental education. But the study's authors claim they took all of that into account and were able to pin the "profound" deficit of cognitive skills that turned up in many messy homes on the disorder itself. So it's not less educated parents, rough neighborhoods, and poor schools that adversely affect children's test performance, it's keeping a messy home. Well, could it possibly have turned out otherwise? The study's authors didn't think so. "It just makes sense," one of the researchers was quoted as saying. "If a kid is in a really chaotic home, it's hard to imagine that they can learn in a normal way." Given that any other findings would have been nearly unimaginable — it's *obvious* that messy homes stunt kids' brains — it's impressive the researchers went through the trouble of running any data through their models.

Actually, messy homes can provide a far more inviting and nurturing environment than highly ordered ones. For one thing, cluttered homes tell us more about the personalities of its occupants than do homes stripped to their carefully arranged essentials. It's the optional, extraneous items we leave lying around that bear the stamp of our quirky inner selves. The authors of the University of Texas study of how people judge others by their rooms take the time in the study to quote from John Steinbeck's *Travels with Charley:*

> As I sat in this unmade room, Lonesome Harry began to take shape and dimension. I could feel that recently departed guest in the bits and pieces of himself he had left behind.

Specifically, the authors note, what Lonesome Harry left behind were laundry receipts, a discarded unfinished letter, an empty bourbon bottle, and other elements of what we'd have to consider something of a mess. "It would seem," the authors go on to say, "that the environments that people craft around themselves are rich with information about their personalities, values, and lifestyles." Unless, of course, the environments are sparse and pristine, in which case we learn only that their occupants are neat freaks.

The writer Caitlin Flanagan has posited that people who are tempted to turn to professional organizers often feel that something is out of kilter in their lives, and they mistakenly attribute the problem to a lack of neatness and order in their homes. She goes on to quote from Cheryl Mendelson's book, *Home Comforts: The Art and Science of Keeping House*, which notes this of home-order enthusiasts:

> They arrange their shoes along the color spectrum in a straight line and suffer anxiety if the towels on the shelf do not all face the same way. They expend enormous effort on what they think of as housekeeping, but their homes often are not welcoming. Who can feel at home in a place where the demand for order is so exaggerated? In housekeeping, more is not always better. Order and cleanliness should not cost more than the value they bring in health, efficiency, and convenience.

Even some interior designers are now explicitly embracing mess in their work. Ilse Crawford, the former editor of *Elle Decoration* who runs an acclaimed London design firm, filled her recent book, *Home Is Where the Heart Is*, with photographs of jammed rooms strewn with hodgepodges of mismatching pillows, scattered clothes, and even litter. Calling the home "a canvas for self-expression," Crawford has explained that her intention is to counter the sparse and overly ordered sensibility that has dominated home interior design and to achieve an effect that feels more relaxed, human, and intimate, with a large measure of what she calls "laissez-faire" — inspired in part, she says, by psychologist Abraham Maslow's self-actualization theory and its appreciation of spontaneity and individuality. (Speaking of home mess and the inner mind, Freud was an inveterate clutterer who jammed an antique collection of some two thousand pieces into his home and office.)

Aesthetic preference and emotional comfort aside, what about physical health? Isn't a neater home cleaner and therefore less likely to harbor disease-causing germs? Not to get hung up on semantics here, but cleanliness usually refers to an absence of grime, which could include stray microorganisms and other biological matter, while neatness implies an absence of clutter and disarray. One could imagine being messy but clean, with spotless items strewn over a spotless floor, or neat but not clean, with a completely stripped down room coated with slime. But it's not unreasonable to assume some overlap between mess and uncleanliness. For one thing, it's harder to clean with lots of stuff scattered around. And let's be realistic: if a person is too busy to pick up around the house, then she may well be too busy to vacuum and scrub with any frequency.

Our society has become somewhat germaphobic. In a poll of more than 3,600 visitors to the ChildFun Web site, two-thirds of respondents said they wash their hands eight or more times a day, and more than a fifth of them wash more than twenty times a day. A fond wish of an increasing number of Americans is to be able to move through the world outside their homes without ever having to touch anything. Mike Herpio is the head of a Finnish company called FogScreen that markets a device that replaces computer or television screens with a nearly invisible slab of water vapor onto which images can be projected. The effect is of an image hanging in midair, and a person can interact with the image — selecting buttons, for example, or punching in numbers — by poking at the image with a finger. For all the interesting applications that might come to mind for a video or computer image that can be instantly conjured up to float in space, Herpio reports that one of the biggest near-term demands is for installing the device in public information kiosks, because people are becoming increasingly uneasy about punching touch screens or keyboards that other human fingers have touched.

The risks are hugely overblown. *Today* sent an infectious disease specialist on a tour of New York City malls, subways, and public bathrooms to swab many of the various surfaces people might touch, dutifully reporting the revolting findings. (Fecal matter on escalator railings!) Slipped in at the end of the segment, almost in passing, was the expert's comment that none of the terrible-sounding microbes found in a busy day of swabbing was likely to cause illness. Germs encountered on the surfaces inside homes are even less likely to be problematic. So don't put too much stock in the advice of home hygiene experts, who not all that long ago urged chucking out messy wooden cutting boards in favor of neat, smooth plastic ones that wouldn't harbor germs — advice that turned out to be exactly backward.

Parents, unsurprisingly, are particularly sensitive to warnings about hygiene. The poll of parents of six- to twelve-year-olds mentioned in the previous chapter found that 96 percent of them "believe that the cleanliness of a child's room is very or somewhat important to their child's health." Germs aren't the only concern; allergy triggers such as dust mites and pet dander are perceived as equally serious threats. Two-thirds of the respondents managed to find time to vacuum their children's rooms once a week or more. It's true, allergens found in the home may exacerbate the symptoms of some of the fifty million children and adults in the United States who suffer from asthma or other respiratory illnesses. But most asthma and allergy experts now maintain that exposure to common triggers can't actually cause these ailments, as was once believed.

Guess what can, though: very clean homes. Researchers at the Curtin University of Technology in Australia found that children exposed to fumes from home-cleaning products, among other chemicals, were up to four times more likely to develop asthma, even when exposure remained within what are currently regarded as safe levels. Another risk factor, oddly enough, is an unusually *low* level of allergens in the home. According to research reported in the British medical journal *Thorax*, children who aren't sufficiently exposed to allergens when they're very young are more likely to develop reactions when later exposed to normal levels. Kids who confront allergens all along, on the other hand, are more likely to become desensitized to them. Those scrubbing their hands and homes with antibacterial cleansers might also ponder the growing body of evidence that suggests these cleansers produce even hardier strains of bacteria than the ones they're designed to kill.

As for children needing neatness and order in their environment to learn normally, that quaint but persistent notion has been discredited. Studying in a noisy, messy, disordered home may seem like a common sense–defying circus trick to those of us who were brought up decades ago in relatively orderly homes run by a full-time homemaker and were conditioned to seek out stillness when in need of concentration. But today, with both parents often working and overtaxed, there is rarely anyone standing over a student's shoulder trying to enforce a neat-and-quiet-work-area rule. And as it turns out, children appear to be able to study comfortably and effectively while listening to music blaring through earbuds, carrying on a dozen simultaneous instant-messaging conversations on the computer, working the cell phone, and fending off the massive, messy pile of books and papers spilling out of a bursting-at-the-seams backpack. In fact, studies have shown that movement and various other forms of stimulation during learning can help create a "memory stamping" effect that aids in retaining information. A Cornell

University study of students allowed to surf the Web *during class* found that the more often students turned their attention to the Web, the likelier they were to get higher grades, and that held true in both lecture and discussion-style classes. Many elementary and high schools, for that matter, don't have libraries any more; they have bustling, buzzy multimedia centers. In short, parents who must choose between spending time maintaining a neat and orderly home, and helping children with homework, attending their numerous extracurricular events, and in general being nurturing and supportive, shouldn't have to labor over the decision.

A Room-by-Room Guide to Worrying Less about Mess

The kitchen: The next time you find yourself contemplating the purchase of a kitchen organizing gadget like the $80 SmartSpice rotating spice rack featuring sixteen identical containers and an integrated alarm-timer and cookbook slot, think instead about buying another one of those fifty-cent items that represent many homes' most important organizing tool: a magnet. In seconds, convert the front of a refrigerator into a messy, invaluable repository of photographs, important bills, shopping lists, and soccer schedules. And then consider these words from Gabrielle Hamilton, owner-chef of the New York City restaurant Prune, writing in the *New York Times* of her visit to her mother-in-law in a village in Italy:

> She only measures anything for my benefit, so I can write it down and make a recipe, but I'm glad every time to see her dump the car keys and daily mail that sit in the pan of the old balance scale and weigh out flour — from her

own wheat! — by throwing little brass weights into the other pan.

When she pulls her old sawed-off broom handle out of the kitchen drawer to roll out the dough, I sigh happily to be so far away, literally and conceptually, from my stainless steel restaurant kitchen where the freezers all freeze to precise Department of Health standards, and there's a knife for turning, for boning, for filleting; there's a wet stone and a dry stone, and the need for improvisation arises rarely.

Closets: According to *Closets* magazine, Americans spend more than $2 billion a year on closet renovations. An array of companies exist solely to provide custom closet-organizing systems and services, typically charging between $1,000 and $10,000, though a heavy-duty closet makeover can run more than $15,000. Unless you truly don't know what to do with your money, could it possibly be worth spending several thousand dollars to get a closet organized? Preprinted clothes-hanger labels, available from a company called Living Order, offer a far less costly way to introduce a ludicrous level of order to a closet.

The bedroom: You rarely use it during the day, you're asleep when you're in it at night, and unless you're heavily dating there isn't much call for bringing guests into it. All in all, the bedroom is a pretty good place to maintain a mess. As some would say, making a bed when you get up in the morning is like tying a shoe after you've taken it off.

The living room: It's the one room that most people keep fairly neat, simply because they use it least often, preserving it for entertaining. In other words, not all that much living goes on in most living rooms. This touches on one of the principles of mess: neatness and usefulness tend to be inversely related. Living rooms are often the sites of CD collections, which can reflect various standards of utility — or none at all. It's easy to make a CD collection look ordered, thanks to the fact that CDs stack or line up so neatly on shelves. Ordering them beyond that can entail several options, as Nick Hornby explored in his novel *High Fidelity*, in which a main character orders and reorders a vast record collection not merely by performer, or type of music, or frequency played, but also by association of the music with life events, such as a particular girlfriend. An important point to grasp, though, is that whatever scheme is used to organize a CD collection, that scheme will render the collection a mess by most other criteria. In other words, if the CDs are organized alphabetically by performer, then they will be randomly organized with regard to type of music. That's another mess principle, of course: to organize in one way is to mess up in another. If you are considering spending hours meticulously ordering a CD collection, you may want to think about the fact that after Apple brought out the iPod, the ideal device for neatly categorizing thousands of songs, it discovered to virtually everyone's surprise that the most popular feature was the "shuffle" capability, which plays tunes in random order. That led to the introduction of the iPod Shuffle model, which features random order play and has been a big seller.

The dining room: Given how rarely most people eat in their dining rooms, who's to say it isn't more useful to use the table as a handy platform for everything from mail to unsorted clothes to business-card collections? Apparently, that is exactly what many, if not most, people do, given that professional organizers say that their most frequent call for help centers on a dining room table submerged under mess.

The garage: A company called GarageTek sends out postcard-style advertisements featuring a photo of a family posing with beaming pride in their newly made-over garage. With its sparse, high-tech decor and pristine monotone surfaces, the garage looks as if it has been prepped as a site for oral surgery rather than for changing the oil in the lawn mower or holding the trash or receiving the kids' baseball gloves and sleds. Does anyone really need a garage that's so neat that the family will be afraid to mar it with actual use?

Cars: Actually, in cars, neatness makes sense. The ratio of time spent in a car to its limited and easily cluttered interior volume — that is, mess-hours per cubic foot — is an order of magnitude higher than it's likely to be in any room in your home or at work. Things left on a car floor can become soiled and torn under shoes, can work their way under a seat where retrieval requires confronting grease and sharp metal, and can even slide under and jam the brake pedal. Things left on the seats can be sat on, can leave stains or soil that can be transferred to passengers' clothes, and can fall out when a door is opened. Because cars are usually closed spaces, spilled food and other substances can eventually produce overpowering and indelible odors. (Advice from National Public Radio's *Car Talk* hosts Tom and Ray "Click and Clack" Magliozzi to owners of cars whose carpeting or upholstery has been in contact with fish or milk products: sell the car.) Loose items can roll and bang around with the car's motion, distracting the driver and masking more important sounds like conversations, horns, and engine rattles. Clutter can bury maps, the car registration, the flashlight, and other items you might need urgently and in the dark. Anything left in the trunk can bake or freeze. Meanwhile, cars are exceptionally easy to clean — a minute or two with an empty shopping bag usually does the trick.

Carve Out Time

Atlanta-based professional organizer Judith Kolberg tells this story:

> A woman hired me to help her organize her office. I showed up at her office and asked her to tell me what she had in mind. She started explaining what she wanted to do with the piles of paper on her desk and where she wanted to put the files, and as she explained it she started putting things away. I just took a seat and watched her. At the end of an hour the office was straightened up, and I had just sat there the entire time without saying anything. The woman looked around, and said to me, "Thank you so much. You're the best organizer in the world."

Kolberg said that while this was a slightly extreme example, she has on other occasions run into people who seem perfectly willing and capable of doing their own straightening, but simply don't take the time to do so until a professional organizer shows up. Kolberg, whose slightly severe looks and dress belie a warm and ranging intelligence, is trained as a social worker and believes the effect that an organizer can have on a client is akin to the phenomenon of *body doubling*. Body doubling is a technique often employed by teachers and therapists of children who have special needs and may have trouble setting themselves to a task in the classroom. Instead of closely helping such a child complete the task, the teacher will simply stand just behind and a bit to the side of the child and remain there mostly silently; in many cases, the simple awareness of being watched over in this way is enough of an aid to keep the child usefully on track with the task. (Perhaps it's a bit like the Hawthorne effect discussed in chapter 3.)

It may be, then, that what people who end up turning to professional organizers lack is not a knack for restoring a bit of order, but the motivation to put aside the time for doing so. If you were conditioned as a child to avoid straightening up until an authority figure made you do so, how, as an adult, could you make yourself take the time? Some organizers recommend assigning fifteen minutes or so at the same time every day or evening to neatening — a way of time organizing your space organizing. But most people should do fine with a more flexible approach. In the end, most of us prioritize tasks and apportion time reasonably well, even if it doesn't always seem that way. If you're having trouble getting yourself to take the time to straighten up, it may simply be that accumulating mess really isn't all that important to you compared to the other things going on in your life. But if you think you're a good candidate for body doubling when it comes to organizing your home, you could always ask a friend to stand over you and offer to return the favor, yielding a combined savings of several thousand dollars.

Eject Some Stuff

There is little question that sooner or later most of us need to get rid of stuff from our homes. We've become masters at acquiring things — Western society, at least, and especially life in the United States, is practically built around acquisition — but there are few external forces that prompt us to expel things other than trash from our homes once they've made it inside. A bigger home may take longer to fill, but people tend to keep acquiring until the pressure of accumulation builds and demands some sort of relief. As anyone who has watched a mess makeover on TV knows, by far the most important element of straightening up is simply getting rid of a vast sea of items that are no longer needed.

But tossing stuff out is difficult for many people. Professional organizers are prepared for this resistance and wield an array of techniques to break it down. These tricks include pushing clients into throwing as many items as possible into large, black trash bags or big cardboard boxes that quickly mask the items and can be whisked away before second thoughts set in, or making the client recall the last time an object was used and predict the next time he'll need it, or having the client keep a photograph of the object as a substitute for the item. One organizer says that when a client exhibits a strong emotional attachment to an item that's a candidate for the trash, she makes the client talk to the item as if it were a friend, to embarrass the client into realizing how silly it is to be overly tied to an object. All organizers reassure clients that they'll ultimately be much happier having gotten rid of the stuff.

But is it really true that people won't regret getting rid of some of the items that are cast out in the name of straightening up? In one TV mess makeover, an organizer rounded up the family's two children and presided over a mass transference of the contents of a large closet of their possessions into boxes for removal. Kneeling on the floor with the kids as they hesitated over old school papers and long-neglected board games and stuffed animals, the organizer kept up a line of chatter about how awesome it was going to be to regain all that space while guiding their hands to the junk box. "This is so liberating," the mother beamed, getting in on the fun. But the children were clearly torn over many of the items, perhaps with good reason. Wouldn't any middle-ager get a thrill out of uncovering childhood drawings and the family Candyland game and passing them on to her own children?

In fact, all kinds of wonderful, valuable, and useful things get thrown out in the name of organizing. Almost anyone over age forty has had the experience of realizing with a pang that their childhood collections of baseball cards or comic books or Barbie dolls would be worth a fortune today, never mind their sentimental value. It's hard to watch an episode of *Antiques Roadshow*, in which marvelous objects hauled in from attics are appraised for fantastic sums, without wondering what one's own great-great-grandparents were thinking of when they neatened up their homes. There's simply no getting around the fact that some of what we discard today represents future lost treasures.

How, then, to decide what should be thrown out and what should be kept? Organizers will tell you to err heavily on the side of chucking out, often offering the justification that if you haven't used the item in a year it must not be useful to you. But this is silly; follow this advice and you'll get rid of items that might have ultimately proved invaluable, like a beloved saxophone, or an heirloom chair you happen to have no place for at the moment, or a gas-powered generator that might come in awfully handy three years from now. A better yardstick than frequency of use is potential value and replaceability. Even if you use the stack of American Automobile Association guidebooks once a year, it's easy to get new ones, so why not chuck them?

Part of the problem is that when it comes to getting organized, people tend to think in terms of Big Bang projects intended to utterly wipe out mess. That leads to the mass excising of a large percentage of possessions, which beside making for a potentially painful experience also increases the chances of throwing out things that will be sorely missed. Instead, why not throw out just enough to restore a comfortable amount of space and order, limiting the carnage to those items that prove no-brainers when it comes to telling the junk from the good stuff? There's no place like home for maintaining some sentimental mess, after all.

As both John Steinbeck and the University of Texas researchers pointed out, our personalities tend to be more clearly expressed in our disorder than in our neatness. When we are being ruthless about ridding ourselves of what naturally accumulates around us and about meticulously straightening out what remains, we are in a sense tidying our identities. The truth is, we are all at least a bit of a mess — and all the more interesting for it.

CHAPTER SEVEN

Mess and Organizations

Out of Order

Louis Strymish was a Harvard-trained chemist at a Massachusetts leather manufacturer when in 1957 he decided to chuck his career to buy what friends and family assured him was the world's worst business. A woman who reviewed books for Boston newspapers had made a small side living out of driving the box loads of free review copies she received from publishers to local fairs and libraries to sell them at a steep discount from the cover price. Tired of hauling books, she sold a garageful of them and her list of contacts to Strymish for $1,000, $500 of which he had borrowed from a friend. "I was buying good will and inventory," Strymish liked to tell people later. "At least I got some inventory." The business would be, he declared, the first step toward opening a bookstore.

Running a bookstore had been a long-standing dream for Strymish, who as a child had been so introverted and so bedeviled by dyslexia, a then-unrecognized disability, that some teachers suspected he was retarded. Largely by sheer force of will, he learned to deal with the jumble of letters that faced him on every page, eventually fashioning himself into a prolific and enthusiastic reader who would carry on a lifelong love affair with the printed word. While earning his degree in chemistry from Harvard, he raised much of his tuition hawking newspapers from the slush near Boston's South Station, wrestling with the *New York Times* crossword puzzle during quiet moments. But postcollege life as a technician in New England's decaying leather industry proved neither emotionally nor financially rewarding. He found himself gravitating toward publishing and was selling magazine subscriptions when he came across the opportunity to plunge into the bookselling business. Or at least into an odd corner of it, one that left him peddling reviewed, damaged, excess stock and other cheap books to fairgoers and librarians as the proprietor and staff of the New England Mobile Book Fair. A year later, with another loan from his friend, he was able to open a small bookstore in the West Roxbury section of Boston, which retained the festive name.

Strymish didn't set up his bookstore to be like other bookstores. To take advantage of his existing inventory, he ran it as a small wholesale warehouse, specializing in bargain books, intended to appeal to librarians and other bookstore owners. Unlike typical bookstore customers, such wholesale buyers are not generally looking for a few particular books or books on a particular subject, and they don't need a cozy atmosphere to facilitate the casual browsing and test-driving of books. So to save time and money, Strymish simply pulled books out of the boxes in which publishers had packed them and plunked them down onto rows of flimsy wooden shelving, leaving them clumped by publisher and bothering to do no further sorting. If a librarian or bookstore owner needed a specific title, author, or subject, he didn't have to be told how to identify the books' publishers via the *Books In Print* catalog, which Strymish kept on hand to supplement his own considerable knowledge of the inventory. The savings from not putting the books in order helped fuel deeper discounts for customers.

Supported by no retail advertising, and displaying only a tiny, uninviting sign out front, Strymish's bookstore wasn't easily mistaken for a conventional one. Still, curious civilians occasionally wandered in off the street, only to be promptly baffled. It wasn't just the chintzy, cramped decor, complete with half-unpacked boxes and piles of unshelved books, that made the place look like a mess. To the typical book browser, the shelves seemed at first to be an undecodable hodgepodge. If one of these customers asked where to find the books on history or auto mechanics or classic literature, Strymish would blithely rattle off the names of a few publishers or point the confused shopper toward *Books In Print*. In a sense, the store was the opposite of another recently opened Boston-area business called Harvey's Hardware. Both stores seemed disordered compared to competitors, if in different ways, but where Harvey Katz was forcing customers at his hardware store to rely on human guides to the confusion, Strymish required his customers to master it on their own.

Many customers fled, of course, leaving Strymish shrugging behind them. But a good number were sufficiently enticed by the cheap prices to stay and browse. And a funny thing happened: once people got the hang of shopping by publisher, they tended to like it. Though the public is mostly oblivious to who publishes which books, when readers start paying attention they discover that certain publishers put out books more likely to appeal to certain tastes. And when forced to browse through a single publisher's books, customers end up stumbling on interesting books they never would have sought out. Word started to get out among book lovers in university-lousy Greater Boston that the small warehouse was a stimulating and rewarding, if slightly goofy, place to stumble through an eclectic and oddly arranged selection of discount books.

Today the New England Mobile Book Fair — or "Strymish's," as it's known locally — stands within five miles of two Barnes & Noble and two Borders stores comprising some 120,000 square feet of direct competition. The squat, featureless warehouse — originally a tennis-racket factory — is surrounded by retail clothing stores and restaurants serving the affluent western suburbs of Boston. With only modest indication of what wares are housed inside, the independent bookstore still outsells each of the four superstores in the area.

A first question might be why, if one was going to set oneself up in a nondescript warehouse, one would bother to do so in a relatively high-priced retail mecca. The answer is that Strymish *didn't* plunk his store in the middle of all this; when he opened it in 1965, a few years after his first store was gutted in a fire, it was a lone outpost of relatively genteel business neighbored by welding shops and lumberyards. The other stores built around him over the years, ultimately proving Strymish to be, on top of everything else, an unlikely visionary of suburban commercial development. (The warehouse today is actually a larger, but no less utilitarian, version of the original.)

Though still a favorite of librarians and other wholesale buyers, the New England Mobile Book Fair is mostly a retail operation now and has been for decades. But don't tell this to the shoppers who pick their way through the dense, dingy, 35,000-square-foot forest of cheap, cramped shelving creaking with some two million titles. Many of the customers think they're crashing a wholesale outlet. What retailer would make it this hard to find a book? Of course, to come to the Book Fair to find a specific book is to miss part of the point. What the store excels at is providing an opportunity to find what you *aren't* looking for. But even so, a customer who is looking for a specific title or a book by a specific author will probably find it faster here than she would in a Borders. Or so argues Jon Strymish, one of Louis's sons. That's because categorizing books by subjects, as virtually all bookstores do, isn't as helpful as people perceive it to be. "If you're looking for a book by Julia Child, you know it's going to be in cookbooks," he says. "But often you'll have trouble guessing what category a book is in." Take the book you're reading right now, for example. Would you have been able to guess how bookstores would categorize it? One Barnes & Noble store manager said she had no idea where it would be stocked, but suggested that was par for the course. The publisher usually recommends a category, she noted, adding, "Sometimes we just take our best guess, and that's where it ends up." A manager at a Waldenbooks store noted that how a book is categorized sometimes depends on which employee unpacks the box.

But since shoppers for a particular book or author at conventional bookstores tend to think they can guess the subject, they usually give it a try first, hunting down the appropriate section and scanning the shelves there for the book, typically failing and trying a different subject or two before giving up and asking an employee. At the Book Fair, the strange organization scheme usually inspires the hunter of a specific book or author to give up at the outset and head straight to the store's copies of *Books In Print* — or more likely to the computer terminals that have since automated that catalog's function — to find the book's publisher. (Within publisher sections, books are alphabetized by author.) "It's like the Dewey decimal system — it might be hard to guess what a book's number is, but it's easy to look it up and go right to it," says Jon. One could rightly argue that an advantage of grouping books by subject is that it gives readers a chance to browse through the books whose topics they're especially interested in. But that assumes people want only books that neatly fall into a standard subject, which is often not the case.

Louis Strymish passed away in 1983, and now Jon, forty-three, owns the company with his brother David. Jon's features are somehow both sensitive and primitive, and they are set over a hulking, slightly stooped frame — the bookstore clerk that time forgot. As he lumbers and lurches down the crazed, narrow aisles at speed, unable to resist grabbing books that are out of place and reshelving them on the fly, he has no trouble clearing a path through the clots of browsers; one mother seems to sense him coming, as if spotting ripples in a cup of liquid, and reflexively scoops her child well out of the way. As in his father's day, a certain amount of customer assistance is available, but the emphasis is on figuring it out on your own. Jon stops to discreetly listen in on a confused first-time customer standing at a computer terminal who has flagged down a harried employee to help him find the work of a particular author. "What was I doing wrong?" the customer asks, as the employee deftly pulls up the author's listings. "It wasn't you, it's the computer," she replies generously and describes what she had done to find them. Then she briskly leads the customer to the shelves where the publisher can be found — the publishers' names are handwritten on irregularly shaped rectangles of paper taped or stapled onto the shelves — and helps him locate the author. Jon grunts, apparently in approval. It has taken a few minutes, but now one more book shopper knows how to deal with the Book Fair system; he may never have to seek an employee's help here again.

But even aside from the leap to computer cataloging, the Book Fair is not a frozen, super-sized incarnation of Louis Strymish's original vision. Actually, it has become a fairly complex business, though it's not the sort of complexity of which a management-consulting firm might approve. Instead, it's now a crazy quilt of a company, a mix of the eclectic, eccentric styles of the people who run it. It isn't a total mess; rather, some aspects of the business are messy in some dimensions, to some extent, and in ways that change over time. You might say it's malleably semimessy.

One of the people who make it so is Steve Gans, the company's chief operating officer and general counsel, the son of the man who twice loaned Louis money in the 1950s to get started. Gans grew up playing with Jon and David and did time as an attorney at a major Boston law firm before he finally recognized in 1993 that Book Fair resistance was futile. A good-naturedly frantic man in jeans and sneakers, Gans operates out of the landing of a stairway that leads to the roof. He tried to requisition an actual room for an office when he signed up, but was told by Jon that God intended actual rooms to serve as places to pile books, and any person who thought he could find space to wedge a desk between the piles was welcome to try. Since Gans's legal work required a certain measure of privacy, he took over the only unburied, quiet eight square feet in the entire vast facility. The only reason that stairway was free, he notes, is because using it for storage would have defied fire codes. Even here, numerous boxes sponge up the little space not taken up by his desk.

As seems to be the case for everyone who works at the company, Gans's job description includes doing pretty much whatever he wants, as long as there's some chance that it will contribute to the business or at least not hurt it too much. Gans started a cookbook publishing company under the Book Fair umbrella called Biscuit Books. "We had no time for it, but we thought we'd have fun with it," he explains. He was inspired by the cookbook sales business David Strymish had already cofounded called Jessica's Biscuit (named after two dogs), which was in turn followed by a coffee bean–sales business that occasioned the importing of an industrial roaster into the company.

The Book Fair's competition is quite a bit steeper now than in Louis's days. For starters there are the superstores, though Gans is relatively sanguine about them, noting that in 1995, the year the first Barnes & Noble and Borders opened up down the road, the Book Fair's sales rose 10 percent. Though the privately held company doesn't release financial information, past comments by the Strymish brothers and Gans suggest that annual sales for the bookstore float in the $10 million range, not including another few million dollars from Jessica's Biscuit. In comparison, average single-store sales for Barnes & Noble and Borders are around half that much.

Amazon.com is another matter. "Amazon costs us millions," says Gans. In particular, Amazon has proved a vicious competitor to Jessica's Biscuit, which focuses on discount online sales of cookbooks. Gans describes how Amazon once dropped its prices on all twelve books featured in Jessica's catalog just a few hours after the catalog was e-mailed to customers. Sales commenced a two-year plunge at Jessica's when Amazon started offering free shipping for orders of at least $25 at the end of 2002, until Jessica's found a way to match the offer. Jessica's has beefed up its call center and fulfillment operation to chase some of Amazon's efficiencies, all while continuing to avoid looking anything like a tightly run organization. It's inventory room, for instance, looks less like one of Amazon's celebratedly hyper-ordered, Segway-scooterized warehouses than what one imagines the inside of one of those warehouse's Dumpsters might look like. Gans assesses it as if realizing what it must look like to an outsider and shrugs. "Okay, it's not as organized as it could be," he says. "But if a customer asks us for a book, our people can find it right away." In any case, he adds, Jessica's can and sometimes does toss in a bag of coffee beans as a customer incentive.

The mother store has quietly undergone change as well, under the laid-back guidance of Jon, who has still found time to build a very modest second career as a photographer of musicians and an even more modest third career as a bassist for bands. He has applied this same mixed focus to stocking an amalgam of new and bargain books that has proved one of the store's signature features. While acquiring a larger selection of new hardcover and paperback books than even most super-stores offer, Jon has maintained a vaster-than-ever collection of the same sort of steeply discounted damaged and publisher's ex-cess books with which Louis Strymish grew the business. To wring out the maximum discount, Jon will often negotiate for a publisher's entire stock of remainder or damaged books, as when he took five hundred copies of Edward Gorey's *The Head-less Bust* — a book that probably saw no order larger than a dozen from any other bookstore in the world.

This sort of going out on a limb for books that have no ob-vious promise of finding an audience — and that aren't return-able to publishers if unsold — is virtually unheard of in the bookselling industry. "The new-book business depresses me sometimes," he says. "It's like a fashion business. What sells is what was pushed on TV this week, and the rest get returned. A bargain book gets sold because someone made a commitment to it out of faith that someone would buy it someday." But the unpredictability of bargain books comes with rewards. The large mishmash of odd books available for a song is not only one of Strymish's big draws, it's also a money machine. Although new books account for 70 percent of the store's revenues, bargain books make up 70 percent of the profits, because Jon gets them so cheaply that he can mark them up as much as 300 percent and still sell them for five dollars or less. In a sense, new books, with their slim margins, are loss leaders at the Book Fair.

Even the Book Fair's signature by-publisher organization is slowly mutating under improvisation and experimentation. Jon lets employees set up subject-oriented sections whenever they feel like it and stock them with whatever books seem appropriate. These categories don't always track the standard ones; there's a conventional travel section, but there's also a tattoo/body art section. Employees sometimes get carried away with categorizing, as when one fellow set up ten different religious sections; Jon himself started to have trouble finding books there, so he scaled it back to two sections. Other employees have set up interesting blends of by-publisher and by-subject sections, so that, for example, a science-fiction section in paperbacks is perched alongside a section dedicated to books from science-fiction and fantasy publisher Wizards of the Coast. Other books never make it into any sort of category — an employee will just randomly lay them out in the sea of bins and unlabeled display cases near the front for a customer to stumble over rather than intentionally look up. "It's a mix of organizing styles," says Jon. "It seems to happen naturally, and it seems to work okay. My goal is to make sure changes don't happen so fast that they can't be reversed if they don't work. But whatever you do, you're going to annoy someone." Actually, it's hard to spot a single customer in the store who looks the least bit annoyed. But then, that wouldn't include those first-timers who even today walk in and find the store so perplexing that they turn and flee.

Organizations are defined to some extent by the way they are organized. The general assumption is that success is related to the degree of organization — more always being better, of course — and to the type of order. This bias extends from the most elemental levels of organizational functioning, such as shuffling paperwork, up through the critical strategic decisions made by senior managers, and applies as well to issues of organizational structure. But as we've seen with people and homes, there are many ways in which order can cause, rather than solve, problems, and many ways to be usefully messy. Here are a few of the ways this notion can apply to different types of organizations.

File This

Despite Pendaflex's best efforts, you'd probably have trouble naming any major innovations in the filing of paper documents since the invention of the filing cabinet. But, in fact, there has been one: the Noguchi filing system. Yukio Noguchi is a Japanese economist revered in his country not only for his intellectual wattage but also for his work in designing and promoting personal organizing systems, or, as he calls the endeavor, "hyperorganization," intended to maximize the efficiency of office workers. Though Noguchi's schemes haven't received much attention outside of Japan, a translator by the name of William

Lise took the trouble to post on his normally obscure Web site what may have been the first English-language description of Noguchi's filing system and was stunned to receive some forty thousand visitors to that page in a single three-week period in 2005.

The gist of the Noguchi scheme is this: every single incoming document, no matter what it is, is placed in a large envelope. The contents are noted on the side of the envelope, which is then placed on its edge on a shelf, so that all the envelopes line up in a horizontal row like books. New envelopes are inserted on the left side of the row, and any envelope that's taken out is put back on the left. After a while, those envelopes that contain the most recent and most often accessed documents will end up on the left side of the row, while the oldest and least used documents will be on the right. In theory, this makes documents easier to access, since they are automatically prioritized by frequency of use. If something seems vaguely familiar about the arrangement, perhaps it's this: Turn the row of envelopes so that the envelopes are stacked vertically instead of horizontally, place the stack on your desktop, and get rid of the envelopes. Now you've got an ordinary pile of papers of the sort that you'd find on any messy desk, where the most recent and most used items tend to end up at the top. So the next time someone tells you your pile-covered desk is messy, you can point out that it's just hyperorganized.

The fact is, no matter how you go about organizing a workplace, others are going to find fault with your scheme. One school administrator describes how the week before school starts in September is always a mad flurry of classroom organizing on the parts of the teachers, even though the classrooms are perfectly neat and organized to begin with. The problem is that the teachers switch classrooms during the summer sessions, and, since no teacher ever seems to find any other teacher's organization scheme remotely acceptable, the rooms — desks, tables, books, supplies, files, wall hangings — always end up being completely rearranged by their summer occupants, which means they have to be re-rearranged again in September when the teachers return to their regular classrooms.

Teachers are just amateurs at organization, of course. How do the real pros handle heavy-duty office organizing? The mother of all document-management challenges may well arise at law firms whose large corporate clients are hit with legal actions. Lawsuits, criminal investigations, and regulatory disputes often begin with a demand for all documents that might be relevant to the action, and document counts routinely mount into the millions. Complying can be relatively easy — it's often just a matter of scooping out the contents of a filing-cabinet forest, putting it in boxes, and shipping it off. The problem arises when it comes time to refile everything. One law firm involved in a major energy-industry legal case recruited a team of workers to handle that odious task after the action. The team spent several days neatly filing away ten file cabinets' worth of documents, and then gave up and randomly stuffed the other 95 percent or so of the documents into the remaining hundred or so file cabinets. On more than one occasion, members of the filing team were asked how to find particular documents, and the reply was always the same: check the first ten filing cabinets. This seemed a sensible answer, for the same reason that the drunk fellow, as the old joke goes, was looking for his car keys underneath the light of a street lamp rather than across the street where he dropped them — it's less frustrating to look for something in the spot where locating it seems possible, even if it's far more likely to be somewhere else. In any case, lawyers at other firms confirm that the careful filing or refiling of a huge collection of documents is not only a waste of effort but also can actually cause more problems than it solves. When an organization is hit with a demand for particular documents, it is typically entirely to its advantage to be able to honestly claim that it has no idea where those documents are, but that the demander is free to pick through a few hundred randomly stuffed file cabinets to find them. Unfortunately for publicly held U.S. companies, filing laxness is no longer an option, thanks to section 404 of the Sarbanes-Oxley Act passed by Congress in 2002, which among other things requires extensive and precise financial-document tracking. According to a survey conducted by AMR Research, the estimated cost of compliance with the act in 2005 — the first full year in which section 404 was in effect — was $6.1 billion. Congress expected high initial compliance costs when it passed the act but assured industry that those costs would quickly go down. Predicted costs of compliance in 2006, according to the same survey: $6.0 billion.

In general, there can be quite a lot of method to the seeming madness of the messy office worker — or the "Scruffy," as David Kirsh likes to say. Kirsh is a cognitive science researcher at the University of California at San Diego who studies messy and neat offices. He's not interested in taking sides in a value-of-order debate but, rather, in simply understanding what is going on when an office is neat or messy. Kirsh, who looks a bit like a cerebral version of Larry of the Three Stooges, spends much of his time bouncing around a small, noisy lab packed with graduate students and computer monitors, including one large-screen display mounted next to a video camera on a wall that presents a view of students bustling around another small lab. The screen is an "electronic window" that lets the occupants of the two labs feel more connected — the other lab is also under his direction and has a similar display and video camera on one wall. This type of virtual link is not unheard of in high-tech labs, but Kirsh's other lab turns out to be literally next door; the electronic window provides precisely the same view as would an actual glass window in the same spot. (Kirsh explains he had wanted a real window, but when quoted a price by the school he calculated it would be cheaper to put up the screens and cameras just to see through to the other side of the wall.)

In long technical papers, Kirsh and his students employ some of the language of anthropologists and computer scientists — *Scruffy* is a term from computer science, believe it or not — to analyze office "activity landscapes." One of the key concepts in Kirsh's research is that of the work *entry point*. What is it in your office environment that helps you figure out how to pick up where you left off or to begin a new task, when you're interrupted, leave the office, switch tasks, or finish a task? "Neats," he's found, depend on a small number of "explicit coordinating structures" such as lists, day planners, and in-boxes to quickly and surely determine what to do next. Scruffies, on the other hand, are "data driven" — that is, they don't explicitly plan out and specify what they do but instead rely on the office environment to give them clues and prompts, in the form of documents lying on the desk, files piled up on top of the filing cabinet, comments scribbled on envelopes, Post-it notes (which, surprisingly, many Neats disdain) stuck here and there, books left open on the floor, and so forth. It may seem wishful thinking to imagine that the environment is up to the task of keeping effective track of workflow in this way, and indeed, Kirsh says that Scruffies tend to at least slightly overestimate their ability to find things in the mess and to underestimate the occasional inefficiencies related to their disordered activity landscapes.

But Scruffies do tend to derive great advantage from the

random prompts around them, noticing for example when a file they weren't looking for proves helpful for the task at hand or suggests an even more useful task. Kirsh likens Scruffy task-opportunism to the shopper who goes to the store to buy lamb chops for dinner but ends up with a great piece of salmon that happens to be on sale. And he points out that there's science to back up the notion that a messy environment is well suited to providing a stream of useful cues. *Descriptive complexity theory*, a branch of information science that characterizes the sorts of resources required to solve certain problems, dictates that the amount of information that can be represented in a system increases with the randomness of the system. This may seem counterintuitive, but it's essentially a generalization of the idea that a messy room says more about its occupants than a neat one. With more things left out in the environment to be arranged in a greater variety of ways, there are more opportunities for gleaning information. An extremely neat office will always look the same, no matter what its occupant has been working on, while a messier office might reflect the occupant's recent activities in a dozen different ways.

Kirsh doesn't try to argue that Scruffies are necessarily more or less productive than Neats. Rather, he concludes that different workers tend to function best in differently ordered landscapes and thus it's a mistake to try to force order on anyone. "People shape their environments over time until it conforms to the way they're comfortable working, even if it seems out of control to someone else," he says. "As soon as you start telling people how to do things, you're customizing their environment for them, and that causes problems." Not only will pushing Scruffies to get organized probably impair their productivity, he adds, but Scruffies will inevitably end up disorganized again anyway. "They're recidivists," he says.

Is the growing dependence on computers making the question of messy offices and desks increasingly irrelevant, as more information migrates to databases, word-processing documents, and the Web? Hardly. As numerous studies have pointed out, the production of paper documents tends to increase, rather than decrease, with computerization, as workers flock to the printer for hard copy. What's more, computer files create a new potential mess, fraught with questions about how they should be named, formatted, grouped, stored, accessed, backed up, and protected, among others. The organizational powers that be often push for strict standards on these points, but others may find that such neatening efforts conflict with or restrict their practices and preferences, leading to tensions and technical problems. When the state information technology chief of Massachusetts announced in 2005 that the state was going to standardize its computer document format to be more compatible with open-source software — software that isn't controlled by a company — than with Microsoft products, loud choruses of support and outrage ensued, closely followed by the announcement of an investigation into the chief's apparently perfectly legal state-funded travel for participation in open-source software conferences, followed by a new state-government announcement that it would work with Microsoft to stay compatible with the company's document formats, followed by an announcement from Microsoft that it would bring its document format closer to an open-source format. In the end, Governor Mitt Romney personally weighed in, concerned that the imbroglio might impinge on his presidential aspirations, or so it was rumored. And this was all over document *formatting*.

But aside from the question of how groups of paper and digital documents are organized, it's also worth noting that a typical digital document is generally in itself neater than a typical paper document. No smudges, no crinkles, no cross outs, and ready to spell-check, justify, paginate, and reproduce perfectly in as many versions as could be desired. It sounds like a big improvement. But consider the discovery in 2005 of an unusually messy handwritten Beethoven manuscript of the *Grosse Fuge*, a find that had music experts swooning and that was sold at auction for $1.95 million, one of the largest sums ever paid for a music manuscript. The exceptional value of the document, as it turns out, was in the mess itself. From auction-house Sotheby's description:

> It is written in brown and black ink, sometimes over pencil and includes later annotations in pencil and red crayon, some added as proof corrections, on ten-stave paper — the staves frequently extended into the margins by the composer. Written on various paper-types the manuscript shows the extent of Beethoven's working and reworking and includes deletions, corrections, deep erasures (occasionally the paper is rubbed right through, leaving small holes), smudged alterations and several pages pasted over the original or affixed with sealing-wax. The passion and struggle of Beethoven's working can be seen graphically: the higher and more intense the music, the larger the notes. As Beethoven pushes the music higher than ever written before, the ledger lines are pushed exponentially towards the upper edge of the paper. It is also evident that Beethoven tried passages out on the piano, or perhaps the desktop. On page 23 of the manuscript, there is a passage of Beethoven's own fingering. It is touching to imagine the ailing and entirely deaf composer running over passages on the piano, music he could scarcely hear, but certainly feel in his fingers.

While the special value of messily handwritten documents might apply to historical creative works, could it possibly have a place in today's office? Absolutely, says Glover Ferguson, a chief scientist at Accenture in Chicago. Ferguson studies ways of usefully imbuing various everyday objects with computer-chip intelligence, and he showed us one of his favorites: a fat, gray-black pen he uses to take notes at meetings. The pen has a tiny sensor at its tip that keeps track of where it is on the paper, so that it can in effect store an image of whatever it writes. It was designed to be used in the field by salespeople, medical practitioners, and others as a way of entering data without having to carry around a fragile and expensive computer, because whatever check marks or letters are written with it can later be converted to digital information, as if they had been typed in. But Ferguson carries it around for a different reason. He wants his words to be preserved in a digital document but also his messy scribbles, just the way he made them. "Every doodle, smudge, or squiggle is a hook on which I can hang memories of what happened in a meeting," he says. "The crossed-out word reminds me of the big debate we had; the arrow reminds me of the steps that led to this important decision. When you end up with only a typed transcript of the notes, you lose all the context and subtleties, and that's the good stuff."

Actually, ordinary digital documents can have a lot of extra information. But it's not the kind of information that's likely to endear them to you. For example, some word-processing programs, and especially Microsoft Word, will hang on to previous versions of your work and even pieces of unrelated files. This extra text doesn't normally show up on your screen, so you probably remain unaware of it, but someone you share a document with might know how to bring it up. In 2005, both the

Democratic National Committee and the United Nations circulated documents that proved embarrassing when critics were able to glean from them information not intended for public consumption. And hidden information in a document from the California attorney general condemning file-sharing software revealed that a movie-industry trade group had helped write it. All of these parties, no doubt, would have happily traded the neatness of digital documents for a few scribbles and coffee stains.

Being too neat with business documents can even present a public menace. When the brakes on all twenty of Amtrak's high-speed Acela trains in the Northeast were found to contain cracks that could have led to a crash, forcing a three-month sidelining of the trains, the problem was eventually traced to an effort to declutter a maintenance manual. The original manual had pointed out the need to inspect the brakes for signs of impending cracks, but Amtrak wanted to put a more concise version in the hands of its maintenance people. Among the snippets cut for the neater, shorter version was the brake inspection warning.

Messy Organizational Structure

Is it a bad idea for companies to grow? That may often be the case in our world of increasingly fast-changing customer interests and demands, asserts Peter Nijkamp, an economics professor at the Free University of Amsterdam who studies the impact of technological change on business. The problem is that company growth typically leads to what Nijkamp calls *path dependency* — that is, a tendency to become locked into a particular way of doing things. "A dynamic market penalizes companies for path dependency," he says. "And that makes creating larger organizations risky."

Though perhaps the problem isn't growth itself, suggests Nijkamp, but the way companies grow. When they become larger, they tend to gravitate to neater, more formal organizational structures and policies geared to push employees to work in neat, efficient synchrony toward common goals. But these very structures are what provide all the friction when it comes to rapid change. The ever-popular "six sigma" philosophy, for example, under the spell of which companies continuously and formally analyze all their processes with an eye to approaching perfection, is obviously not conducive to quickly throwing together a new business unit to rush out a product for a market that springs up overnight and that may disappear as quickly. Merely deciding to attack a new market can be a torturously prolonged process in larger companies. And sometimes, ironically enough, the fault lies largely with postmodern, network-style organizational schemes that companies have embraced as less-restrictive antidotes to the classic pyramidal hierarchy. In these newer schemes, the lines of reporting can become comically complex, to the point that it becomes unclear if anyone is really in a position to make a decision. IBM, for example, in the 1990s adopted a management structure that took the form of an eight-dimensional matrix, whose working presumably would have been perfectly transparent to anyone conversant in string theory. And companies keep taking on new, ambitious organizational schemes as they grow, partly out of fear of the alternative — that the organization will behave in unpredictable, uneven, uncoordinated, messy ways — and partly because they provide senior management with a sense of real accomplishment. Adding to the drive toward new, more ordered schemes is the observation that corporate performance invariably gets a temporary boost from them, thanks to a sort of organizational placebo effect. It's an offshoot of the Hawthorne effect, mentioned in chapter 3 — the principle that almost any purposeful change in a work environment tends to be temporarily effective. But the fact is, almost any highly ordered organizational scheme is ultimately going to be a poor fit for the dramatic swelling and collapsing that characterizes most markets these days.

In contrast, consider Scientific Generics, located in Waltham, Massachusetts, and Cambridge, England. It's a three-hundred-employee firm that has no real "main" line of business. The company provides some consulting services, but mostly looks for interesting unserved niches in any market, creates units to develop or acquire technology aimed at those niches, then does whatever seems most profitable with the technology: licenses it, builds a business unit around it, spins it off into its own company, partners with an established company, or just lets it die should demand wither or fail to materialize in the first place. Over the past seventeen years, Scientific Generics has created or partnered in some seventy companies and business units whose products range from display screens to toys to medical devices. Sometimes the new lines of business generate new lines of business. That's what happened in 1998, when a business unit developing a sensor-equipped stylus for Palm-like handheld devices spawned a unit that developed position-tracking devices for automobiles. "Companies usually focus their R&D [research and development] only on their existing strategic needs," says Geoff Waite, the company's vice president. "That makes them less idea-rich, and they miss opportunities."

The basic thinking behind this more freewheeling sort of structure is to focus on new, "spin-up" business units that quickly pop into existence when an opportunity presents itself and then compete for resources within the company. If the spin-up thrives, it's allowed to quickly expand without limit, pulling whatever it needs from other parts of the company, even if doing so hurts the rest of the company. If it doesn't thrive, it's quickly put out of its misery. It's a different way of thinking about a company — not as a seamless whole, but as a fractured conglomeration of transitory, semi-independent units, some leaping into being and growing quickly, others withering away, with employees and funding flowing freely and fast between them. University of Milan researcher Mario Benassi refers to spin-up-friendly companies as "modular" companies, and espouses three basic principles for them: growing in pieces instead of holistically; being as quick to shrink or get rid of logy pieces of the company as to invest in the promising ones; and being prepared to reorient its efforts around any of the pieces. "Modular companies are more focused, and faster," he says. "They can quickly get rid of activities they're not interested in anymore." Traditional companies, by contrast, tend to be so fixated on preserving the same core business that potentially hot new markets are poorly served — if they are served at all. As challenging as coming up with promising new spin-up ideas may be, the hardest part of the process may be to quickly close down those ideas that don't show signs of panning out. Nijkamp says a company with a spin-up failure rate of 60 percent would be doing quite well, suggesting that the key is to keep a high churn rate. In that light, the spin-up concept starts to look a little less like brilliant business planning and a little more like trial and error.

You don't have to be high-tech to take advantage of the spin-up concept. Smart fashion and sporting goods firms also whip up new, independent brands to surf the trend of the moment. Large advertising agencies typically comprise dozens of smaller ones that address various industry niches. And savvy restaurateurs like Stephen Starr in Philadelphia (Pod, Buddakan), or Danny Meyer in New York (Union Square Café, Gramercy Tavern), grow not by making individual restaurants bigger, nor by opening clones of the same restaurant, but by creating entirely new concepts to add to their strings of properties, occasionally closing or reinventing existing ones when their cachet fades.

Messy Innovation

Half-Life 2, the blockbuster computer game from Valve Software in Bellevue, Washington, first became available over the Internet in late 2003. Valve hadn't actually released the game — the code had been stolen by hackers, who posted it for free downloading. Online piracy has become fairly routine, of course. But what happened next wasn't: Valve customers worldwide got to work hunting down the thieves. Why would a bunch of online gamers, notorious for disrespecting niceties like copyrights, go after the glorious liberators of the program they had so eagerly awaited?

The answer has to do with where some companies are now turning for innovation. Thanks to globalization, the search for creative solutions may be the most important issue facing U.S. businesses today, insists David Audretsch, director of the Institute for Development Strategies at Indiana University, and author of *The Entrepreneurial Society*. China alone has mustered a vast trove of capital investment and cheap labor it is skillfully wielding to undercut U.S. manufacturers of everything from socks to electronic chips, and service firms are under attack as well. "You're not going to be able to compete on price," says Audretsch. "You're going to have to live off of having a new idea that other companies around the globe don't have." A company that's just taking care of business, doing all the things that used to guarantee success — providing high-quality products backed by great service, marketing with flair, holding costs down, and carefully managing cash flow — is at risk of being flattened if it isn't also an innovation engine in the style of a computer or nanotechnology company.

So where are all the bright ideas supposed to come from? Holding companies back has been a rigid approach to innovation based on a classic, neat division of labor in which R&D is carried out by scientists and engineers in the labs of high-tech companies. What we need now, says Audretsch, is a messier concept of innovation that enables any company to tease it out of any employee, as well as from external stores of expertise such as boards of directors, venture capital firms, suppliers, and partners. Consider a company called Three Rivers in Mesa, Arizona, which markets wheelchairs with easier-to-turn wheel rims, a hand-powered exercycle that controls video games, and other innovative products for the disabled. Like most smaller companies with a modest staff — Three Rivers has six full-time employees — the firm can't afford to hire dedicated researchers. So the four-year-old company scours university research labs specializing in "human engineering" to dig up ideas it can license. "Our expertise is in deciding if there's a market for a new type of product, and in taking a lab prototype and developing it into a marketable, manufacturable version," says cofounder and president Ron Boninger. He adds that Three Rivers contracts all its production to outside manufacturing firms — and cajoles them into coming up with not only manufacturing innovations but also suggested design changes to make products more reliable and cheaper to produce. One manufacturing supplier, for example, figured out a way to make oval aluminum wheelchair wheel rims by squeezing heated aluminum out an oval hole like toothpaste instead of the far more expensive molding process other manufacturers offered.

One of the best sources of innovation for companies may be the one that's furthest from traditional, engineering-lab-driven R&D: customers. The computer gaming community has been a leader in this regard. Take Valve, for example. Not long after the company opened shop in 1996, managers noticed that a number of skilled enthusiasts had hacked into the shoot-'em-up game's code and created modified versions with more exotic settings and weapons. At first appalled, the managers quickly realized that the customized games were winning new fans, so they provided new software that made it easier for fans to go to town on "mods." One extensive mod became so popular that the company "in-housed" — hired — the modder and spun off the new version as a separate product. "Having people constantly adding to the product extends its life and fills out all kinds of market niches that the original product wouldn't have reached," says Lars Bo Jeppesen, a researcher at the Copenhagen Business School in Sweden who has studied how customers contribute to products at Valve and other software companies.

But it's not just software companies that can usefully blur the line between customers and employees. Take Van's Aircraft, an Aurora, Oregon, manufacturer of small, personal airplanes that are shipped as kits to be assembled in customers' garages. A thriving community of Van's enthusiasts, meeting online as well as at "fly-in" gatherings, collaborates on and swaps designs for plane modifications and accessories, ranging from alternative engines to cockpit sunshades. The five top managers at Van's spend a combined twenty-five hours a week online checking out customers' doings, says general manager Scott Risen, along with untold hours at fly-ins to get a firsthand look at some of the innovations. The best ones are incorporated into the planes or offered through the company's catalog of accessories. "We offer all kinds of items designed by customers," says Risen. "If we see something we like in an airplane, we find out who made it and ask them if they'd let us market it." The company is flexible about the arrangement, offering either to buy the rights to the innovation outright or to serve as a distributor for a commission. One popular recent addition to the catalog, for example, is an electronic switch that performs a previously cumbersome adjustment to wing flaps with just a touch of a button; a customer makes the device and Van's takes orders for it.

Some types of products readily lend themselves to customer input by virtue of a sharing-oriented community whose members are quick to roll up their sleeves, notes Sonali Shah, a University of Illinois at Urbana-Champaign business school professor who studies innovation in user communities. Windsurfers, inline skaters, and skateboarders have been inventing and driving the evolution of new products for many years, she notes, initially sharing their ideas with each other and with companies through events and magazines and more recently online. "Car tuners," who rig up small cars with exotic gadgets to extract spine-snapping performance, feed ideas via the Internet to the thousands of companies that make aftermarket components and inspire the major manufacturers: Ford and Honda have brought out versions of their Focus and Civic models, respectively, that incorporate modifications pioneered by tuners. And even disease sufferers are banding together on the Web to shoulder some drug-company responsibilities: when the Food and Drug Administration forced GlaxoSmithKline to take a drug for irritable bowel syndrome off the market because of side effect risks, an online community of IBS patients successfully lobbied the FDA to reconsider.

Getting an online community of customers to shoulder some of the work for a company is often as easy as asking. That's all Valve had to do. It posted a message on its Web site asking fans to help catch the code thieves, and hundreds got to work. It may seem unlikely that customers are eager to take on tasks for which even well-paid employees may not always show great enthusiasm, but that's the big surprise revealed by the community-driven, rather than company-driven, world of open-source software: what might be drudge work to an employee will be a thrilling challenge to some civilian out there. "Companies spent the '90s in a race for talent, and paid whatever it took to retain the best people, but never ended up getting most of their energy," says Steven Weber, a University of California at Berkeley professor researching how open-source principles apply to businesses and government. "Open-source projects get about twice as much energy from people." After all, how many automobile engineers would be honored to be charged with developing a better cup holder? But customers sick of cleaning spilled coffee would line up for the job, asserts Weber. They certainly don't hesitate to take on jobs like providing technical support to one another — one of the main activities of many online communities.

Teasing out innovations from customers may only require providing them with the right tools and instruction. Statistics software vendor StataCorp in College Station, Texas, for example, gives customers the software needed to create new types of statistics reports and then makes the new versions available to other customers. Anvil Cases, a City of Industry, California, manufacturer of highly protective shipping cases, provides customers with detailed directions and diagrams for designing a case's interior to fit the complex shape of a particular video monitor, say, or musical instrument. The company then hangs on to the designs to make cases for future customers with the same monitor or instrument.

As is often true with messier approaches, coordination and goal setting present challenges. Customers may help out a company, but that doesn't mean they can be ordered around like employees. For one thing, managers have to appeal to customers' internal motivations instead of simply telling them what to do. "To get productivity from them, you have to give up control," says Eric Raymond, president of the Open Source Initiative, and widely considered one of the leaders of the open-source movement. Other requirements for managing nonemployee contributors, adds Raymond, include being quick to respond openly and honestly to questions and setting up a means for giving public recognition of their efforts. "People will go through astonishing amounts of effort to get that reward," he says. Ironically, the ultimate reward is often that of offering a job — some customer-contributors are motivated by the notion that their effort might be treated as a sort of audition. Like Valve, Van's Aircraft has "in-housed" talented customers. Not that customers can be expected to provide an unbroken stream of great ideas. Most ideas won't be useful, says Shah, and it will be up to managers to separate the grains of wheat from the piles of chaff. "Companies that can recognize which customer innovations are the ones that the market needs will have a real competitive advantage," she explains.

And companies that have won the loyalty of an online customer detective force — well, they'll do even better. As Valve's director of marketing Doug Lombardi explains, the hackers who stole Half-Life 2 were tracked down by the game's fans and arrested six months after the company asked for help. "This game had been in development for five years and cost us tens of millions of dollars," Lombardi says. "It was nice to have the help."

Messy Information Systems

In 2004, the FBI abandoned work on a computer system on which it had spent more than $150 million over a five-year period. In the ensuing finger-pointing over the derailed system, which was supposed to allow agents to share information about cases with each other and with other agencies, congresspeople lined up to declare they were shocked — shocked! — to learn that this much money could be wasted on a project that didn't do the job. They had forgotten, apparently, that the Federal Aviation Administration, the Internal Revenue Service, and every branch of the military, among many other federal entities, have lost far more on big, dead-end technology projects.

It's tempting to pass off such costly mishaps to the inability of lumbering, bureaucratic government agencies to manage projects, but the fact is, having a money-devouring information system go feet up is more the rule than the exception at almost any sort of organization — it just doesn't get the press if it's a private company's blunder. "More than half the large, custom systems that are started never reach users," says Joseph Goguen, a computer science researcher (and colleague of David Kirsh) at the University of California at San Diego. "Usually they're just canceled, but sometimes they're declared a success and then not used." Even small and midsized businesses build these clunkers by the tens of thousands, he adds — and often blow a larger percentage of revenues on them to boot.

To an outsider, runaway computer projects may smack of

incompetence on the part of the project's managers. But even companies with gilded technology reputations get pulled into mammoth failures — IBM, for example, was accused in the mid-1990s of helping burn $1.5 billion of taxpayer funds in a futile effort to revamp the nation's air traffic control systems. And indeed, Goguen notes that when experts studied the costs of fixing failed computer projects, they found that only about 20 percent of the costs were related to problems with programming or system design. Another 20 percent or so was related to the project's failure to address the needs the organization had stated. But about 60 percent of the costs went into the real culprit: the organization's failure to figure out what its people really needed from the project. "The developers end up designing and building the wrong system," says Goguen, "and they don't realize it until they're almost through."

You might have thought that taking into account what people want from a computer system is the easy part, rather than the killer. The problem is that computer systems are usually highly ordered, relatively inflexible entities that must be worked with in specific ways. People, on the other hand, tend to work in a variety of less predictable ways. Sometimes these messier work styles are simply ignored by the people who build information systems, under the assumption that if a system is potentially useful enough, people will adapt themselves to it — a terrible assumption, as it turns out. In other cases, user work styles are investigated but ultimately misunderstood by the computer specialists who do the investigating. Either way, the result is essentially a mismatch between the way computer systems are organized and how people are organized.

Taking a less ordered approach to building computer systems can help. For example, information technology projects often begin with interviews of managers and potential users of the new system — an obvious first move for the well-organized system builder. But Justin Hectus, a director of information for Los Angeles–based law firm Keesal, Young & Logan, points out that a funny thing happens when you ask people point-blank about the way they work. They get it all wrong. People tend to be unaware of the eccentric ways in which they organize their own work processes, he says, and make all kinds of poor guesses about how a computer system would best help them. To get it right, Hectus and his staff become office ethnographers, unobtrusively shadowing managers and other employees for days on end to observe firsthand how people work until they've obtained a feeling for the needs of those who will be dependent on the system. "We spend significantly more time studying how people work than we do on the actual programming and development," he notes. One behavior his group observed among the company's eighty lawyers and paralegals, for example, was the frequent frantic effort to try to enlist someone — anyone — in the firm to help out with a sudden, overwhelming influx of tasks. Realizing that lawyers had tremendously irregular workloads and no good way of smoothing out the spikes, Hectus's department put together a system that lets everyone in the firm keep track of everyone else's workload via mobile device, so that a lawyer who's swamped in court can see at a glance who in the firm is experiencing a lull and may be available to help out for a few hours or days. It was a system that no one had specifically asked for but that everyone was glad to have.

A related problem, says the University of California's Goguen, is that people will often state with great confidence what they want from a system, until they actually see the results, at which point they change their minds. The trick, he says, is to find a faster, cheaper, and messier way to uncover that sort of mind changing, rather than going through a long, complex, orderly system-development process to reach the same point. When Goguen's students took on the task of developing an on-line system for a local jazz festival, for example, he had them sit down representative users in front of a cardboard box on which handwritten pages were taped, providing a zero-cost simulation of a first iteration of the system. One of the several discoveries that came out of the sessions was that the jazz fans, who tend to be older, preferred easier-to-read large type on the "screen" — a simple change that if left undiscovered would have required redesigning the entire Web site.

But even when systems developers do a good job of figuring out exactly what users really do need and want from a system, projects can still fail. The problem, notes Danny Shader, founder and CEO of mobile applications provider Good Technology in Santa Clara, California, is that companies operate in a disordered, fast-changing business environment. As a result, firms sometimes end up with systems designed to meet their now-outdated needs of eighteen months ago. "If you give a developer a snapshot of your business to work with, you're going to have a problem," says Shader. The solution, he explains, is to assume that systems, no matter how they're designed, are going to fail to meet users' needs in some ways, and to build into them the capacity for frequent and extensive modification. Such messy systems may not initially perform as many functions as a rigidly designed system, but in the end they'll prove far more useful.

Contracts need to be messier, too. Organizations frequently turn to consulting firms for major computer projects, enlisting long contracts that spell out in great detail exactly what is supposed to be delivered at the end of the project. That simply forces the consulting firm to drive single-mindedly toward those specifications, without necessarily having much regard for how users will appreciate the results when it's all over. Instead, some firms are starting to offer an "optional scope" contract that is actually a conglomeration of flexible minicontracts, each one of which covers the work for a few months or other limited period of time. At the end of each period, the client has the option to activate the minicontract for the next period of time, to walk away from the entire remaining deal, or to renegotiate the next minicontract based on problems with the intermediate results or changes in the organization's needs. In a sense, the contract is being written on the fly. That encourages everyone to watch out for and correct brewing mismatches on an ongoing basis and allows them to cut short losses if things are going far wrong. Of course, doing so may very well throw a number of monkey wrenches into the normally orderly development process and make for a lot of zigging and zagging, and may even add costs, delay deadlines, and limit functionality compared to the original specifications. But it probably beats having to listen to a bunch of congresspeople expressing outrage at your well-organized incompetence.

Chapter Eight

Messy Leadership

Elbert "Burt" Rutan's career trajectory hasn't followed that of a typical manager. Now a successful CEO, Rutan's job in the late 1960s found him in an F-4 Phantom jet fighter that was tumbling to the ground. Never before had an out-of-control F-4 avoided crashing, but this time, thanks in part to Rutan's skill, the plane recovered. Rutan wasn't a fighter jock; he was an engineer who had been asked to figure out why the treacherous aircraft was flying pilots into the ground in Vietnam. While his fellow engineers attacked such tasks with calculators, Rutan insisted on considering the problem in the air. The near-fatal experience not only led to a critical F-4 modification, it also confirmed for Rutan a notion he had held ever since he had built model airplanes as a child. The way to make a better aircraft wasn't to sit around perfecting a design, it was to get something up in the air and see what happens, then try to fix whatever goes wrong.

Despite what happened in the F-4, that policy isn't as dangerous as it sounds. There are plenty of ways to test a suspect aircraft without risking life and limb — like lashing the wing or tail of the aircraft to a truck and driving it at high speed down a highway to get a feel for how it behaves, a technique Rutan mastered in the early 1970s when he started his own company designing cutting-edge experimental aircraft for amateur builders and pilots. Not that Rutan is afraid to wrap his hand around the control stick of a finicky plane; he had his pilot's license before his driver's license. Rutan is sort of an action nerd, and even today, at sixty-three, he cuts a figure that is somehow both dashing and just a little bit goofy — part Evel Knievel with even bigger sideburns, part Bill Gates with a slight drawl and leather jacket. In 1982, Rutan founded an aircraft design and prototyping company called Scaled Composites, which now sprawls through a village of corrugated-metal buildings in a windblown patch of desert in Mojave, eighty miles northeast of Los Angeles.

What are Rutan's management rules for keeping the firm on track? He insists he doesn't have any. "I don't like rules," he says. "Things are so easy to change if you don't write them down." Rutan feels good management works in much the same way good aircraft design does: instead of trying to figure out the best way to do something and sticking to it, just try out an approach, and keep fixing it. He does allow, however, that he's evolved a few rough, guiding principles for his company. One is not to worry so much about the formal background of the engineers he hires or to look for the sorts of specialists normally sought after by aerospace companies. Instead, he looks for people who share his passion for aircraft design and who can work on anything from a fuselage to a door handle or are willing to learn how. He then gives those people free rein.

Another Rutan principle is that it's useful to have everyone questioning everything the company does all the time, and especially to have people questioning their own work. Rutan makes sure that when employees point out their mistakes, they're applauded rather than reprimanded.

A principle he applies to himself is to avoid spending a lot of time running the company. He long ago trained his board of directors not to waste time asking administrative or financial questions he can't or won't answer. An eight-person management committee, of which he is a member, guides the firm. But Rutan mostly keeps busy by picking out the one or two projects that interest him — there are usually a dozen or so going on at any one time — and joining those teams as a designer.

Downplaying up-front design, not matching employees' tasks to their experience and training, eschewing specialization, creating a culture that glorifies questions and mistakes, refusing to act like a CEO — how has all this worked out for Rutan? The one-hundred-employee Scaled Composites managed eighty-eight consecutive profitable quarters in an industry that is perennially profit challenged. The firm's regular clients include NASA and most of the big aerospace companies, and it is known as the go-to concern when a need arises for an aircraft that flies higher or faster or farther or more nimbly or less expensively than any other has. Scaled Composites has never lost a test pilot and has rolled out twenty-six new types of aircraft in thirty years, at a time when giant aerospace companies struggle to get a single new aircraft out in a decade.

Rutan's unwillingness to stick with rules, overplan, constrain employees, or do anything the way it was done before served Scaled Composites especially well when the company set out to design and build the first private-sector, reusable spacecraft. In 2004, Scaled's *SpaceShipOne*, boasting an almost outrageously novel design that includes rotating wings and a rocket engine running on rubber and laughing gas, safely flew more than one hundred kilometers up into the edge of space and back twice in a week. That feat earned Rutan's team the $10 million Ansari X-Prize, and the job of creating a five-passenger space vehicle for Virgin Galactic, the company set up by Virgin Atlantic Airways' founder Richard Branson to carry paying passengers into space. Scaled Composites will remain in control of the project because, in Rutan's words, "It's way too risky to turn this technology over to another group and let them manufacture and operate it." He's simply seen too many aircraft companies sink projects under the weight of rules, planning, routine, and oversight.

It's easy to assume that it takes a strong manager to run an orderly company and a weak one to let a company become somewhat messy and disorganized. And it's true that a manager who's unwilling or unable to provide guidance, inspiration, or other forms of leadership is likely to see her organization devolve into unproductive disorder. But as we've seen, organizations can be messy in highly useful ways. And some managers are adept at cultivating this sort of productive disorder, though it hardly stems from weakness. Let's take a look at some of the ways in which managers have profitably allowed various types of disorder to slip into their organizations.

Patient Mess

A manager who recognizes an opportunity to apply a usefully messier touch to an ordered organization can face skepticism from employees, directors, and customers. In that situation, starting with just a piece of the organization rather than the whole can help lower the perceived risk and provide a proof of concept that paves the way for broader changes.

Patrick Charmel, the forty-four-year-old CEO of Griffin Hospital in Derby, Connecticut, has recognized the effectiveness of that approach. For the better part of a decade, the community hospital had been losing patients to hospitals in more affluent communities. Finally, the Griffin board of directors decided to invest in building a new obstetrics wing. Charmel and his management team commissioned a survey of women who had recently given birth, asking them what they would like to see in an obstetrics unit. The answers came in: Mothers wanted not only their husbands in the room during delivery, but also their children and their own parents. They wanted rooms that didn't look like hospital rooms. They wanted double beds, so their husbands — or whoever — could sleep next to them. They wanted Jacuzzis. They wanted big windows and skylights. They wanted large, comfortable lounges where the family could gather at all hours. They wanted nurses who constantly paid close attention to them and doctors who always followed up on problems.

A bit taken aback by the colorful and daunting list of requests, the rangy, soft-spoken but direct Charmel decided to see which of these sorts of needs were being met by the competition. He had one of the hospital's female managers stuff a pillow under her dress, and the two of them visited every obstetrics and maternity ward within an hour's drive, posing as expectant parents who wanted to tour the facilities. The rest of the management team researched obstetrics wings around the country. The answer: no hospital they could find addressed these sorts of requests. Charmel decided Griffin would come as close as it reasonably could to responding to the wish list that had come up in the survey.

The first step, presumably, would be to heavily winnow down and prioritize the list. Some of the ideas, like allowing children in delivery rooms, seemed goofy. Some, like skylights, seemed frivolous. Some, like Jacuzzis, seemed downright dangerous, since it is widely known that bathing during labor carries a risk of infection. As for double-size hospital beds — well, they didn't even exist. And how was the hospital supposed to change the behavior of doctors and nurses, who tend to be fiercely protective of their routines? It's one thing to give hardware shoppers the sort of messy completeness they're looking for; it's quite another in a hospital. Besides, prioritizing and focusing are basic functions of senior management. Funds, time, skills, and other resources are in limited supply, but ways in which they can be spent are not. Prioritizing is one of a manager's primary means for imposing order on a large, messy universe of demands.

Which is why Griffin's board was shocked to hear Charmel argue for skipping the winnowing, focusing, and prioritizing, and, instead, just going ahead and doing everything on the list. "We asked them what they wanted, and they told us," Charmel said of the mothers. "Now let's just give it to them." The board reluctantly said okay, though Charmel wouldn't be allowed to spend more per square foot than other hospitals spent on average on their facilities in the state.

The new obstetrics and maternity unit had rooms where families could gather. It had skylights. It had a Jacuzzi. (Research revealed that the concern over infection while bathing during labor was a myth.) It had custom-built double beds. It had birthing-helper classes for children and grandparents. And it had "primary-care nursing" — each patient was the responsibility of a single nurse who would make sure that all of the patient's needs were met and that the doctors were taking care of business. The wing came in on budget, thanks to heavy leaning on contractors and suppliers, and creative corner cutting that included buying some of the furniture on sale at local discount stores. More important, patient response was immediate and enthusiastic. But some of the nurses complained to Charmel about the loss of routine and order in the wing. Swarms of families and friends were using the communal rooms for pizza parties or late-night card games. "Excellent," replied Charmel. "That's what the room is there for." Husbands were showing up after working late shifts and climbing into the double beds with their wives, waking up mother and baby. "What's going to happen when we discharge her tomorrow?" reasoned Charmel. "He's going to come home from the late shift and wake up his wife and baby. As long as they're not complaining, we might as well let them get used to it here." Many of the nurses and obstetricians grumbled about the new, unconstrained patient demands on their time and attention, and some left. But as word of the strange new wing got out into the medical community, top-notch obstetricians, including younger doctors and female doctors often favored by expectant mothers, started actively seeking out Griffin. Obstetrics admissions doubled.

"Can we build an entire hospital like this?" Charmel asked the senior management team.

The surveys went out, and the list of demands came rolling in. Patients wanted nice furniture. They wanted full kitchens. They wanted carpeting. They wanted nurses near their beds essentially all the time — elderly patients often press the call button not because anything is wrong but to make sure someone is out there, just in case. They wanted unlimited visits at any time from anyone and everyone. They wanted their pets to visit. They wanted fish tanks. They wanted spouses or family members to have beds so they could sleep right there in the room with them and help take care of them. They didn't want to get lost in the halls. They wanted double rooms so they wouldn't be alone, while at the same time wanting privacy. And they wanted a better understanding of what was happening to them medically. Once again, Charmel pushed for doing it all, no exceptions.

Today, visitors to Griffin Hospital are greeted in the lobby and escorted by a staff member to make sure they don't get lost; signs and pointing are banned. The corridors are carpeted; special wheel bearings were brought in to keep gurneys from bogging down in the thick pile. L-shaped double rooms were custom designed to keep each patient out of sight of the other for privacy while affording both a window view. Some are "care partner" rooms, in which family members who help provide care are allowed to stay with the patient on couches that fold out into double beds. Nurse workstations are scattered around instead of centralized so that every patient can look out from his or her bed and see a nurse sitting some fifteen feet away. No room is more than one hundred feet from a well-stocked, home-style kitchen, open to all patients and visitors twenty-four hours a day, where muffins are frequently baking. Patients are encouraged to look over their charts, as well as literature about their illnesses, and are asked to take part in a detailed "case conference" with doctors and nurses the day after admission. For those who want to learn even more, a lay-oriented medical library is open for patients to browse and study, often alongside doctors leafing through medical journals. The hospital couldn't get health clearance for patients' pets, so it brought in specially groomed and trained dogs to make rounds. The fish tank in the psychiatric ward is made of bulletproof glass to satisfy security regulations.

Patient satisfaction soared to 96 percent, a level virtually unheard of in the hospital business, and admissions have risen an average of 2 percent a year. Griffin's no-prioritizing, no-winnowing approach has become a product in its own right.

Some forty hospitals a year each pay Griffin $3,000 to give administrators and caregivers tours of the facility, and more than one hundred hospitals pay $15,000 a year to become members of Planetree, a Griffin-owned organization that helps hospitals duplicate the Griffin model. Not a bad result for scaling up the benefits from a single wing to a whole hospital's worth of messy management.

Hacking out a Compromise

As with human couples, a union between neater and messier organizations can lead to tensions. It takes skilled managers to work out the sorts of compromises that can preserve much of the messier organization's useful disorder while avoiding dysfunctional clashes — and ideally help the neater organization open up to at least a little disorder.

It would be hard to find a more improbable candidate for the job of mess ambassador to orderly companies than Miguel de Icaza. In the early 1990s, de Icaza was a long-haired, boisterous undergraduate at the Universidad Nacional Autónoma de México, where he stumbled on computer bulletin boards used by programmers in the open-source software movement — the approach to software development that hinges on free distribution by a loose confederation of independent programmers scattered around the planet who communicate via the Internet. De Icaza quickly made a name for himself in the open-source community writing deft, useful programs such as spreadsheets, as well as by hacking into the heart of Mexico's largest supercomputer to demonstrate its vulnerability. After blowing a job interview at Microsoft in 1996 by lecturing managers there on why open-source software is better than Microsoft's, de Icaza enlisted hundreds of volunteer open-source programmers around the world to join him in writing GNOME, a program that layered a Microsoft Windows–like, easy-to-use graphical interface over the arcane commands previously needed to use open-source software. A critical step toward bringing open-source software to the masses, GNOME was an enormous hit, adopted by tens of thousands of users as well as by Hewlett-Packard, Novell, Red Hat, Sun Microsystems, and several other mainstream software companies that compete with Microsoft and its hugely dominant Windows software.

In 1999, de Icaza and a friend founded a company called Ximian, in Cambridge, Massachusetts, to develop more open-source programs and to get paid by companies for customizing and supporting the software. Then in 2000, de Icaza was struck by a vision — on a box of cornflakes. The box offered a free computer game that, like most software in the world, ran only on Windows. There was no denying it: as long as Windows remained so dominant, most programmers would write their programs to run on it instead of writing open-source software, further perpetuating Windows' dominance. What would level the playing field, de Icaza realized, was a set of programming tools that would let programmers write software for both Windows-based and open-source-based computers. Backed by $15 million in venture capital, de Icaza set Ximian and programmers around the world to work on the project straightaway, calling it *Mono*, Spanish for "monkey."

In 2002, Brady Anderson was a top programming manager and a sixteen-year veteran at Utah-based software manufacturer Novell, a large, old-line, Windows-based software company whose moribund product line had been losing more than a tenth of its business every year. Novell executives thought one way to stanch the flow might be to partner with hot young open-source software companies, so it dispatched Anderson to the slushy streets of Cambridge to check out Ximian. When Anderson entered the Ximian office, he saw little to encourage him. It looked more like a dorm than a place of business — a messy playground for water-pistol duels between young hippies over which a large, inflatable moose head presided. It was a far cry from Novell's hushed maze of cubicles, where interaction meant a meeting in a conference room at 9:00 a.m. sharp.

The picture seemed even less promising when Anderson laid eyes on de Icaza, a boyish, T-shirted fellow, rail thin in a way that suggested either extraordinary aerobic fitness or nutritional obliviousness. But de Icaza quickly proved an agreeable host — mellow, chatty, amiably confident, and surprisingly noneccentric. He articulated his plans and ambitions for Mono with something akin to religious fervor, and Anderson, to his own surprise, found himself agreeing with everything de Icaza said. "From that conversation, I decided we'd do most of our development work in Mono," Anderson says. He returned to Utah and told other Novell executives he had seen and heard the future of their company. Meanwhile, de Icaza, who had previously rebuffed several other large companies that had come courting because he doubted their commitment to open-source software, told his Ximian colleagues that he had sensed a kindred spirit in Anderson. The next year Ximian became part of Novell.

But how would Novell, a company long accustomed to developing software with tightly organized groups of employees in neighboring cubicles, mesh its operations with a company that relied on a loose band of maverick in-house hackers who did their best work at 2:00 a.m. and communicated mostly online and a few hundred volunteer programmers around the world who did whatever they wanted to whenever they felt like it?

De Icaza knew that, for starters, Ximian would have to neaten up some. "To integrate the companies, we had to let go of our culture of independence," he says. Ximian and its forty employees agreed to move into new, more buttoned-down offices in Cambridge with — shudder — cubicles and conference rooms, though at least the moose head made the trip, too. De Icaza was used to coming in at noon to start work, but now he gamely staggered in for early-morning meetings. With Novell employees on the team and to keep Novell investors apprised of progress, project schedules had to be more clearly defined and responsibilities more tightly delineated. "Now one of my motivations is that I'm being paid to do this, and I have to deliver products," de Icaza says. On the other hand, he still has been able to hang on to many of his less-ordered management techniques. He relies on a crew scattered around the world, managed almost entirely through online communications. He hires not through résumés or interviews but by offering jobs to open-source contributors whose online work he admires. And he still usually works noon through the small hours of the morning when an absence of early meetings allows, and lets others at Ximian keep the routines that work best for them.

Meanwhile, Anderson was determined to bring some of de Icaza's high-bounce, messy style to Novell's staid culture. He repeatedly brought de Icaza out to Novell's headquarters in Provo, where de Icaza was encouraged to walk around and spread the gospel of open-source attitudes. Matt Asay, a business office director at Novell, concedes it took people a while to get used to "this Bohemian invader," as he refers to de Icaza. "People were uncomfortable at first, they didn't like it," he says. But changes started to take hold. Anderson's programmers, who had always worked out project details in conference rooms or over the walls between adjoining cubicles, gradually became comfortable posting their work online day to day and letting programmers they had never met take shots at it over the Internet. Instead of standardizing a single method to solving a software problem, Novell programmers learned to tolerate the messiness of multiple approaches among project programmers. "If there are three different ways of getting something done, Miguel won't take a stand," Anderson says. "It's not efficient, but if you tell someone they can't do it their way, they'll probably drop out."

Novell has since thrown itself completely into open-source programming. In 2004, the company even shifted its corporate headquarters from Provo to Waltham, Massachusetts, twenty minutes from Ximian. The changes saw the company's stock price double from its level before the Ximian acquisition. Novell has more recently had some down quarters, not because of having slipped into the open-source camp, but in large part because so many other companies have been following its lead. Within eight months of Novell's announcement of its new open-source commitment, three of the largest players in the computer industry — IBM, Sun, and, of all companies, Microsoft — announced the transfer of significant chunks of their respective product lines to the open-source world.

De Icaza's and Anderson's efforts to fuse the messy world of renegade programming with the highly ordered one of cubicle-rat software development may have helped set the future of computing for years to come.

Cooking up a Mess

Entrepreneurs who create companies from scratch have a distinct advantage when it comes to building in disorder. They needn't overcome the inertia of entrenched processes, employees used to doing things a certain way, or a sea of investors of which some subset will always object to the risks of straying from the planned, consistent, and orderly. If an entrepreneur can come up with a helpfully disordered approach to some aspect of the business, there's simply less friction to keep her from implementing it.

Disorder is not the first thing to come to mind when one enters the stately art deco building across from Manhattan's Madison Square Park that houses the restaurant Tabla. But things start to get mildly and interestingly mixed up inside the restaurant, thanks to a decor that genteelly blends wood, mosaics, and metal in swooping architectural forms, simultaneously suggesting the exotic and the familiar. This mix turns out to hint at the blur in the menu, which features standards of upscale Western cuisine, such as lobster, veal, and bass, filtered through a mesh of Indian-and-otherwise-Asian-accented treatments, ranging from coriander-and-coconut curry to lotus roots and green cardamom. The blending of styles seems to work: a $75 prix-fixe charge has not deterred crowds at Tabla, and this in a city where Indian food is heavily associated with $10 meals in Second Avenue joints. There's no restaurant like it in New York City.

Which is actually a little odd in and of itself, considering that Tabla is technically part of a chain of eight New York City eateries in the Union Square Hospitality Group, founded and run by restaurateur Danny Meyer. None of the restaurants has any visible connection to the others in terms of decor or menu. One is a burger-and-shake stand, one a high-cuisine classic, one a jazz club, one a museum café, and so on. Other restaurant owners can rightfully boast if just one of their restaurants survives five years in New York's viciously competitive eating scene. But Meyer has not only kept all of his restaurants afloat, he has seen four of them make it onto the Zagat Survey's list of top ten restaurants in New York.

There is a link between the diversity among the restaurants in the Union Square Group and their success. If other restaurant groups don't outright clone their eateries, they at least generally work off a theme, such as following the latest trend in food, or sticking with high-end nouvelle style, or pitching at families. Meyer's model for how to develop a great restaurant, in contrast, thrives on inconsistency. The first step involves finding a partner who has a personal vision for a restaurant. Meyer's own vision resulted in the Union Square Café, considered by many to be the best restaurant in New York, and Tabla was the inspiration of former Union Square chef Michael Romano, now a full partner of the group. The rough vision is then turned over to a chef eager to spin it into a fully imagined experience, with full autonomy to shape the menu as he sees fit. Each restaurant becomes an independent corporation co-owned by the group, the partner, and the chef. In fact, the only constraint that Meyer and his company place on the venture is that it be different from everything else out there, and the more different, the better. In some cases, the vision draws on a familiar idea, but it never ends up with a conventional result. Susan Salgado, a director with Meyer's company, offers the group's "Jazz Standard" as an example. "Jazz clubs are usually dark, dingy, and have lousy food," she says. "So our jazz club is clean, roomy, with excellent food."

The group is so determined to maintain each restaurant's individuality that it even eschews such obvious opportunities for economies of scale as standardizing paper products. The group is not entirely hands off, though. For one thing, it provides some computer, accounting, marketing, and administrative services to all the restaurants. More important, Meyer urges a loose operational philosophy for the entire enterprise — one aspect of which is that managers shouldn't be autocrats in the restaurants. It sounds like a reasonable constraint, but it can take some getting used to for top chefs, who are typically trained in the French tradition in which the head chef is absolute, heavy-handed ruler, if not raging tyrant. Tabla chef Floyd Cardoz stops by our table and tells us he too came up under the "abusive chef" model, and had to adjust. "I like it this way better," he says. One reason Meyer insists on nondespotic chefs is out of respect for employees, whom the group generally treats well; its policy of providing free health and dental insurance and 401k plans, for example, is generous by any standard and off the charts in the restaurant world. But even more important, Salgado explains, Meyer wants the kitchens of his restaurants to be scenes of rampant and collegial improvisation, not dictatorial consistency and rigidity. Cardoz notes that he often works without recipes, wielding some twenty-one different spices. "I just play," he has said of his approach to creating dishes.

An emphasis on improvisation is in fact a larger part of the Meyer philosophy and applies at least as much to how servers interact with customers as it does in the kitchen. In Tabla, waiters seem to be almost prowling through the restaurant, on the hunt for a customer who might in some way need attention. But they prove to be neither brusquely hyperefficient nor fawning; rather, they are relaxed and engaging. Diners who mention that they are having trouble deciding between two dishes might be surprised to find their waiter bringing them small dishes of each. A $35 glass of dessert wine that tempts but is ultimately judged too big a splurge might end up on a table anyway, a waiter's gift. These are the sorts of delightful shocks that engrave a dining experience into memory. To make sure waiters are good at improvising them, the Meyer philosophy includes the notion that traditional serving skills be somewhat downplayed in the hiring process. "We're looking for people with the emotional capacity to deliver hospitality," says Salgado. If they care and can express it in creative ways, the rest can be taught, figures Meyer.

But a restaurant can't run well as a glorious mess of improvisation. At any one time, as many as fifty dishes are in some stage of preparation at Tabla, and they have to be completed and delivered to tables with impeccable timing — a mechanically complex process that, if marred in any way, will ruin a dining experience no matter how brilliant the menu or engaging the waiters. In most restaurants, waiters typically do what they can to avoid extraneous interactions with customers, so they can focus on getting a correctly prepared dish to the right diner at the right time. But Meyer wanted to indulge and even encourage happy surprises at the customer end. To do it, he realized, the waiters would need to be able to rely on a highly ordered, highly predictable system of preparing and delivering food, leaving them free to improvise with customers on everything else. And that notion of a measure of randomness supported by a layer of order is the final pillar of the group's philosophy.

At Tabla, for example, exhaustive, explicit systems are in place for preparing ingredients, setting up the tables, running drinks, and assigning customers and waiters to tables: each waiter oversees two tables, each table at a different stage of the meal. An "expediter" in the kitchen essentially serves as a highly ordered interface between the improvisation in the recipes and the improvisation at the customer end, tracking by clipboard every order that comes into the kitchen and every dish that goes out to make sure the dozens of dishes are prepared and dispatched at the right time and in the right order. To fine-tune the systems and confirm that customers are getting the right sorts of surprises, the entire Tabla staff meets three times a day, for as long as an hour and a half per meeting, coordinating responsibilities and ironing out wrinkles. "Danny's model for a restaurant is a jazz ensemble," Salgado explains. "There's a background theme that's predictable, and the instruments can improvise around it."

In other words, the pleasurable surprises that make Meyer's restaurants unique depend on the kind of order that's standard in the restaurant trade. But as in life, it's variety that's the spice.

More Messy Successes

Messy Goliath Even when small companies become large ones, they can continue to reflect the personalities of their founder-leaders, and that can be especially true with regard to the level of messiness ingrained in the culture. One interesting example is the contrast between Microsoft and Apple Computer. Apple tends to get better press and word of mouth than Microsoft does, in part because it is the underdog to industry-dominant Microsoft, and also because Apple has won the devotion of fans of its products' high style. Because of Apple's status as David to Microsoft's Goliath, it's also tempting to imagine that Apple is the freewheeling, improvising rebel while Microsoft is a lumbering, rigid bureaucracy. In fact, Microsoft has always operated in a usefully messy fashion, while Apple is the picture of rigid order. Considering Apple CEO Steve Jobs and Microsoft chairman Bill Gates, it would be surprising if it were otherwise.

Jobs is famously a fastidious, turtleneck-only control freak widely known to rage at his teams when they've diverged from precise goals and schedules. Gates is known for encouraging independent teams to go off in many, often conflicting, directions, and is more tolerant of delays and changes. (And Gates could never be accused of fastidiousness in appearance, though he has neatened up a bit in recent years.) Apple has always focused on and driven toward a single, narrow goal — originally a more stylish PC, and then, when Apple couldn't make much headway there, an emphasis on stylish multimedia devices, most notably of late the iPod. Microsoft, meanwhile, has tried to enter virtually every corner of the computer world, from PCs to corporate servers to application software to multimedia to search engines. Apple keeps its developing products under tight wraps until it is ready to introduce them with a big bang as fully realized gems. Microsoft often throws together, under little secrecy, buggy, ill-functioning first versions of products, and then keeps fixing, shifting, and tweaking them until they're the most popular out there: The company's Xbox 360 video-game console, rushed out in a first version prone to crashing and even electrically frying, still went on to win an enthusiastic following. And Windows, Word, and Excel are now such utterly dominant products in their fields that it's easy to forget they were sneered at as unmitigated disasters in early incarnations. Apple finally scored a large hit with the iPod, but by early 2006 analysts were predicting the iPod would soon be losing market share.

A Few Good Messes The U.S. Marines operate under the same sort of rigid, pyramidal hierarchy as all the armed forces, which generally means that every officer has three officers reporting to him or her, right down the line from generals to corporals.

But when critical situations — especially combat — render the chain of command a cumbersome source of delay, Marines at all levels know from training that they are expected to seize whatever decision-making responsibilities are needed to get the job done. That's why when Marines meet for a premission planning session — never earlier than the night before a mission as per "plan early, plan twice" — the mission orders are given in loose form, describing broad goals and restrictions rather than specific actions. Why specify rigid actions when the fast-changing dynamics of battle are likely to render them irrelevant? If war is a mess, than warriors should be messy, too.

Messy Portfolios An entrepreneur can be usefully messy in ways that aren't reflected in the messiness of any one company. The disorder can instead manifest itself over multiple companies. But a skilled entrepreneur can find ways to benefit from the sprawl. Take David Slawson, whose past ventures have included, in order, a burger joint, a massage therapy practice, an alternative health care school, a clean-air car manufacturer, an ecology cable channel, and an herbal supplement distributorship. Most recently, Slawson founded and ran a company called Stirling Energy Systems, which builds solar energy power plants, and he's won $3 million in grants from the U.S. Department of Energy and a preliminary agreement to provide a major utility with up to $2.7 billion worth of electricity over twenty years, with another $1.4 billion under close discussion with another utility. One reason he won contracts is that, unlike many alternative power ventures, Slawson has been able to establish a track record of attracting private investment, averaging $2 million a year for nine years. The secret to his fund-raising? Slawson taps into the vast, affluent crowd of alternative health care and environmentally conscious contacts he gradually amassed through all of his other ventures, many of whom are also fans of clean power.

It's tempting, in considering these examples, to try to extract rules that lay out the secrets of effective, messy leadership and management. But the truth is, every manager who successfully incorporates a degree of mess into her organization seems to do it differently. And that's really part of the point, of course. Mess is about flexibility, variation, inconsistency, and the unexpected. If there were a single right way to do it, it wouldn't be messy. The best advice to the would-be disorder-savvy business leader: go and find your own way to mess up a company.

CHAPTER NINE

The Politics of Mess

Organization is a marvelous thing. What could be more
organized and more marvelous a spectacle to behold than a
Nuremberg rally, with its flags, its trumpets, its serried ranks of
thousands or tens of thousands of organized human beings, all
shouting exactly alike, all thinking the same thing.
— RALPH ESTLING, *SKEPTICAL INQUIRER* COLUMNIST

Cities once grew helter-skelter, with buildings sprouting wherever money could be raised for their construction, and with little regard for what sorts of edifices and dwellers might end up as neighbors or for how roads might have to wind, constrict, and fracture to navigate them. Paris circa 1850 exemplified this unconstrained, disordered approach to urban development. Almost an M. C. Escher maze of cramped alleys and skewed rows of apartment buildings, the dizzyingly disorganized city yet managed to harbor notable parks, palaces, monuments, and museums, not to mention holding a worldwide reputation as one of civilization's cultural and social apexes. But growing annoyed with the ubiquitous crowds, the traffic bottlenecks, the lack of sewers, and the slums, among other features of Parisian life, Napoleon III authorized Baron Georges-Eugène Haussmann in 1853 to straighten out the big mess. The personally hyperfastidious Haussmann embarked on a half-billion-franc urban makeover that included essentially razing the heart of Old Paris and taking down or refashioning some 60 percent of the city's buildings, forcing much of the less affluent population to migrate out. He slashed a dozen broad, long, straight boulevards into the city in the form of spokes radiating from the Arc de Triomphe, intended both to provide grand views of various landmarks and to demarcate and physically separate neighborhoods, slicing the city into twenty arrondissements. When it was all over, Haussmann had provided a new paradigm for generations of European and American urban planners to come. The designer city: a vast, three-dimensional work of art to which a population — or at least the subset of the population with sufficient taste and means — could happily accommodate itself.

Plus ça change, sighs Joel Kotkin, a feisty and amiably cranky expert on the growth of U.S. cities and a senior fellow at the New America Foundation, a public-policy think tank. Kotkin says Haussmann's artisto-intellectual descendants today find some expression in New Urbanism, a movement that picked up steam in the New Economy of the late 1990s and continues strongly despite the bursting of that bubble. New Urbanists argue for cities that each have a dense urban core serving as an engine of attraction, thanks to stylish apartment buildings; bustling business centers jammed not with shipping docks and smokestacks but with advertising agencies, telecommunications consulting firms, and other employers of "the creative class"; and most important to pedestrian-oriented designer alleys lined with coffeehouses, bookstores, restaurants, and art galleries. Surrounding this bustling core, say New Urbanists, should be outer "rings" of suburbs and exurbs dedicated to vast crops of apartment buildings, town houses, and houses, connected to the city's attractions by light rail lines that radiate like spokes from the core.

This neat, highly ordered conception of the city, which has influenced urban planning in Boston, Washington, San Francisco, Seattle, and many other U.S. cities, is perfect, says Kotkin. Perfect, that is, if you're anything like the sort of people who become experts in urban design and follow movements like New Urbanism. By which Kotkin means advanced-degreed professionals who love hip, urban life — New Urbanists pass the word *hip* around like a holiday confection — and who are relatively affluent, cultured, design conscious, work focused, craving of high stimulation, and as likely to take root in ideas as in places. They are also inclined to start families later in life and keep them small, if they have children at all. In other words, urban designers tend to want to make cities over in their own image. "They're building ephemeral cities for the nomadic rich," as Kotkin puts it.

What a dense, stylish urban environment and its predominantly residential outer rings do not provide, says Kotkin, are what most of the 36 percent of Americans who are currently raising children, plus the tens of millions more who help raise or plan to raise children, want: single-family houses, with enough land for a wildflower meadow (all right, a lawn), that are reasonably close to jobs, shopping, and entertainment. Such homes could in principle be located in the innermost ring of a New Urbanism–designed city, but only at an enormous premium, because competition to live near the richly endowed core will always be fierce and apartment buildings will hold sway. The vast majority of house owners will be relegated far into the outer rings, a long train ride from the resources that are the point of the New Urbanism exercise. Indeed, the U.S. cities that New Urbanists point to as the most livable are the very ones that seem to be driving families out. San Francisco has the lowest under-eighteen population percentage of any big city in the United States, about 15 percent. Less than 23 percent of households in Boston and Atlanta include children under age eighteen. In Seattle, children are outnumbered by dogs. Portland, Oregon, has hit its lowest level of children in eighty years. San Jose has been closing schools each year. "We've moved from stigmatizing people without children to celebrating them," says Kotkin.

A better model of a city for the family oriented — that is, for the people who carry out much of the actual living in and around cities rather than planning them — would be to take the New Urbanism core and all its rings, add more houses and a wider range of businesses, and throw them into a big shaker to undo all that planning and order. Pouring out of the shaker would be a rambling, widely varied blend of villagelike clots of semisuburbia snuggled right up against urbanlike clots of businesses and apartment buildings. What America needs, says Kotkin, is more sprawling, mixed, blurred, disorganized cities. What America needs is more cities like Los Angeles.

Kotkin lives in the Valley Village section of Los Angeles, a sea of small but pleasant houses pierced along a few axes by strings of strip malls. Strip malls are the bête noire of city planners, but Kotkin has some affection for them. L.A. strip malls, he says, are microversions of the New Urbanism city core, made affordable and geographically accessible to families and reflecting a broad range of tastes and ethnic identities. As an example, he points out a restaurant near his home that offers a clever blend of Japanese and American food amid eccentric decor. There's no long wait for a table, it's reasonably priced, and you won't find many like it anywhere else, Kotkin says, though you'll find some sort of unique strip-mall restaurant in neighborhoods throughout L.A., along with office buildings, warehouses, and machine shops. Strip malls and micro–industrial parks may not be stylish or lovely, but they nicely meet the needs of local residents in far-flung neighborhoods.

What's more, notes Kotkin, Los Angeles's disorder exists on multiple scales. Studding the city's minivillage landscape without much rhyme or reason are bigger chunks of urban and suburban development, ranging from a modest sky-scrapered downtown area to genteel Bel-Air to the Lincoln Heights barrio to carnivalesque Venice, along with pockets of culture both high and pop, ranging from the Getty Museum to Universal CityWalk — a cartoonish, family-oriented parody of a New Urbanism city core. Getting around via the city's dense maze of roads is perhaps not much easier than it was to get through Paris 160 years ago, but that reflects the wide, disorganized distribution of L.A.'s resources and attractions. "Life is unstructured, and a lot of it is best discovered just driving around," Kotkin says.

To design out this sort of messiness, says Kotkin, is to cut out the hearts and souls of cities and replace them with something that's clever and appealing but that ultimately fails to resonate with most of the population. The drive to create ordered urban utopias comes not from the public at large, he says, but from what he calls "the chattering class" — academics, journalists, and highly paid consultants who have something to gain from the notion that cities need to be carefully thought out and planned. This is an unexpected gibe from someone who, having held fellowships at Pepperdine and other universities and having written several books and innumerable magazine articles, has committed more than his share of chattering, but Kotkin notes that his own chattering must be of a different sort, given how frequently he's been vilified in print and elsewhere by his fellow chatterers. Besides which, he adds, he has only a high school degree. In any case, the most discouraging resistance he gets is from his current students at the Southern California Institute of Architecture, most of whom are irrepressibly eager to impose their designs on the canvas of a disordered city. "They all want to be Haussmanns," he says.

Kotkin can always point out that Haussmann was fired by Napoleon III in 1870. Not only had the financial cost of Haussmann's massive makeover proved a painful burden, but Parisians by and large keenly missed their sprawling, messy city.

Mess and disorder, and our biases against them, are woven into the fabric of society. The ways in which we as individuals and institutions forge relationships, achieve advantages, fight, protect ourselves, help each other, communicate, govern ourselves, heal ourselves, assemble our infrastructures — all this and more is modified, compromised, and enriched by the degree and types of disorganization tolerated in each instance. The role of disorder in any one of these areas could be the subject of many chapters, so this tour of mess "politics" — to employ the term in its broadest possible meaning — will by necessity be selective and superficial. But even a smattering of examples will show that just as people and organizations are messy and ordered to different extents and in different ways, so too are cities and nations.

Mess Around the World

The United States

Americans like to think of themselves as being a diverse, free-thinking, and independent lot, and of the United States as a nation unburdened by excessive political and social order. It's true that the United States can fairly be called a blended nation, thanks to a history largely dominated by immigration from around the world. Even those who take the trouble to trace their ancestry back to the Pilgrims are defining themselves through their immigrant roots. Home of the pizza bagel, America offers a vivid mix of ethnic identities that provides a sort of national ethnic metaidentity in its own right, and holds open opportunity and mobility where many other countries fall into categorization by socioeconomic classes.

On the other hand, the United States works awfully hard these days to keep people out of the country. A 2005 survey by scientific research society Sigma Xi revealed that nearly 60 percent of postdoctoral scholars at U.S. universities who aren't U.S. citizens have had trouble getting back into the United States after traveling outside the country. This despite the fact that foreign postdocs may be the best value in our workforce. The survey indicates that they work longer hours and are paid less than their already hardworking, low-paid U.S. counterparts, while publishing 30 percent more of the sort of high-powered, innovative, technical and scientific research that helps drive the U.S. economy. And where the government leaves off in its efforts to squelch the influx of global blood into the country, others are prepared to take up the slack with enthusiasm, as witnessed by the Arizona-based Minuteman Civil Defense Corps, which recruits armed citizens to patrol the border with Mexico. According to a poll conducted by Rasmussen Reports, Americans are evenly split on whether this sort of thing is a good idea, leaving open the question of whether their reverence for independence and opportunity is better represented by the illegal immigrant struggling against the odds to find work or by the gun-packing vigilante eager to track him down as a hobby.

One of Americans' proudest traits is a quickness to stand up to the sort of abusive authoritarianism often required to assert firm, consistent, uniform order over a people. The self-perception of this don't-tread-on-me mentality was particularly reassuring after World War II, when U.S. psychologists lined up to explain that the German character contained a subservience that allowed strong-arming by a sociopath such as Hitler, whereas the American character clearly did not. Yale researcher Stanley Milgram set out to prove it in 1961 with an experiment in which an actor would instruct a subject to inflict increasingly severe "electric shocks" — the subject didn't know the shocks were faked — to another person in the name of research into learning and memory. Milgram envisioned first demonstrating that Americans would shrug off such pathological guidance and refuse to electrocute an innocent victim, and then that just-following-orders Germans would readily get with the program. As it turned out, there was little point in going to Germany; every single one of the American subjects was successfully pushed into applying what he or she believed was a jolt of 300 volts, a level labeled "Danger: Severe shock," to the screaming victim, and two-thirds of them continued to up the juice to an apparently lethal level of 450 volts when ordered to. In one variation of the experiment, a third of the subjects obeyed orders to physically force the victim's hand into contact with the shock-delivering mechanism.

On a less gruesome note, but one that perturbs on a more constant basis, America shares with most developed countries a problem with noise pollution. Aural noise, at least to the extent that it's random, is a form of mess, and can be highly distracting — though that's not necessarily the problem in an inarguably and constantly noisy city like New York, since the brain is quite good at filtering out constant noise. The bigger problem is that as noise grows louder, it starts to become a health hazard. Times Square's sustained decibel level of 89 — one of the loudest found in any major city in the world — is regarded by experts as high enough that prolonged exposure can cause high blood pressure as well as threaten permanent damage to higher-frequency hearing. In 2004, Mayor Bloomberg openly declared war on New York's noisiness; *New York* magazine made noise a cover story; and U.S. representative Nita Lowey, whose district borders the city on the north, helped spearhead an effort to pass federal noise restrictions on cities. But in the end, New Yorkers may actually have relatively little to whine about. The real cacophony in the United States isn't from subways, traffic, jackhammers, and street vendors; it's from tractors, combines, and threshers, so much so that three-quarters of farmers in the United States suffer from hearing loss. For them, a visit to New York City might be a chance to grab a little relative peace and quiet.

Germany

Hans Rindisbacher, a professor at Pomona College outside of Los Angeles, was crossing an empty intersection on foot one night when a passerby on the sidewalk behind him started shouting angrily at him. "Are you color blind?" the man roared, pointing at the red DON'T WALK sign. Rindisbacher was momentarily taken aback — there was, after all, not a car in sight — but then remembered he was visiting Germany, where even minor transgressions of regulatory, business, and social conventions can lead to loud confrontations.

Germans often yell in public at perfect strangers, as well as at neighbors, over what they perceive as the flouting of proper order, says Rindisbacher, who grew up in German-speaking Switzerland and now specializes in German studies. You can expect to be dressed down by whoever happens to be near you for walking on the wrong path, ordering at the wrong window, or placing the wrong kind of trash in the wrong bin. This can be unsettling for visiting Americans, who back home might be annoyed at the fellow who slips into the twelve-items-or-less line with fourteen items, but typically would not criticize a stranger's behavior out loud. Being a visiting foreigner who doesn't know the ropes won't win you much slack in Germany, either, notes Rindisbacher. In fact, he says, Germans tend to be even more expressively annoyed at the noncompliant behavior of people they perceive to be clueless outsiders.

Rindisbacher suspects that Germans' outspokenness toward those who don't do things a certain way dates back centuries to the tradition of guilds — organizations of craftsmen who kept tight control on the training and employment of workers in most fields, be it bricklaying or accounting. A career in a guild-dominated field meant first being taken on as an apprentice who could expect to be browbeaten for years by a demanding "master" intolerant of the slightest deviance from his meticulous techniques. Eventually, the apprentice would become a master expected to treat his own apprentices in exactly the same way. Though the guilds are long gone, their impact is still felt in Germany via powerful labor unions and a body of workers' rights regulations that makes it exceedingly difficult for companies to fire or transfer a worker, let alone get them to do things differently. While looser, more dynamic American-style business practices are starting to take hold in Germany, says Rindisbacher, the how-dare-you-not-do-it-this-way culture is tough to kill and spills beyond the workplace.

The German expectation of order has also been associated with the peculiarities of the German language, which, unlike English, is a highly structured and consistent one with few exceptions in grammar, spelling, or pronunciation. English, for example, permits a certain amount of improvisation in how the parts of a sentence can be arranged, but German demands sticking the verb at the end of a sentence so that a listener or reader must sometimes wade through a long, complex parade of nouns, adjectives, and prepositions before finally getting to find out what the fuss is all about. Having to learn to speak in this somewhat rigid and ponderous fashion surely has an effect on how people think, or so the theory goes. Actually, this once widely accepted link between the German style of thinking and its language had fallen out of vogue over the past few decades, but it is being reasserted by scientists in the wake of brain-scan studies that seem to support the notion of strong language-thinking links.

There may be another language-related reason why Germans can be less tolerant of mess than others: they don't really have a word for it. The closest is the word *unordnung*, which means "unorder," but that leaves Germans able to think of mess only in terms of what it is not, rather than having a concept for mess as a condition in its own right. It's like understanding *coolness* only as "unwarmth." It may be harder to appreciate something when the only way to conceive of it is as the absence of something else, especially when that something else is generally cherished. Many English words and phrases that refer to mess-related concepts and processes are utterly untranslatable into German in any meaningful way, adds Rindisbacher. *Yard sale* is an example. Relatively few Germans have yards or garages, he notes, and if they did, they wouldn't have hundreds of excess possessions with which to fill them, let alone expect others to buy them.

The strong brand of environmentalism one encounters in Germany also has a whiff of excess order to it, says Rindisbacher, particularly when it comes to recycling. A pile of undifferentiated trash feels to some like a form of uncomfortable lawlessness, in that it invites the close proximity of items that don't normally belong together. "There's nothing wrong with a piece of fruit, a pair of underpants, and a teddy bear, but if you throw them together then you have something awful," he explains. "It violates the social order of everyday objects." The sorting of trash required for recycling restores some of this order, he notes — and Germans, as a rule, recycle with zeal.

Germans aren't less mess-friendly than Americans in all ways. For one thing, says Rindisbacher, they tend to be more relaxed than Americans about their work schedule, taking more breaks, lingering longer at social meetings, and knocking off sooner. They can also be highly innovative — especially when they're expected to be, as in the case of automobile and other engineers. And when it comes to waiting in line, they are free-wheeling to an extent that would appall most Americans, says Rindisbacher, often forming shapeless swarms beside cash registers, shouldering in front of each other, and walking around barriers intended to keep crowds queued. That's not because they don't respect the rules for lining up; it's because there *aren't any* widely accepted rules for lining up. Rather, everyone seems to have their own.

Incidentally, though Milgram was too horrified by his results with Americans to take his "shocking" experiment to Germany, other researchers performed it there and found that German subjects were 30 percent more likely than American subjects to administer to innocents what they believed were lethal levels of electricity.

France

France has long taken an unusually ordered official view of the various ethnic variations among its citizens and permanent residents, and especially among immigrants. It has essentially maintained that such variations don't, or at least should not, exist. In the United States and the United Kingdom, it would be unthinkable for the government to refuse to acknowledge the cultural and religious differences of its immigrants; these nations at least pay lip service to the benefits of diversity and have in many ways recognized the appropriateness of affirmative action. Germany and Austria tried to finesse the challenge of accommodating immigrants by allowing for two categories of resident: the full citizen and the "guest worker," the latter category implicitly making room for the immigrant who might behave differently and have different needs, if at a cost of having to give up some rights and benefits. France, on the other hand, simply decreed that French citizenship confers a national identity that subsumes any other. As a result, the government not only refused to consider any special programs or allowances for immigrants who might face discrimination or other difficulties, it even refused to specifically survey immigrant populations or in any other way study the situation. The government did, however, take the trouble to regulate mosques — there are only six mosques with minarets in the country — and ban the wearing of religious head scarves in schools, moves that did not sit well with the country's five million Muslims, nearly a tenth of the population. Many of them live in the poor neighborhoods that surround Paris, the contemporary embodiment of the first outer rings that originated when Haussmann's makeover sent the poorer residents of Paris packing and left them disconnected from the city, and where today unemployment among workers under age twenty-five runs near 50 percent. It was, of course, these young Muslims who initiated more than two weeks of intense rioting, first around Paris and then all over France in 2005, shaking the country to its core and battering its image worldwide. That produced a serious mess, but apparently the suburban residents had long been considered messy anyway, at least by President Jacques Chirac, who in 1991 openly referred to the problem of "the noises and cooking smells" emanating from the homes of immigrants there.

Foreign visitors to Parisian parks are sometimes surprised to be accosted by a uniformed guard who brusquely tells them to get off the grass, or, if they have children, to remove them to another section of the park altogether, despite the absence of signs warning of any restrictions. The visitors are not being gratuitously harassed; they are being welcomed to an essential element of French society: assuming that something is prohibited until you have positively ascertained that it is not. Though the French are fairly maniacal about distributing garish red and white *INTERDIT* — "prohibited" — signs in every nook and cranny of the country, their numbers pale in comparison to the catalog of acts one must simply know are prohibited. Rollerblading in public, touching certain merchandise in stores, not having a passport or identification card on your person, running to catch a Metro, driving with your parking lights on during the day — these and countless other infractions can result in tickets, arrest, or forcible ejection from your immediate location. The French, for their part, find foreigners — and especially Americans — exceedingly childish in their petulance over being taken to task for not complying with any of a bewildering, unpredictable, and seemingly gratuitous multitude of odd restrictions. That's because the French themselves are acclimated to the pervasive concept of *interdit* as preschool students. There are a number of children's books dedicated to explaining to tots why the endless stream of *interdit*s they are already encountering is critical to the smooth functioning of society. Here's how the book *Interdit, Toujours Interdit, Mais Pourquoi?* (Prohibited, Always Prohibited, but Why?) puts it:

All around us and in our daily lives, it seems as if there isn't anything that's not prohibited. It's enough to make you wonder if you have any rights at all! But actually, the prohibitions are essential, and there's a bright side to them. What's the point of all the prohibitions? . . . What would our lives be like if everything were allowed?

It's a reasonable notion, up to a point. Children have to learn not to run out into the street or eat candy by the pound. But the idea that children must be conditioned to embrace a ubiquitous and often arbitrary array of restrictions imposed on every aspect of life seems a uniquely French one.

On the other hand, the French do make use of a colorful vocabulary of mess, including *pêle-mêle*, which the English language has borrowed as "pell-mell," and especially *bordel*, or "brothel." The latter is commonly employed with enthusiasm in the form of *"Quel bordel!"* and translates into English as "What a mess!" The French are not alone here. The use of words that mean brothel to also signify mess turns out to be nearly universal. The middle-Persian word *balakhaana*, which meant "an upper room," eventually made it into Turkic and thence to Russian, Polish, Yiddish, Hebrew, and Lebanese, among several other Eastern European and Middle Eastern languages, in the form of *balagan*, which today is widely used to mean both "brothel" and "mess." (All English got from the deal was the word *balcony*.) Meanwhile, the Old Indo-European word *bherdh*, or "wooden plank" and later "a shack," became *bordel* in French, *burdel* in Polish, and *bardak* in Russian and Hebrew, again used to mean both "brothel" and "mess." English ended up with *board*, though also *bordello*, which sometimes stands in for mess in the United Kingdom, but not in the United States. Italians use *casino*, literally "a small house," to mean both "brothel" and "mess." One can't help wondering, in looking at this long-standing and widespread verbal intertwining of brothels and mess, if being messy didn't at one time carry a more interesting and provocative aura.

Japan

A midlevel manager at a U.S.-based subsidiary of Japanese industrial giant Fujitsu was brought to Japan to visit the home offices of his division and was taken to an enormous room of several dozen desks arrayed in a distinct and neat, if a bit asymmetrical, fashion. The desks, which had no partitions separating them, were all that served as offices for the division's managers, a host explained to him. The manager was impressed that senior executives made do with the same office facilities as the most junior of employees, but also noticed that the higher-ranked managers were grouped on one side of the room and had more space around their desks. He suddenly realized that the desks were set up in exactly the arrangement of the division's published organizational chart. Every time a manager arrived at work, glanced up from his desk, or got up to go to a meeting or the bathroom, he would be unambiguously reminded of where he stood in the organization. Still digesting this odd fact, the U.S. manager was whisked to a meeting of a dozen or so Japanese managers, presided over by a vice president. When a lively discussion sprang up over a proposed project, the vice president put his chin on his chest, closed his eyes, and soon started snoring audibly. Even more astonishing to the U.S. manager was the fact that no one else at the meeting seemed to find the snoozing worth noting. When the discussion died down, the vice president awoke, inquired about the results, gave his blessing to it, and ended the meeting. The manager learned later that the vice presidential nap wasn't indicative of a lack of interest or a sleeping disorder, but was rather a common solution to a knotty management problem. In a society that insists on both group consensus and deep respect for the opinions of superiors, how can group decisions be reached at meetings without either excluding the boss or failing to defer to his opinion? Easy: the boss kicks off the meeting, falls asleep, and wakes up when consensus has been reached.

Japan is one of the most order-obsessed nations in the world, and keeping a society functioning in the face of all that rigid organization and neatness can require a fair amount of resourcefulness. Some of the order is by necessity. Thanks to high population density and urban real-estate costs, most families must make do with tiny apartments. But with affluence comparable to that of Americans, Japanese families typically have a great many items to stuff into their small space. To avoid a genuine clutter crisis, Japanese often sleep on beds that are rolled up and put away in the morning, maintain storage areas under their floors and in their ceilings, and in general keep things in their place. They are also quicker to get rid of old possessions to make room for the new, and since buying other people's used items is considered a bit crass, the only option is simply to trash them. As a result, the curbs of Japanese streets are often piled with some pretty nice "junk." Japanese trash in many towns is further neatened by draconian trash-sorting requirements that include up to forty-four different categories of items that must be kept separate, such as chopsticks and bottle caps. Those who mix up steel cans with aluminum ones or who fail to wash and dry their used handkerchiefs before trashing them can expect to receive stern written warnings from trash-prowling volunteers who can, in some cases, get repeat offenders evicted from their homes.

The adherence to order in Japan sometimes seems irrational.

Some parking garages won't accept motorcycles, simply because they're not cars. On a Tokyo street on a rainy day during rush hour, where one's view can encompass ten thousand people, it can seem as if every single one of them has the same black umbrella. The Japanese also tend to be highly time organized, to tragic result in 2005 when the engineer of a Kyoto-bound train one minute behind schedule — a significant deficit in Japan — increased the train's speed to at least eighty miles per hour on a section of track with a forty-five-mile-per-hour speed limit. The train jumped the tracks and plowed into an apartment building, killing seventy-three people and injuring more than four hundred others. The country's rigid social hierarchies are reflected in its language, which allows for at least four different levels of politeness in manner of speech, adjustable for the genders, ages, and relative social, family, or business position of the speaker and listener. (The system can be cumbersome in the case of conflicting hierarchies, as, say, when a younger brother is the boss of an older brother at work, in which case the older brother would use deferential language with his brother at work but superior language elsewhere.) The written language relies on three separate systems of characters: one for the grammatical elements of a sentence, as well as for the names of some plants and animals and for anything that needs to be written phonetically; one for the hundreds of foreign words that have become a regular part of the Japanese language; and one for everything else. Japan also has a sort of caste system that leaves more than a million of its people essentially ineligible for better jobs, and in some cases better homes, simply by virtue of their ancestry.

But the Japanese can be messy in some ways by other countries' standards. Tokyo and some one hundred square miles around it represent one of the great urban sprawls of the world, a vast, dense, largely undifferentiated mixture of residences, businesses, heavy industry, and even farms, some of which lap right up against the edges of Tokyo proper. Visitors to Tokyo often think they're being teased when they're told that most buildings have no address, in the sense of a street name and number, but it's true; addresses refer only to a complex, irregular, and nearly useless system of districts and subdistricts. The only reliable way to find a building is to have someone familiar with it specify directions there by landmarks.

Weapon of Mess Destruction

The world can only assume that terrorists are eager to get their hands on a nuclear bomb, which if detonated in a city could flatten most of it, kill millions, and threaten an entire region of a nation with drifting radioactive fallout. True nuclear bombs require either plutonium or uranium. (*Dirty bombs*, which are several orders of magnitude less destructive, merely scatter around any sort of radioactive material.) Building a plutonium nuclear bomb is probably beyond terrorists' means, but a crude nuclear bomb based on uranium probably isn't. The bigger challenge to terrorists would be getting their hands on the needed fifty kilograms or so of "highly enriched" uranium — uranium that is extensively processed to have unnaturally high levels of unstable atoms. The bad news is that there are several plausible ways they could acquire the stuff. The good news is that the atomic instability that makes radioactive materials potential weapons also provides a critical tell: in any given second, some tiny fraction of the atomic nuclei in a chunk of enriched uranium spontaneously blows apart, hurling tiny bursts of energy called gamma rays into the environment. Enriched uranium, in other words, announces its presence, at least if someone's listening nearby with the right equipment. And herein lies an opportunity for a mess-savvy government to foil a nuclear plot.

The United States uses several types of sensitive detectors to foil attempts to smuggle enriched uranium into the country. At border crossings, airports, and seaports, for example, detectors examine cargo for gamma rays and for lead and other heavy-metal shielding that suggests someone might have something to hide from a gamma-ray detector. Detectors are also placed around major roadways leading into some large cities, sometimes at toll plazas. The problem is that, knowing about the detectors, terrorists are likely to enlist an ingeniously messy and very simple countermeasure. They'll hide a small, shielded sample of uranium in the middle of any of the thousands of densely cluttered cargo containers or trucks that can enter a seaport or border crossing or city during a busy hour, when agents and detectors tend to be overwhelmed checking out the many containers and vehicles that contain harmless items that can trip detectors. "Bananas, Fiestaware, beach sand, Coleman lanterns, smoke detectors, kitty litter, Kaopectate — these are all naturally radioactive," notes Carl Czajkowski, director of a program to test new radiation detectors at Brookhaven National Laboratory. Or a terrorist with a chunk of uranium can simply avoid official border crossings, seaports, and major entrances to cities, and sneak in through unobserved routes.

That leaves the government with two possible strategies. First, it could attempt to impose more order on would-be uranium smugglers by spending hundreds of billions of dollars to better seal up America's roughly twenty thousand miles of coastline and borders, and hundreds of billions more fencing off major cities, except for a few closely watched entrances, and then forcing each and every vehicle and container that passed through any of these points to undergo a thorough scanning — a process that would bring our borders, seaports, and transcity traffic, along with the economy, to an utter standstill.

A second strategy would be to match the messy behavior of smugglers by scattering detectors around more widely. Detectors are already available in the form of devices the size of cell phones, and these could be issued to all government workers and even to millions of civilians, and placed throughout public areas. Lawrence Livermore National Laboratory is working on a networked system of radiation detectors and cameras capable of identifying a vehicle carrying enriched uranium at highway speeds, and scientists at Pacific Northwest National Laboratory have come up with a flexible glass fiber detector that can be embedded in asphalt roadways. Installing these sorts of devices in large enough numbers nationwide might cost hundreds of billions of dollars right now, but a more random, smaller-scale deployment around cities could be affordable and offer a better chance than now exists to finger any rogue uranium. What's more, unlike the cost of sealing up borders and cities, the costs of detectors are rapidly plunging. A bigger challenge would be dealing with all the false alarms from innocently radioactive materials, including the radioactive substances in the blood of about one in twenty-six hundred Americans at any particular time because of a medical procedure. But new generations of detectors are emerging that can better differentiate between uranium and, say, kitty litter.

Any scheme to significantly improve our chances of spotting enriched uranium is going to carry a staggering price tag and still leave us with large holes and inconveniences. Perhaps the most useful way to apply the concept of mess to the terrorism threat is to recognize that in terms of national security, at least, we have been enjoying an extraordinarily neat and ordered way of life in the United States, and like all highly ordered systems it is therefore highly vulnerable to disruption. Lawrence Wein, a professor at the Stanford Graduate School of Business who studies port security, says that Americans must on one hand be psychologically prepared not to exhaust their resources trying to stop what may be inevitable but highly confined attacks, such as a dirty bomb or a suicide bomber, and on the other hand get the government to do whatever it takes to try to head off the catastrophic ones, such as a nuclear bomb or an anthrax outbreak. It is indeed a grim form of mess triage, but if it helps stop an almost inconceivable disaster, there's little to recommend against it.

Road Mess

A mile from the intersection of the Boston area's celebrated Routes 128 and 9 is a narrow, two- and sometimes three-lane road with a wicked curve that runs past department stores, upscale specialty shops, and good old Strymish's bookstore. This retail spread is sufficiently attractive to consumers throughout the area that traffic conditions along the cranky road range from sluggish to stop and go.

In the late 1990s, senior managers at the Stop & Shop Supermarket Companies reasoned that, since so many shoppers passed through that spot already, why not also throw in a really big supermarket? Predictably, the local community, based in the town of Newton, objected on the grounds that the addition of a giant supermarket would send area traffic over the top. No problem, responded Stop & Shop; the company would happily subsidize the conversion of the road into something a little more comfortable for the hubbub it channeled. Instead of two or three cramped lanes, the area could be served by a wide, modern, four-lane road with entrance and exit ramps and carefully timed traffic signals.

The concept of replacing older roads that have become overrun with more traffic than they were designed to handle with new, larger, straighter, more carefully organized ones seems perfectly sensible and has been a staple of traffic engineering and urban planning going as far back as the road itself. You'd think that of all the things a municipal, county, state, or national government could do, improving roads would be a surefire winner. There's just one small drawback to the approach: traffic frequently gets worse after a larger, more carefully planned road is put in.

The reason is simple. When a better, wider road is constructed between two points, it doesn't just service the cars that were traveling between those points all along, it also attracts new drivers who are impressed with the traffic-handling capabilities of the better road. And not only does an improved road attract travelers, it also attracts residents who want to live nearer to good roads and businesses that want to be nearer to a passing stream of potential customers. Now, one might reasonably argue that this sort of development can be a good thing from some points of view, but it doesn't alter the fact that traffic increases. The injection of this "induced traffic," as traffic engineers call the increase, more often than not wipes out whatever improvements in traffic flow the new road offered, and then some. University of California researchers who studied roads in thirty urban counties discovered that for every 10 percent increase in the number of new lane-miles, traffic increased by 9 percent. Another study estimated that expanding roadways in the Greater Cincinnati area caused congestion to jump by up to 43 percent. In the case of Stop & Shop's planned improvements, estimates suggested the new road would see at least eight thousand additional cars per day, enough to nearly gridlock the area. Narrower, windy, busy roads unbothered by precisely spaced entrances and exits and by cleverly timed lights may be a bit of a mess, but they'll get people where they're going faster than wider, more organized replacements clogged with neat, highly regulated traffic jams.

The failure to account for induced traffic is only one reason traffic ordering schemes can go wrong. More generally, says Alan Horowitz, a traffic forecasting researcher at the University of Wisconsin at Milwaukee's Center for Urban Transportation Studies, traffic planning is hard to get right because all kinds of things tend to go screwy in ways that planners couldn't possibly anticipate, including shifts among political forces, lurches in the economy, and changes in where people want to live and work. "Thirty-five years ago I thought it was possible to play SimCity with traffic planning — you just plot land use and where people wanted to go, and you magically had a perfect transportation system," Horowitz says. "I eventually learned you have to go with the flow. We're constantly working in response mode to random and disorganized inputs." The best way to plan roads, he adds, is to "build the seemingly disorganized patterns into our planning." In other words, if people's driving needs are messy, it's not inappropriate for road systems to be somewhat messy.

In the case of Stop & Shop's proposed road project in Newton, the city's board of aldermen wisely declined to provide the votes needed to approve it. But the company's lawyers did their homework and came up with another neatness-based political gambit. It turned out that the board hadn't complied with an obscure paperwork requirement when it filed its decision, leading a court to rule that the company could go ahead and build its store and "improve" the roads. It seemed as if all the stars of excess order were aligning, until a local superhero of mess came to the rescue. New England Mobile Book Fair's Steve Gans coauthored a brief to help sway the Supreme Judicial Court of Massachusetts to rule against Stop & Shop, killing the project.

The building of wider, more carefully planned roads is not the only sort of traffic-neatening attempt that backfires. Many neighborhoods have discovered that speed bumps, intended to reduce accidents by forcing cars to make their way through in a slow, measured fashion, sometimes invite precisely the opposite sort of result. Some drivers are oblivious to the bumps until they are upon them, at which point they slam on their brakes, risking a loss of control or a collision with a closely following car. Other drivers discover that speed bumps actually provide less of a bump at high speeds than at moderate speeds, because the jolt to the wheels comes and goes so fast that the shock absorbers essentially don't have time to transmit it to the frame of the car. A stream of skidding, colliding, and speeding traffic is hardly what the installers of speed bumps had in mind.

A fix to the speed-bump problem seemed at hand in the 1990s when engineers at a traffic laboratory in the United Kingdom endeavored to restore order through more careful design. The result was the *speed hump*, a spread-out version of the bump that transmits a bigger jolt at higher speeds and less of one at moderate speeds. Humps were an immediate hit in the United Kingdom, Australia, and Canada and have caught on to some extent in the United States. But in recent years, numerous experts have come forward in all of these countries to argue that speed humps are more likely to contribute to injury and death than to prevent them. The biggest problem is the slowing of emergency vehicles, especially those carrying cardiac patients, whose chances of surviving drop with every wasted second. In London, which installed more than twenty thousand speed humps, the humps have been cited as a factor in the city's unusually poor survival rate for heart attack victims. Not only do humps slow fire trucks on their way to fires, but the jolt on a ponderous fire truck that can't or won't slow down is severe enough to have caused permanent spinal injury to firefighters. Buses designed with low floors to accommodate disabled passengers are especially vulnerable to damage and severe jostling, even at low speeds. The U.K. transportation lab that developed the hump now encourages communities to consider alternatives.

Not all projects intended to bring order to traffic make traffic worse. Most Boston-area residents who drive into the city or to its airport can attest to the fact that the "Big Dig" roadway project, largely completed in 2004, has shortened travel times, in some cases considerably. Many experts warn that the improvements, which included the construction of a new tunnel under Boston Harbor and a major highway underneath the city, will yield to renewed congestion in the coming years, but only time will tell. In the meantime, Bostonians can mull over the Big Dig's cost of neatness: $14.6 billion, or twice the cost of the Panama Canal in constant dollars. Considering the Big Dig project was highly controversial at the originally approved price tag of $4 billion, it's hard to imagine that there would have been much support for the project if anything approaching the true cost had been forecast.

But even if the delays return, the city will still have something to show for the billions. A major component of the project was tearing down an elevated major artery through the city and building in its place a New Urbanism–style pedestrian mall, accessible to outer-ring residents via several light rail lines.

CHAPTER TEN

Optimizing Mess

Anyone who has spent much time in midtown Manhattan has witnessed out-of-towners standing on the corner shifting uncertainly when a brief break in traffic sends the regulars scurrying across the road, as if the glaring DON'T WALK signals were red capes before bulls. Even visitors from most other big U.S. cities — people, in other words, who know a thing or two about hustle and bustle — end up aghast at the willingness of Manhattanite pedestrians to charge through vehicular gauntlets in blatant disregard of traffic signals and crosswalks. New York mayors Giuliani and Bloomberg each cracked down in turn on the city's jaywalking culture, assailing it variously as dangerous, disruptive to the carefully regulated flow of traffic, and even a form of petty crime that contributes to a general sense of lawlessness.

Whether jaywalking leads to muggings or drug abuse is a question beyond the scope of this book. But do jaywalkers thwart the efficiency of neatly timed pedestrian and traffic signals? If that were the case, then the most pedestrian-heavy sections of Washington, DC, Tokyo, London, and other cities where there is relatively little jaywalking should be models of people-movement efficiency compared to New York. But they aren't. As pedestrians in these cities congregate on corners waiting faithfully for a WALK signal, they form a large crowd. The crowd crosses together when it gets the signal and tends to remain together as it oozes down the block, a pig in a python limited by the speed of the slowest pedestrians in the group. When the crowd reaches the next intersection, it swells further. These waxing clots of pedestrians can clash with one another, block sidewalks, and even grow large enough to create a pedestrian-vehicular gridlock.

The crowds move more smoothly in Manhattan, thanks to the fact that jaywalkers thin them out by acting as a sort of relief valve. That's not to say that an increased disregard for traffic signals is always an improvement — traffic flow in Mexico City and Bangkok, for example, is chronically hobbled by an overabundance of jaywalkers. But blending a measure of jaywalking into a mostly orderly system of signal-regulated flow works fairly well.

A modest level of messy walking may not only get the crowds through the city faster, it probably saves lives. Though statistics on this point are hard to sort out, a search of newspaper accident reports seems to support the notion that in the United States pedestrians are more likely to be struck by cars while in crosswalks than when outside of them (assuming there's a crosswalk in the area). This makes perfect sense, even if it seems unjust. Crosswalks are typically at intersections, where vehicular traffic is converging and often turning from four or more directions. Pedestrians who are legally in the crosswalks often stare straight ahead as they walk — the sign has told them to proceed, so they assume they must be safe. But if pedestrian signals carried small print, they might reasonably read, WALK* *very carefully, keeping a close eye out for drivers on the cross street who have a green light and may be hurtling around the corner, not to mention distracted, drug-or-alcohol-addled, and sociopathic drivers who aren't prepared to give way even to legal crossers

Jaywalkers, on the other hand, generally don't need to be told to watch carefully and move nimbly. They also usually don't have to worry about traffic coming from more than one direction at a time, because they're either crossing midblock, away from intersections, or at intersections while the DON'T WALK signals are glowing, which means cars on the cross streets are stopped at red lights rather than turning into surprised crosswalkers. Perhaps all this is why police in New York City, as well as in Boston, where legend has it the term *jaywalking* originated (*jay* being slang at one time for a hick), rarely hand out jaywalking tickets. Be warned, though. In Singapore, jaywalking can get you six months in jail.

Analyzing Mess's Pros and Cons

Whether in business, at home, or in navigating New York's streets, messier isn't always better — it's all about achieving the *optimal* level of messiness. People and organizations tend to be biased toward excess neatness and order, which is why this book has been pushing messiness. But people and organizations aren't usually at their best when they're highly messy in all ways or highly neat in all ways.

There are plenty of exceptions. Pharmacies and ATM machines aren't likely to thrive on mess. Mosh pits and demolition derbies, on the other hand, might suffer from even a little order. But more often, people and organizations are at their best when they've achieved an interesting mix of messiness and order. In this sense, mess and disorder can be variables to be played around with, placing you on a frontier for experiment, rather than on a treadmill for rotely increasing neatness and organization. The formula for experimenting with mess is simple enough and works in personal, institutional, and technical contexts: Try being a little messier in some way, and see if there's an improvement. If there is, try a little more. Keep going until you get the sense that somewhere along the way things got worse, at which point you might want to try being a little neater. You get the idea.

The reason there are optimal levels of mess is simple, from a theoretical viewpoint. As you increase the messiness of a system in some way, you'll obtain certain benefits (in such forms as flexibility, serendipitous connections, and savings in the cost of neatness) and suffer some drawbacks (typically in conventional inefficiencies). Take, for example, that old favorite, the messy desk. As a desk becomes a little messy, more documents and other items may end up usefully at hand in sensible piles with few disadvantages, instead of filed away and forgotten. As the desk becomes messier, more items may be usefully at hand, but now it may also become harder to locate others. By the time the desk becomes buried under a single massive mound, the situation has presumably become dysfunctional.

The advantages and disadvantages to increasing mess don't kick in smoothly and steadily. With most systems, adding a little mess tends to lead quickly to some big advantages with few drawbacks. As the mess grows, the rate at which the advantages grow tends to slow and eventually trail off — a desk that's already pretty messy doesn't become a lot more useful when you add a bit more mess to it. Meanwhile, the rate at which the disadvantages accumulate will eventually start to take off — a very messy desk with just a small amount of open workspace can dramatically leap into utter uselessness when a little additional mess takes over that space. The result is that as mess is added to a system, the disadvantages will at some point start to overwhelm the advantages. That's why, for example, a little jaywalking can be a good thing, and ubiquitous jaywalking can be a big problem.

Remember, too, that mess levels can often be varied in multiple dimensions. In some cases, the mess levels can be experimented with independently — so that, for example, you could neaten up your office a bit without messing up your tightly scheduled day. In other cases, changing the mess level in one dimension will force changes in another — as when, for example, you start scheduling your day more tightly and realize you no longer seem to have quite enough time to maintain an immaculate personal appearance. In fact, a formal analysis of any system's multidimensionally optimized mess levels would be a formidable task. Suffice it to say, you're better off just playing around with mess and seeing what happens.

When Buses Fly

Ed Iacobucci often had to travel several times a week as CEO of Citrix Systems, the $750-million computer-server-software company he founded in 1989. In doing so, Iacobucci was regularly irked by the fact that business travelers who fly between smaller cities waste a lot of time making connections at one or more "hub" airports that serve bigger cities. It wasn't just a slight inconvenience; the lost time turned what otherwise might have been a day trip into an overnighter. Why couldn't airlines fly people directly between small cities, so they could get back home to their families by evening?

Three reasons, as it turns out. One is that on any given morning, there's likely to be at best only a handful of people who want to fly between any two small cities — barely enough to fill a tiny, slow, inefficient, weather-sensitive propeller plane. Second, traffic between most pairs of small cities wouldn't be steady or predictable enough to support a tiny plane's worth of regular routes and schedules — there might be four people one day and none the next. And finally, how would an inter-small-city airline set fares, given the likely variation in day-to-day traffic? A fare that would be profitable with four passengers could be a big money-loser with just two fewer passengers. One could always charter a small jet for the trip, of course, at a typical cost of about $5,000 or more for a journey across a couple of states, but that was hardly a universal solution to the problem.

Pondering these obstacles led Iacobucci to pose another question: could an airline operate with routes and schedules that changed day to day? Free of fixed routes and scheduling, planes could be dispatched in response to the constant and messy ebb and flow of customer demand. The trick would be to find a way to do it not as a pricey charter or "air taxi" service, whose aircraft are each booked for the needs of a single party, but as a genuine airline whose aircraft carried groups of independent passengers.

To answer that last question, let's start with another: would you rather be served by a bus that runs relatively infrequently but is always exactly on schedule, or one that runs more frequently but is sometimes five or so minutes late? Bus riders generally say that timeliness is the most important aspect of service. But timeliness is a surprisingly complex issue. When a bus repeatedly arrives late at its stops, transit departments usually simply schedule a later arrival time for the bus, which translates to slower, less frequent service. But it turns out that riders don't mind lateness much if they're warned about it. One study in London — a city of inveterate bus riders — found that people rated their level of satisfaction with bus service twice as highly when they were told about impending late bus arrivals. "The big question for many riders is this: 'Do I have enough time to run to Starbucks?'" says Matthew Rabkin, a research analyst for the Volpe National Transportation Systems Center, a transit think tank in Cambridge, Massachusetts. For that reason, a growing number of bus transit systems are tracking buses' locations via global positioning system (GPS) transmitters, and transmitting arrival predictions to electronic bus-stop signs, Web sites, and even cell phones. Alleviating riders' frustration with late buses then frees up planners to schedule more frequent, if messier, service.

Why, indeed, should buses run on regular schedules at all? Thanks to the transit "smart cards" with which many riders pay, as well as to onboard sensors that can track how many people get on and off a bus, the schedule for a route can be varied day to day or even, in theory, over the course of an hour as ridership climbs and falls. Buses on routes with unexpectedly low ridership can be diverted on short notice to routes that can better use them. For that matter, why should buses always be confined to their precise routes? Buses aren't stuck running on tracks. In Maryland's traffic-clogged Montgomery County outside of Washington, DC, GPS-equipped buses are monitored in a NASA-style control room by operators who can direct bus drivers off their routes to get around traffic jams, and even ease their way by remotely triggering green traffic lights for them. (Who says traffic lights have to be on a rigid schedule?)

Come to think of it, why have fixed routes in the first place? With GPS systems, onboard computer displays, and control centers equipped with space-age route configuration software, transit systems could constantly reconfigure bus paths to get closer to the positions of those people who actually want a ride at any particular time. In eastern Prince William County and the Manassas area in Virginia, anyone can phone in and request an "off-route" pickup from certain buses. Off-route drop-off points can likewise be requested. Other areas that offer some degree of flexible routing include Madison, Wisconsin, Salt Lake City, and suburban Detroit, and many others are looking closely at it.

Thus, the bus world offered a sort of precedent for Iacobucci. But translating the concept of flexible routes and scheduling to an airline is tricky. A big airline typically offers about fifty routes to serve some thirty cities, but it would take some sixteen million routes to provide direct flights between every possible pair of about the same number of cities, never mind the hundreds of cities a flexible-route, small-city airline would have to service — and all while filing and sticking to flight plans, getting matched up with crews, and following meticulous, heavily regulated maintenance schedules. In addition, intercity business travelers need reliable reservations, not just a strong hope that a plane will be available on the morning they need it. As for setting fares, that's not an issue with buses, where the cost per rider is often pocket change. Flying, in contrast, is relatively expensive, and the price of a ticket would have to be at least in the ballpark of regular airline tickets, while reflecting potentially wild variation among passenger loads.

At first, a small-city airline service seemed a lost cause to Iacobucci. But when he left Citrix in 2000, he found himself thinking he might be able to pull it off. For one thing, a company called Eclipse Aviation in Albuquerque, New Mexico, was working on a new class of six-seat aircraft called a *microjet*, which would carry six people with nearly the speed, efficiency, comfort, and weather-insensitivity of a big jet. Meanwhile, computer technology had advanced to the point where, Iacobucci believed, the massive mixing-and-matching chores required to figure out where to send each plane each day could be crunched out quickly and affordably enough.

Most important, Iacobucci dreamed up a business plan that added a measure of order to the messiness of flexible-schedule-and-route flying. "DayJet," as Iacobucci has named his airline, will let customers specify which cities they want to fly between on what days, at which point DayJet will figure out the routes it will need to fly to most efficiently serve the greatest number of customers on a given day, and what prices it needs to charge each passenger to make a profit. Bear in mind that the big airlines tear their hair out simply over having to figure out their optimal fixed routes every few months. DayJet's computers will work it out hour by hour, with countless times as many possible routes.

Critically, DayJet won't merely be figuring out a single, set price for a flight — it will offer each customer a menu of two or more prices based on how flexible the customer can be with regard to departure time. Basically, travelers will get a discount for giving DayJet a little wiggle room on timing, because that will increase the chances that DayJet can fit them in a plane with other passengers who want the same route on that day, dramatically lowering the airline's per-passenger costs. In this way, DayJet will essentially rejigger its scheduling and prices every time the phone rings. "We keep everything suspended as long as possible in a state of flux and disruption," says Iacobucci. "We don't freeze the schedule until the last possible moment." It's a form of order that will continually be messed up and then reordered. Iacobucci calculates as an example that DayJet will be able to fly passengers from Montgomery, Alabama, to Danville, Virginia, in two and a half hours for about $600, compared to five hours and $350 on a cheap commercial flight with a plane change, and $4,000 for a one-and-a-half-hour charter-jet ride.

It's something to think about while you kill time in Chicago waiting for your connecting flight to Appleton, Wisconsin.

Search Us

A mess can be rewarding as the object of random browsing, as for example at a flea market, through a stack of Sunday newspaper flyers, among the boxes of a departed loved one's mementos and documents, or at a café well situated for people-watching on a busy street. The Web is a giant mess, too. Aside from a few notable exceptions, such as Web censorship in China and the prosecution of Web gambling promoters and pornographers in the United States, anyone can put up any sort of Web site they want. There is no inherent unifying or overarching structure to the aggregate content, other than the technical rules followed in making the content displayable and the Web site reachable through an address.

But the sort of roam-and-scan browsing that works well in a flea market isn't really an option with the Web. There's no easily accessible list of all Web sites to browse through, and even if there were it's hard to imagine how a list of more than eight billion Web pages could be arranged to allow your eye to be caught by the pages likely to hold interest. Eight billion, if you're wondering, is the number of Web pages Google claims to *index* — that is, sort through to allow searching for text. By enabling you to hunt down Web sites containing certain words, Google and other search engines impose a form of order on the Web that makes fantastically useful what would otherwise be paralyzingly cluttered and inaccessible.

Google's impact is moving beyond Web text searches as it throws itself into shopping, maps, books, and images. It could even spill into the physical world, as the growing availability of tiny, dirt-cheap chips with built-in radio transmitters is expected to create an opportunity for Google to let people call up the exact location of their car keys or their children. Imagine being able to simply toss things into your attic without any concern for any form of organization, and then going to Google when you needed one of the items to call up its position within the attic. In short, Google is a wonderful way to get your hands on a specific piece of information out of a vast trove that no one has to waste time putting in order.

Googling has become such a routine, comfortable, and seemingly effective part of everyday life, that it's easy to overlook its drawbacks. One of them is what Bret Rappaport calls "the shade-tree problem." (Rappaport, as you may recall, is the natural-landscape-championing lawyer from chapter 2; he tends to put things in floratic terms.) Imagine, he says, a paralegal in a law firm asked to research case law relating to a Texas client's ire with a neighbor whose tree has grown to overhang the client's lawn, preventing part of the lawn from getting enough sun to survive. The paralegal would likely run to Lexis — the legal world's version of Google — and enter in the keywords *tree, lawn, neighbor,* and *shade.* A few cases pop up and are dutifully handed over, wrapping up the chore in five minutes. But thirty years ago, says Rappaport, the paralegal would have hit the Texas law books, running her finger over topic listings and indexes, perhaps intending to look up *trees*, but noticing there are also sublistings for tree houses, oaks, and bushes. In leafing through the book to check out some of the indicated cases, other cases leap out as interesting and possibly relevant. Perhaps it takes half an hour, but in the end the paralegal uncovers what turns out to be the most useful case in the books, one in which a vine invaded a neighbor's swimming pool, and in which the words *tree* and *lawn* never appear. What's more, this more prolonged and varied hunt has imbued the paralegal with a bit of perspective and even expertise in the subject that could come in handy in this case or another one. Over time and many such hunts, the expertise will extend to a range of topics. In other words, the very imprecision and inefficiencies of the conventional search process compared to Googling provides better results and a measure of enrichment, if at a cost in time.

A number of search engines have tried to get around the flaws in Google-style exact-match searching. Clusty.com is one of many that use "clustering," a technique that returns not just Web pages that match your exact queries, but also other search categories that might be fruitful. Thus, a search on *hot dog*, for example, yields a suggestion to look at Web pages related to sausages, Coney Island, and recipes — the sorts of categories that you might run across if you were browsing through a directory for *hot dog*. A company called Fast offers different search engines — some based on technology developed to help the U.S. military hunt down information useful in combating terrorism — that can derive a certain amount of meaning and context from the text it scans. That might allow it, for example, to distinguish sites that label certain movies as "bombs" from sites that offer recipes for homemade bombs, and to throw in sites that include the word *explosive* but don't mention the word *bomb.* A firm called Cymfony provides a search service that scours blogs as well as the Web to track down information with a particular subjective content — for example, in searching out references to a company, it can distinguish those that praise the company from those that flame it.

There are also innumerable search engines that specialize in a subset of the Web or in searching specific non-Web databases, and these engines often prompt searchers to dig deeper by enlisting specific criteria. A prominent example is Amazon.com's book-searching engine, which allows one to search its catalog with an eye for, say, Spanish-language books on ghosts published in 2003. (You can then follow up by checking each book's Amazon listing to see which offers the most words per pound.) A number of companies are working to make video searchable. IBM, for one, struck a deal with the NFL in 2005 to do so with all NFL game films, allowing a coach to call up in five seconds, for example, all of an upcoming opponent's third-down plays with four yards to go for a first down — the sort of task that had previously taken six hours. And then there's the search engine BananaSlug, which adds a random search term, such as *coral*, or *justice*, to your specified search terms. Strange as it sounds, you simply have to try it to appreciate its utility.

Some of these techniques work by trying to impose more order on the search process than Googling does and some less. One manager at the search company Fast routinely draws on a portfolio of thirty different search engines to track down information. In the end, there probably will never be one search technique, or one particular level of order, that will always prove appropriate or sufficient for dealing with a giant mess, especially one as gigantic as the Web. And somehow, that seems fitting.

Electronic Chips to Poker Chips

Changeable versus Cheap Chips Products that contain electronic chips usually use one of two basic types: hardwired chips, in which custom circuitry is engraved onto the chip, or programmable chips, which provide a range of standard building-block circuits that can be assembled by a software program — though not in an efficient way — into circuitry that performs the product tasks. The trade-offs are straightforward. Hardwired chips can cost $10 million, take years for design and manufacturing tooling, and can't easily be changed later on — but because they're so fixed and highly ordered, they're extremely fast, and once the up-front work is done they cost as little as pennies each to produce. Programmable chips, on the other hand, require little up-front investment and are easily designed and modified, but the drawback to all that messy flexibility is that they can cost $100 or more each to make and are typically tens of times slower than custom chips. But why choose? Increasingly, companies are turning to chips that combine a certain amount of custom, hardwired circuitry with a modest level of changeability. These semicustom, semimessy chips allow them to bring fairly high-performance products to market more quickly without prohibitive costs, either up-front or per-unit. *Purchasing* magazine predicts that by 2008 the market for semicustom chips will jump tenfold from its 2003 level to $1.4 billion.

Tender Smackdowns The various incarnations of cage, or no-holds-barred, fighting — in which two opponents have at each other with few rules, usually in a fenced-in ring, until one of them is twisted or pummeled into submission — have been widely perceived as gory, vicious, sadistic, and extremely dangerous events featuring brutal psychopaths. Famously branded a "human cockfight" by Senator John McCain, the sport has been the subject of frequent outraged magazine and television news pieces, and thanks in part to McCain has been outlawed in all but one state at one time or another. But the notion that cage fighting is more dangerous and brutal than boxing, a widely admired sport that is routinely and cheerfully covered by the same networks and publications that cluck at cage fighting, would have to come as news to the family and friends of Leavander Johnson, a lightweight champion boxer who died after a fight in September 2005 — the second boxer to be killed in a boxing match that year and the fourth to suffer serious brain damage. Over the years, some twelve hundred boxers have died from injuries sustained in the ring. The toll for the entire history of no-holds-barred fighting: the death in the Ukraine of an American fighter in his first bout, who hadn't been allowed to fight in the United States because he had been known to suffer from black-outs during training and who succumbed after four blows to the head. To be sure, there have been far more boxing matches than cage fights, making statistical comparisons difficult. But there's good reason why boxing should prove more dangerous on a fight-by-fight basis. Cage fighting may be messier than boxing in most ways, with its elbow strikes, kicks, and choke holds, and especially because of the frequency with which blood is drawn and then splattered by blows to the head — often to an opponent on his back — from fists covered with just thinly padded half-gloves. Boxing, in contrast, is relatively neat, featuring stand-up punching only, with heavily padded gloves. But here's the catch: boxing's repeated punching to the head wreaks havoc on the brain. The heavily padded gloves do a great job of minimizing gashes, ensuring longer fights that won't be stopped because of superficial bleeding, and allowing more opportunities to land blows to the head that drive the brain against the skull. (A knockout is a mild form of brain damage, one from which the brain may never entirely recover.) Middle-aged former boxers often speak with slurred words and with other difficulties or are palsied, because the mess in boxing is all inside the head, where the body is most vulnerable and least able to heal itself. The editors of the *Journal of the American Medical Association* have stated that 75 percent of boxers with twenty or more professional bouts are observably brain damaged. No cage fighters, in contrast, have been diagnosed with severe or chronic brain damage. Perhaps if all this were better known, no-holds-barred fighting might win over more boxing fans like Senator McCain, who reportedly was ringside in Las Vegas in 1995 to watch the boxer Jimmy Garcia receive fatal brain injuries.

Shake That Thing Pilots, like automobile drivers, want aircraft that handle predictably and provide precise control. Jet manufacturers have obliged over the years, producing control systems, often computer assisted, that make planes respond smoothly to the pilot's every input through the control yoke. Actually, they initially did *too* good a job of it. When an airplane moves too slowly, it risks losing its lift and plunging. One of the traditional tip-offs to this potentially calamitous loss of lift is a yoke that shakes, a sure sign that something serious is amiss, but in higher-tech planes there's no such inherent yoke "feel" to the impending drop. Planes often have warning horns, lights, and even computer voices to signal a dangerous loss in speed, but when a pilot has let a plane get too slow it's often because some other sort of emergency is stealing his attention — a cockpit fire, for example, or a close brush with another plane — and one more warning sound or light can go unnoticed. So manufacturers have now put back in a little of the erratic behavior they had taken out, in the form of a mechanism that causes the yoke to shake when the plane is about to lose its lift. This added mess plugs a problematic hole in an otherwise beneficial neatening.

The Silicon Mouse Cornell researcher Michael Shuler realized that a big reason drug effects are hard to predict is that when a drug is taken it's whirled on a wild, high-pressure ride through the body, where it can be broken down by the liver, absorbed by the intestines, and held on to by fat. Testing drugs on cells in a test tube is too neat, leaving out most of the chemical interactions that take place on the true ride. Testing them on animals and people is too messy, because there are too many interactions with hard-to-observe organs to get a clear picture. That's why, after a typical ten years and $800 million of this sort of research per approved drug, we still end up with Vioxx and many other drugs that get pulled off the market for unforeseen side effects — and no one knows how many hundreds of potentially terrific drugs never see the inside of a pill bottle because of flawed testing. Shuler and fellow researcher Greg Baxter came up with a compromise: a silicon chip that looks like an electronic one, except carved with shallow chambers and snaking channels lined with living human or animal tissue, through which artificial blood and a test drug is pumped. The chip mimics many of the messy effects of organs while preserving a neat, observable means for seeing what's going on. Pharmaceutical giant Johnson & Johnson has already signed on to put the chip through its paces, and some experts predict it could lop $100 million off the cost of testing a drug, not to mention eliminating the deaths of millions of lab animals each year.

The Other World Series Poker has become hugely popular in recent years, with more and more Americans pouring leisure time into honing their talents at the table. But how much does skill matter? Luck — that is, randomness — seems to play the larger role, at least to judge by the fact that no player has won the World Series of Poker main event more than once since the 1980s, when only dozens of players competed. Indeed, only two players have managed repeat appearances in the final round of nine players since the number of competitors hit five hundred in 2000. Perhaps as a result, some enterprising individuals — inspired in large part by a desire to operate poker Web sites legitimately in the United States, where online gambling is illegal — came up with a truly skill-only, no-luck version of the game. No-luck poker is set up like tournament bridge, in that the players at one of the multiple tables (real or virtual) are given the same hands as the players at other tables. Each player is then evaluated not against the other players at the table — who after all have different cards — but against her counterpart with the same hand at a different table. The game emerged in 2003, and since then has gone pretty much nowhere. The original Poker.com, a company that dedicated itself to marketing the most prominent incarnation of the game, ran out of money in 2004. (The current owner of the Poker.com Web site does not offer no-luck poker.) *News flash:* people *like* the fact that poker is a combination of skill and randomness. Those who want to keep luck out of it can play chess or, well, tournament bridge. Those who want to keep skill out of it can play roulette.

CHAPTER ELEVEN

Messy Thinking

Once a year, several dozen amateur astronomers head into the Arizona desert to stalk faint, smudgy celestial prey from dusk until dawn. There, at a scrubby site, the observers swing their portable telescopes to and fro at nebulae, star clusters, and galaxies while the temperature plummets and coyotes jeer from the distance. When the observers train their lenses on a particularly hard-to-see galaxy poised to disappear below the horizon, the more experienced members of the group do something surprising. They jiggle their telescopes. You might have thought that someone struggling to discern the elusive, wispy whorl of a distant galaxy through an eyepiece would seek utter stillness. But, as one of the astronomers explains it, a faint object is sometimes easier to make out in a telescope not when the object is fixed and stared at, but when it's dashing around the observer's field of vision.

People tend to imagine that they are getting the most out of their brains when their thoughts are well organized and focused, when they are able to clearly spell out their goals and intentions, and when the confusing world around them has been sorted out according to a distinct scheme. But actually, the mind is built around disorder on several levels, ranging from the processing of raw sensory data to the juggling of complex ideas. Our brains evolved to function in a messy world, and sometimes when we insist on thinking in neat, orderly ways, we're really holding back our minds from doing what they do best. In fact, it is when our brains seem to be efficiently putting the world around us into perfect order that they are most likely to be leading us astray.

Random Brilliance

A Web-marketing consultant named Steve Nelson was brainstorming with managers from a car insurance company when the group became stuck in its efforts to come up with a theme for a new advertising campaign. None of the ideas that had been kicked around seemed satisfying, and no one seemed to have any additional ones to suggest. Car insurance marketing is a constrained subject; the insurance is always sold on the basis of price, convenience, and claims support. The company was hoping to take a different tack, but the team kept circling back to the same old approaches. After a minute or so of heavy silence, Nelson reached into his briefcase, pulled out a stack of handmade cards, and asked a manager to pick one and read it out loud. "Blue," read the manager. Okay, blue, said Nelson. Let's work with that.

Blue. Sad. Feelings. Happiness. Fear. Fear of what? Fear of . . . car accidents. Who's afraid of car accidents? Mothers are afraid of car accidents. Sell to mothers, instead of to men looking for price, convenience, and claims support? Sell on what? Helping them to not be afraid of car accidents? Helping them to not *have* car accidents. Safety. Sell on safety. Provide safe-driving tips. A car insurance company that helps its customers avoid accidents by encouraging them to drive more safely.

The safe-driving campaign ended up a big hit. A single random word had helped kick off a shift in the team's thinking from aiming at the traditional buyers of car insurance to targeting a different influencer in the household with a pitch that resonated. Nelson, as it turns out, is a big fan of the power of random words; he's the founder of BananaSlug, the search engine mentioned in chapter 10 that adds a random word to search terms. Though his day job is helping to run Clear Ink, the digital marketing firm he cofounded, Nelson is a former programmer and likes to keep his hand in it by developing various software projects as a hobby. He's written computer games and put together other Web sites for fun, including SpellWeb, which enlists the Web to gauge the relative popularity of two different terms or of two different spellings of the same word. In 2003, when he was casting about for a new project, a ukulele-playing friend happened to mention that he found it difficult to uncover interesting Web sites about ukuleles via a Google search, because the pages that came up near the top of the search results were too generic, the full list of some two million pages was far too big to browse, and he couldn't think of a useful way to narrow down the list. Nelson suggested just randomly adding an interesting word to the Google search, and the results proved so satisfying that Nelson created BananaSlug. (The Fighting Banana Slug is the mascot at Nelson's alma mater, the University of California at Santa Cruz.) Of course, another way to find the most interesting Web sites is to have experts exhaustively search them out and put them in a list, which is how BananaSlug came to be named one of the top one hundred Web sites by *PC Magazine* in 2005.

Why does adding a random word to a Web search produce

more interesting results? Nelson suggests it does so for three reasons. First, it adds an element of "relevant surprise," in that a Web site that prominently incorporates a random word will probably address a topic that strays from the focus you had in mind — but will still have some relevance to you, because it also prominently incorporates your search term. Second, it's more likely to pull up unusual Web sites, because a Web site that manages to address two concepts that have little to do with one another will probably be at least a bit idiosyncratic. (To avoid bland random words that goose the results a bit, BananaSlug offers a choice of categories of more colorful random words, including animals, themes from Shakespeare, and urban dictionary.) Third, it will probably pull up a varied group of Web sites, because whatever odd link a Web site finds between two different concepts is not likely to be the same link found by another Web site. "If you're searching for, I don't know, tennis stars, and you add the random word *poodle*, you're probably going to get a pretty interesting group of sites," says Nelson. (He had randomly tossed this example off the top of his head, but it turns out to be nicely illustrative. On a straight Google search for tennis players, the first sixty results are almost all lists of players. When *poodle* is thrown in, the fourth entry is about a book on the nature of consciousness, the fifth is an interview with David Bowie's bass player, and the thirteenth an article on the mathematics of wobbly tables. BananaSlug search results are often weirdly compelling in this way.)

Nelson is hardly the first to suggest enlisting random concepts to free up creativity. In fact, "seeding" brainstorming and other idea-generation efforts with random, unrelated, or randomly combined ideas is virtually doctrine in a substantial creativity industry comprising consultants, books, software, and Web sites. The essence of the creativity problem, as Nelson explains it, is that it's easy for a person's thinking to get into a rut, and simply trying to think her way out of it may be no more effective than a car's wheels spinning in the mud. Innovation expert Robert Sutton, the Stanford professor mentioned in chapter 1, advocates random input into task solving, putting it this way in his book, *Weird Ideas That Work:* "No matter how hard people try not to think about their past experiences, irrational prejudices, and personal preferences, much research shows that these and a host of other biases have powerful effects." Meditating on almost anything that's not directly related to the problem at hand can serve to yank you away from these biases and out of a creativity rut; random inputs happen to work well because they're almost guaranteed to be unrelated. A random cue, in other words, defocuses the mind and serves as an antidote to consistent thinking — focus and consistency often being the enemies of creativity.

Although tossing a random concept into your brainstorming may pull you out of a thinking rut, it won't necessarily plunk you directly down on a fruitful conceptual path. It could easily — and in fact probably will — lead you to a new dead end, in which case you can try a new random concept. But even though you can't count on serendipity, it's more likely to find those who are open to disorder. Working off-the-subject words or concepts into your thinking is simply one way to prompt discovery. Messy behavior is another, as proved true for Alexander Fleming when he stumbled on penicillin. And Fleming's serendipitous breakthrough was far from unique; messy lab work has often led to major scientific insights. The 2000 Nobel Prize in chemistry for the discovery of electrically conductive plastics was the culmination of a scientific trail that began when a researcher managed to mismeasure the amount of one ingredient in a chemical mixture by a factor of 1000. The first Nobel Prize in physics was awarded for X-rays, discovered when Wilhelm Röntgen happened to notice a mysteriously glowing screen in his laboratory after he had been promiscuously shooting electrons around the area. Another physics Nobel went to two Bell Labs researchers who stumbled on a strange, staticky radio signal that they later determined is the leftover radiation from the Big Bang that gave birth to the universe. Charles Goodyear came up with the process for vulcanizing rubber after a pot boiled over on his stove. According to the ten hits from a search of "discovered by accident" combined with the random word *companion* at BananaSlug — more manageable than Google's 98,800 results for "discovered by accident" — other discoveries prompted by random events include that of nylon, an asteroid spotted in 2002 that shares the Earth's orbit, LSD, polyethylene, and the artificial sweeteners saccharin, cyclamate, aspartame, and sucralose.

Clearly our minds are prepared to do some of their best work when they're diverted, one way or another, from what we intend to focus them on. Think about that — but only for a minute.

Mentally Neatening the World

No matter how messy the world is, we humans seem determined not to see it that way. We enlist all sorts of schemes to avoid having to accept disorder and randomness, but when viewed logically these appear to be glitches in our software. A few examples:

Fabricating Justice Psychologists have long been aware that people tend to assume anyone who suffers a misfortune probably deserved it in some way, a phenomenon known as the *just-*

world hypothesis. The man who dropped dead of a heart attack at forty-five must not have been fit; the woman who was raped was probably engaging in risky behavior; the homeless person must not have really wanted to get a job. The notion that terrible things can befall utterly innocent people, which of course happens all the time, is one that forces us to confront the messiness and randomness of life, and we manufacture excuses to deny it.

Neatening Sights and Sounds Our brains are uncomfortable with visual disorder, or so it would seem, considering how hard it is to look at an ink blot or a cloud without making out a figure of some sort. And filmmakers know that a movie soundtrack doesn't have to be precisely keyed to the action on the screen for the audience to perceive it that way; in fact, even a random tune played along with a film will seem synchronized to it.

Rashomonic Memory Most of us have had the experience of learning from a relative or friend that an event we've long remembered with perfect clarity did not in fact take place in that way, or at all. Our memories aren't precise recordings of what we've taken in from the world; rather, they are heavily massaged tableaux constructed by our brains based partly on reality and partly on what we need, want, or expect reality to be — a way of retroactively neatening the world. That this process can produce heavily flawed recollections is borne out vividly in National Transportation Safety Board reports of investigations into airplane accidents, which often detail highly conflicting eyewitness accounts. People tend to be utterly unfamiliar with the sights and sounds of a struggling aircraft — unlike the experience of car accidents — and the brain, having no useful template by which to sort things out, apparently assembles an inaccurate scenario that the brain's owner will nonetheless cling to with utter conviction.

Neatening Chance Where would you rather put your quarter? In a slot machine that just now paid out $1,000 or in an identical machine that has been fed hundreds of quarters since it last paid out big? Most people would go for the second machine, intuiting that the machine is "due" to pay out. But that's flawed reasoning. Slot machines are meticulously designed so that every pull of the lever or press of the button provides exactly the same odds of paying out as a pull or press on any other machine of the same model. The pattern of payouts is for all practical purposes completely random, and there's no useful information to be gleaned from past payouts when it comes to picking the "right" time to drop in a coin.

Part of the problem is that the public tends to have a poor understanding of probability and how it plays out in real-world situations. For example, many people would figure that if five coin tosses in a row result in heads, it's more likely than not that the next one will yield tails, though of course the odds are really always fifty-fifty. But for gamblers, there's another phenomenon in force. Gamblers are highly prone to thinking that they can give themselves an edge in whatever game they're playing and readily adopt distorted views of the world in order to guard their belief that they can profitably assert order over randomness. According to James Whelan, a University of Memphis psychology professor who codirects the school's Institute for Gambling Education and Research, dedicated slot-machine players become so convinced that the machine into which they've been popping coins is due to pay out that some players will wet themselves rather than take a bathroom break and risk having another player reap the supposedly imminent payout.

The belief that you should stick with a machine that hasn't paid off in a while is a crude form of a gambler's *system* — a scheme of play that enables one to see gambling as less subject to randomness in general and to unfavorable odds in particular. Some systems are simple and straightforward, such as always betting on the favorite in a horse race, while others can be more involved. John Grochowski, a gambling-odds expert who writes widely on casino games, has described this roulette system, for example:

> One close friend likes to extend play at roulette by betting on black plus an equal amount on the third column. Eight of the numbers in the third column are red, so my friend covers 26 of the 38 numbers — all 18 black numbers plus eight red. If a black in the first two columns shows up, he breaks even, winning on black but losing the column bet. If one of his eight reds turns up, he makes a one-unit profit, winning a 2-1 payoff on the column while losing on black. But if the ball lands on one of the four third-column blacks, he wins triple — even money on black, plus 2-1 column.
>
> Of course, there's the pesky matter of the 10 red numbers he doesn't cover, plus 0 and 00. Any of those dozen numbers bring a double loss.

This may not make much sense if you're unfamiliar with roulette, but you can get the larger point: a system can enlist various betting gymnastics to obscure the essential fact that no matter what you do, the odds are against you in the long run. In the case of roulette, as Grochowski notes, the odds are tilted 1.0526 to 1 toward your eventually losing *regardless of how you bet*. (Unless you also throw in a so-called basket bet on 0, 00, 1, 2, and 3, in which case the odds are worse.)

Whelan and his colleagues at the institute have studied gamblers and their systems at some length. He notes, for one thing, that gambling systems are often based on erroneous and irrational beliefs that are encased in assumptions with a more factual basis. A prominent example is blackjack card counting, which in its simple, most popular form involves keeping mental track of how many cards with a value of ten have been played since the deck was last shuffled; if the number becomes unusually high or low, that knowledge can indeed be used to improve the chances of certain bets paying off. But what amateur card counters typically remain resolutely blind to is the simple fact that while counting can improve the odds by a fraction of a percent, it isn't enough to put the odds in the player's favor; the game remains a losing proposition by roughly half a percent, depending on the casino's rules and the player's ability to adhere to perfect strategy. (There are more complex forms of card counting that can in theory tip the balance in the player's favor by up to 1 percent, but they require extensive training, facility with numbers, and confederates to disguise your betting patterns, since casinos will toss you out and may even ban you if they catch you at expert card counting.) Another popular system that can be applied to almost any sort of gambling involves temporarily increasing the size of your bet every time you lose, under the correct reasoning that doing so can in theory counteract any losing streak by ensuring that when a winning bet finally comes in it can be large enough to put you back into the black. The flaw in this case is that eventually a freakishly long losing streak will require such a large bet to make it up — the number can easily climb into the thousands and even tens of thousands of dollars — that the player will run out of money, or the house will refuse a bet that large, leaving the player with a potentially astronomical loss. Some players enlist the simple system of riding winning streaks until they end, in the hopes of gaining maximum advantage from them, while others adopt a policy of always walking away in the middle of winning streaks, to avoid giving the gains back to the house, though neither strategy will alter in the slightest the odds of winning over the long term.

In the end, all permissible gambling strategies are flawed and fail to erase the casino's, racetrack's, bookie's, or lottery commission's edge. And yet, notes Whelan, gamblers not only have faith in their systems, they also become wrongly convinced that their records of earnings and losses bear that faith out. That's because of a psychological phenomenon known as a *confirmation bias:* when a person wants and expects something to be true, he tends to pay special attention to and to remember whatever confirms the expectation and is more likely to ignore or forget what contradicts it. In other words, the brain steps in and tidies up our view of the world so that it jibes with how we expect the world to behave. Whelan and his colleagues have performed studies in which they compare gamblers' actual wins and losses to what the gamblers report at the end of six months. "Gamblers are very reliable when it comes to reporting on how many days they gambled, which days they gambled, what games they played, and almost everything else about their gambling," he says. "The one thing they seem to have a really hard time remembering accurately is how much they won or lost. The vast majority reports results that are highly biased toward winning." (Whelan notes that when he drives his daughter to school in the morning, they adopt a system of "thinking green" in order to influence traffic lights, and he reports it seems to help.) Heavy gamblers are more likely to believe in systems than are occasional gamblers, Whelan has found, and hang on to the beliefs more tenaciously. In fact, contrary to popular belief, casinos welcome the simple version of card counting at blackjack tables, knowing that the more gamblers are convinced they can overcome the randomness of a game through a system, the more they will gamble. That's why some casinos *teach* card counting. Even educating heavy gamblers about the irrationality of and flaws in their systems doesn't seem to help them control their gambling, Whelan discovered in one study.

The brain's proclivity for gambling systems is probably a side effect of what may have evolved as a sometimes helpful hitch in our powers of reasoning, suggests Whelan. If we were always good at recognizing our powerlessness to control randomness — that is, if we fully accepted how disordered the world is — we might too often become paralyzed by indecision or hopelessness. Being quick to imagine that we can assert order and improve the odds to a greater degree than we actually can is what often inspires us to act boldly. The entrepreneur who starts up a new restaurant, the infantryman who kicks down a door in an insurgent hot zone, the comet-hunter who wakes at 3:00 a.m. to sweep her telescope across the sky, the CEO who engages in strategic planning — in each case there is, to a greater or lesser degree, an element of casting a blind eye to uncontrollable randomness. The line between foolishness and adventurousness is sometimes drawn after the fact. Fred Smith, the founder and CEO of FedEx, has celebratedly claimed that he owes the rescue of his then nascent, money-losing company from near bankruptcy in 1974 to a winning night of blackjack in Las Vegas. Too bad he wasn't able to share his system with the thousands of foolish gamblers who lost their shirts that night.

Categorize This

As almost any parent can attest, a five-month-old infant need only run into two or three dogs before he has formulated a mental category for them, to store alongside the categories of caregivers, strangers, food, and toys. At first, dogs might be lumped in with all animals in the infant's mind, but soon dogs, cats, squirrels, and other intriguing creatures are all given their own subcategories. We are literally born categorizers and for good reason; there isn't enough time when we encounter each new entity in the world to go through the process of carefully observing and analyzing it so that we can finally decide if we need to pet it, eat it, flee from it, or smile at it. How much more efficient to quickly determine what easily flagged characteristics certain entities have in common, come up with some useful generalizations about this group of entities, and then apply those generalizations to every new entity that seems to fit. It's got four legs, fur, a wagging tail, floppy ears — that's enough to know you're probably going to get sniffed and licked and maybe snapped at, too, if you pull too hard on one of those ears.

The urge to categorize hardly abates as we grow older. An eleven-year-old is virtually a categorization engine, wrestling with in-groups and out-groups at school, and then coming home to sort out a baseball-card collection or a scrapbook. Grown and employed, we rely on categorization throughout the day in our jobs as we file, departmentalize, hire the winners, and fire the losers, leaving the office at the end of the day to catch a museum exhibit of impressionism, expressionism, fauvism, or Dadaism. It's surprising what some people will take the trouble to categorize. The Kama Sutra offers a typology not only of lovemaking positions, but also of love scratches, including the half-moon, the tiger's claw, the peacock foot, and the hare's leap. Northwestern University's medical school has long maintained a carefully organized collection of some 170 "anomalous" fetuses. There are museums of lawn mowers and of toilet-seat art.

While it's hard to imagine how we'd get through the day without relying on our sorting skills, categorization is not without drawbacks. It can be used as an instrument of irrational prejudice, for example. Physiognomics, or the characterization of personality and character types via measurements of the face and body, was once a respected science in some quarters, and under Nazi rule it was applied murderously. Our interest in categorizing can lead us to view the world in oversimplified ways, as when political candidates become regarded primarily as liberals or conservatives. As soon as we put an entity in one category, we risk failing to notice its potential utility in another one. Stick a book in the business section of a bookstore, for example, and readers who aren't specifically interested in business aren't likely to find it, no matter how much nonbusiness material is in it. And, as with all forms of order, categorization can be frustratingly relative. The directors of the National Museum of the American Indian in Washington, DC, went through the trouble of seeking input from the members of twenty-four different tribes as to how items relating to their tribes should be grouped and annotated. On their advice, the items, which range from dolls and animals to tobacco and corn, are displayed not by typical artifact categories of strict chronology or historical events but, rather, by their significance to tribal stories and beliefs, and are supplemented by a range of information from computers and tribal members at hand around the exhibits. The museum opened in 2004 to a blast of largely scathing reviews from experts who were appalled at the unconventional categorization of items. *New York Times* critic Edward Rothstein called the exhibit style "pure pap," explaining on National Public Radio: "I would wager that there are any number of scholars of American Indian history who know far more about these tribes than the elders of the tribe."

A good example of the sort of problems that categorization can cause is one that has become a signature annoyance of modern life: the voice menus that businesses and other organizations make you wend your way through when you call them. A Forrester Research study concluded in 2005 that fourteen out of fifteen companies' automated voice-response systems deserve a flunking grade. Another study indicated that a mere 16 percent of callers felt "completely satisfied" after calling with a problem, while a whopping 73 percent felt "customer *rage*." (Given that many of us are making these sorts of calls on cell phones in cars, perhaps we can guess how some of that rage manifests itself.) If companies' Web sites are doing a better job, customers don't know it; according to a study by technology consultancy Gartner, customers with a problem are three times more likely to call up than visit the organization's Web site, and of those who do try the Web, nearly two-thirds will give up and call anyway. In other words, those detested voice menus have become the primary means by which customers communicate with companies. Businesses see this as a real dilemma — or at least they ought to. On the one hand, a call involving a live agent is at least five times as expensive on average as one handled by a voice-response system, according to Forrester. On the other hand, companies whose voice systems enrage customers are being penny-wise and pound-foolish, given that studies have shown that up to half the callers who end up dissatisfied decide to take their business elsewhere.

The problem with voice menus is that they are crude categorization engines, intended to get you to quickly characterize yourself as needing one of several neatly defined types of assistance. That's swell when your needs fit into one of the menu's main categories. If you want directions to a store and its business hours, for example, no problem — just press 3, and you're taken care of. That's why the ATM machine, another type of categorization engine, has become a model of self-service; almost everyone who uses one either wants to get cash or make a deposit, so the machine can be designed to gracefully handle those neatly defined chores. The breakdown occurs when a customer feels her need doesn't fit neatly into any of the menu options. Say, for example, you want to change the address to which your phone company sends its bills or report that the silverware set you bought has too many spoons and not enough forks. Businesses can't fit the dozens or thousands of different types of possible customer-service requests into a voice menu, or even come close, without forcing customers to slog through multiple levels of choices likely to leave them confused, stuck, and unassisted. That's why the end result is typically the one considered the worst of all possible worlds: the bailout, or the request to speak to a live agent.

The frequency at which voice-menu systems run into categorization failure leading to bailout can be surprising. You'd think, for example, that asking customers to categorize themselves geographically by punching in their zip codes would be a no-brainer. But Marco Pacelli, who runs a company called ClickFox that specializes in fine-tuning customer-response systems, discovered that about a fifth of one client's customers were bailing out of a voice-response system at the zip-code request. As it turns out, even zip codes don't make for a neat category; people calling from their offices are often confused about whether to enter their business or home zip codes. And it's downhill from there.

It's not a trivial problem. When a customer bails out of an automated system, the organization has not only failed to save agent costs, it has also irritated the customer before the agent says "hello." Yet customer expectations of being quickly and usefully categorized by voice-menu systems are so low that 37 percent of people who reach one of them press 0 immediately, according to a 2004 study by market research firm Harris Interactive. The popularity of this sort of preemptive bailout has led to an escalating battle between instant bailers and companies that don't want callers bailing out before giving the system a chance. To prevent instant bailing, many businesses simply take away the zero option; if you press 0, you're told it's not a valid option. But there's almost always *some* way to get the system to kick a caller to an agent, and many callers become determined to figure out what it is. There are even extensive cheat sheets posted on the Web that list the sequence of button-pushes and spoken phrases needed to bypass the voice systems for a surprisingly large number of organizations. You can get past the Fidelity NetBenefits voice menu, for example, by first pressing 1, and then pressing # up to seventeen times. Barking "help" repeatedly every time the system asks for input does the trick on the Sears repair line. For Cellular One, press 4, say "agent," then press #. (*Tip:* ignore any admonishments from a system that your responses are invalid or not understood; the system is usually keeping track.)

But bailout, whether premature or not, isn't just a problem for organizations hoping to save on agent costs. It's also often a loss for the caller. That's because voice menus typically have a secondary purpose beyond trying to serve a customer entirely automatically — namely, to determine what *sort* of agent, out of a field of many specialists, is most likely to be able to solve the customer's problem when the system can't solve it. Partly because of premature bailout, but also because voice-menu systems simply aren't very good at getting customers to usefully self-categorize, customers often get to a live agent only to find themselves in a second level of hell. Studies show that once customers with complaints are transferred to a person, there's a 50 percent chance they'll be transferred a second time — at which point the chances that they'll decide never to do business with the company again jump by 30 percent.

One solution is for a business to try to at least roughly categorize callers before the voice-menu system answers the phone. That can sometimes be accomplished automatically by matching the caller ID against customer databases to check on the customer's profile and history. For example, an insurance company's system could distinguish between an existing customer who recently filed a claim and thus probably wants to check on its status, a customer who hasn't recently filed a claim and thus is likely to want to either file one or to update his policy, and a caller who isn't in the database at all and thus must be a prospective customer. Armed with this first level of categorization, the company could then provide a short and more relevant menu to the caller, and if the caller bails out, the company can pass the call on to the sort of agent most likely to be able to help. In some cases, the organization may not even want a prescreened caller to have a shot at a voice menu, because the organization and the caller may have differing ideas of how the caller should be categorized. Take, for example, a well-heeled bank customer who calls in with the intention of self-categorizing as someone who wants to check account balances; the bank, on the other hand, may prefer to categorize this caller as someone who needs a little quality time with a salesperson in the mutual funds department. One study found that high-value credit-card customers are 30 percent more likely than other cardholders to ditch their card company over being kept on hold. So the next time you're forced to spend twenty minutes waiting to get through to an agent at a company, you wouldn't be paranoid to suspect that customers whose business the company values more highly than yours are getting through right away.

In most cases, though, callers can't be precategorized with much precision or reliability. After all, Wal-Mart has no good way of guessing why someone is calling, regardless of what they might have recently purchased. For most organizations, then, little can be done to greatly improve their voice-menu systems, other than biting the bullet, getting rid of the systems, and restoring the answering of phones to well-trained human agents capable of handling callers' messy requests and needs.

Listening to Your Inner Mess

For anyone outside the science world looking in, it's easy to get the impression that progress happens steadily, through the purposeful collaboration of scientists forging ahead along a grandly envisioned path. In fact, though, science itself is more often a big mess, lurching along in fits and starts, plunging headlong into dead ends here, unexpectedly bursting into fruit there. Not only is what ultimately seems to be the right path rarely envisioned ahead of time, it may in fact be just retroactively, after decades of work and many chance encounters and other random connections, that anyone realizes there had ever been any sort of path at all.

A good example of the disordered progress of science is that of the study of disorder or at least of a contemporary branch of it. It's a branch that owes much to Frank Moss, a bearded, chunky, and — unusually for his field — folksily spoken physicist at the

University of Missouri in St. Louis. Moss used to study the behavior of low-temperature fluids, but by 1979 he had become bored with the field and took a sabbatical in the hopes of rekindling his excitement for the scientific hunt. Leafing desultorily through a random collection of research papers, Moss, then forty-six, stumbled on an obscure one from a group of Belgian researchers that set off a spark for him, though he couldn't at first say why. The paper theorized that adding randomness could make a physical system work better. Though the paper didn't identify any such systems, the theory seemed plausible enough to Moss. After all, Einstein's work on Brownian motion had long since been expanded and applied to the world of high finance, to the extent that a cornerstone of the global economy was the ability to consistently make vast sums of money every day on the movements of markets, not in spite of the essential randomness of the markets but *because* of it. If randomness could be made to pay off there, why not in physical systems?

Actually, there had been glimpses over the years of disorder's potential utility in the world of things. Some photographers knew, for example, that a picture taken in low light would sometimes stand out more clearly if the image was superimposed over that of a busy random background. And the designers of early radios had found that slightly mistuning them increased the static background but also brought in the music more clearly. These happy-noise observations — *noise*, that is, in the technical sense of a disordered signal — were very much the exception, though, and regarded as little more than curiosities. The engineering world's attitude toward noise was clearly established in the 1930s when electrical engineers were trying to perfect the vacuum tube, which enlisted a hot stream of electrons to amplify a weak electronic signal. As the tubes became increasingly sensitive, engineers listening to the results over loudspeakers began to hear an odd sound in the background, reminiscent of bursts of rain landing on a tin roof or of a load of shotgun pellets clattering into a wall, a baffling sound dubbed *shot noise*. Shot noise turned out to result from the random motion of electrons, analogous to the random molecular surges that cause a grain of pollen to dance in water; the engineers were literally listening to disorder. *Noise* eventually became a generic term for random signals, by which time it had already been declared an enemy of electronics so that ever since circuits have been designed to minimize it.

Mulling over the Belgian paper, Moss wondered if there might be systems that demonstrate noise can be helpful in ways that had been overlooked. Plowing through stacks of obscure scientific journals, he finally stumbled on his system: turtle eggs. A paper described how outside temperature can determine whether the eggs of the European pond turtle produce male or female hatchlings. If the temperature were to remain steady, or vary more in one direction than in the other, broods would tend to be all of one sex, placing the species in an awkward position. Fortunately for the pond turtle, temperature usually fluctuates fairly randomly, leaving the turtles with mixed-sex broods. Moss was struck by the apparent fact that the turtles had evolved not merely to withstand noise but had actually come to depend on it for the survival of the species. "I knew right then and there what I wanted to do with my career," he says. Moss crammed his modest laboratory with vintage analog electronic equipment of the sort that increasingly digitally minded engineers and physicists were eager to dump; the older equipment had good old-fashioned knobs that could be delicately twisted to dial in just the right sort of noise. (Designer noise comes in colors: a slowly fluctuating signal is called *red noise*; *blue noise* is a signal that rapidly fluctuates; *pink noise* is a combination of red and blue noise; and *white noise* is a broad mixture of all sorts of fluctuations.) Moss became one of the world's experts on noisy electronic circuits, attracting funding from the U.S. Navy, which is always looking for ways to improve its ability to electronically detect and hide the noisy signals left by submarines against a literal sea of other noise.

In 1982, a second theoretical shot was fired on behalf of useful noise by an Italian group trying to figure out what triggered ice ages every hundred thousand years. The onsets tended to coincide with a wobble in the Earth's orbit that occasionally brought the Earth farther from the sun, but calculations clearly indicated that this variation was too small to effect a major climate change. Their conclusion: climatic noise, in the form of random temperature fluctuations from changing ocean patterns and other weather systems, is amplifying the effect of the orbital wobble.

That a random signal could amplify a weak, ordered one seems as counterintuitive as the notion of enhancing a piano sonata by inviting a cat to walk across the keyboard, or indiscriminately grabbing spices off a shelf to improve a delicate sauce. But picture the sort of heavy, wall-mounted electric switch that mad scientists' assistants are always dramatically throwing in old horror movies. Now imagine that the assistant needs to throw the switch back and forth repeatedly in order to make his master's experiment work — but the switch is sticking, and the assistant is too weak, by a hair, to get the job done. Suddenly an earthquake strikes, randomly heaving the room this way and that, while the assistant continues to struggle to push the switch back and forth. It's not hard to imagine that some of the heaves will provide just the extra oomph needed to enable the assistant to throw the switch one way, and others will allow him to throw it back. Most of the heaves will do the assistant no good, of course, but that doesn't really matter, as long as there's a good chance that *some* of the heaves will be useful and that the other, useless heaves won't interfere with the task. That's the essence of *stochastic resonance*, as the Italian climatologists named the phenomenon. A noisy signal occasionally randomly lines up with a regular signal to get the job done, and when the two don't line up no harm is done.

Moss wondered, could stochastic resonance be important in other systems? A colleague in a naval research institute had asked Moss to help him create electronic circuits that mimicked the way groups of brain cells "fired" in response to certain signals. Moss suggested trying to get stochastic resonance to work in these brainlike circuits. Sure enough, adding noise to the original signal made the artificial brain cells ten times as sensitive to the signal. Though the experiment seemed far afield from anything neuroscientists were working on, Moss's colleague presented the results at a neuroscience conference. When he put up a slide showing an unusually shaped graph of how the artificial neurons fired in response to the noise-enhanced signal, one researcher in the audience leaped to his feet and shouted, "I've seen that diagram before!" As it turned out, the idiosyncratic graph was identical to graphs that had come out of research over the past two decades into the way the brains of monkeys and cats recognize flashing lights and audio tones. Researchers had long been puzzled by the unusual nature of the firing pattern of these actual brain cells. In particular, no one had been able to explain why the cells didn't always immediately fire when exposed to a flashing light; sometimes they didn't fire until the second or even the third flash. Moss was able to offer a simple explanation: if the firing relied on stochastic resonance, with its strong component of randomness, then you would expect the firings to be a bit hit or miss.

But where in the brain would the noise needed for stochastic resonance come from? One set of experiments later provided a possible answer, at least in the case of hearing. In the leopard frog, the fine, hairlike structures in the inner ear called cilia, responsible for turning the mechanical energy of sound into electrical impulses for brain cells, vibrate not only in response to external sounds but are also tossed about by the Brownian motion of the molecules in the fluid around them. When experimenters damped or enhanced this random signal, the auditory brain cells connected to the cilia stopped firing in the presence of sound. Apparently, the frog's auditory system has evolved to depend critically on exactly the level and type of disorder naturally found in the fluid of the inner air. Moss himself suspects the brain actually *manufactures* noise in some cases to help stochastic resonance along. That remains to be proved, though he notes that in one study researchers found that human ear cilia churn out about ten times more noise than would be expected. "Noise is ubiquitous in neurons," he says. "Wherever you stick a probe in, you get noise."

There have since been a number of studies suggesting that different types of noise in general, and stochastic resonance in particular, are important to brain functions, including the sensory systems of cats, crayfish, electric fish, and humans. One experiment, for example, demonstrated that people tend to be more adept at multiplication problems when exposed to auditory noise. Peter Tass of Germany's Research Center Jülich, widely considered one of the world's foremost neuroscientists, has been using state-of-the-art brain scans to investigate the role stochastic resonance may play in the human visual system, along with the possibility that noise might somehow be enlisted to improve the impaired vision of stroke victims.

The notion of a medical prescription for noise is not as far-fetched as it may seem. Jim Collins, a biomedical engineering researcher at Boston University, had been thinking about applications for stochastic resonance when he came to consider the fact that about one in ten Americans over age sixty-five are seriously injured in falls every year, and some thirteen thousand of them die of complications from these injuries. Aside from the toll in suffering, it's a $19 billion burden on the health care system, according to a study by the Centers for Disease Control. One critical component of balance, Collins knew, is the transmission of sensory information, from the foot to the brain, about sudden instabilities, allowing the brain to dash off quick compensatory commands for leaning or foot repositioning. But that foot-to-brain signal weakens with age as nerves become less sensitive. Could stochastic resonance help? Collins constructed a vibrating platform and studied how well people balanced on it when it was set to mildly vibrate compared to when it was still. "The vibrations enabled seventy-five-year-olds to balance as well as twenty-three-year-olds," says Collins. Working with a spin-off company called Afferent, Collins has helped design vibrating insoles for shoes that in early testing appear to provide the benefits of the vibrating platform. The insoles also seem to help diabetic patients feel the early onset of foot ulcers; because these patients often lose sensation in their feet, the ulcers frequently remain undiscovered until they're untreatable, leading to some eighty thousand foot and leg amputations each year and to treatment costs of more than $4 billion a year in the United States alone. Collins says Afferent is even looking into shoewear that could improve balance for athletes and construction workers, as well as vibrating grips for golf and tennis rackets that would provide better ball control.

Knowing that the brain is not merely comfortable with but actually *thrives* on a background of disorder may make it a little less mysterious that cell-phone listeners are uncomfortable with silence, that children can knock out their homework in noisy homes, and that jiggling a telescope helps an observer pick out a faint object. Stochastic resonance might even provide another way of looking at how mess can play a useful role in daily life. When you invite a certain amount of disorder into your rooms, your job, and your calendar, you can reasonably hope that by sheer chance the random zigs and zags of mess will occasionally line up with your goals — furnishing you with, from a heap of papers on a desk, a document that connects two unrelated projects; steering you to the person who unexpectedly solves your problem; sending you down a tiny street past an unfamiliar store where you spot the item you didn't even realize you needed so badly. Much of the time the mess won't do a lot for you, of course. But how much will it really hurt?

CHAPTER TWELVE

Pathological Mess

O n the first day of spring in 1947, a New York City pa-
trolman was dispatched to a decaying Harlem man-
sion to investigate an anonymous report of a dead body within.
No one answered his knocks, the doors were locked, and the
first-floor and basement windows were grilled, so the officer
called for a crew to break down the front door. Waiting behind
it was an impassable blockade of stacked furniture and boxes,
intermingled with a strange assortment of other items, including parts of a sewing machine and a wine press. The clutter appeared to fill every cubic foot of the entire first floor of the
house. A ladder provided access to a second-story window, but
entrance was denied there, too, by a prodigious volume of
tightly packed junk, consisting in no small portion of bundles of
thousands of newspapers. The crew began to haul out the newspapers, along with a startling array of items in various states of
disrepair, including a baby carriage, gardening implements, and
umbrellas. As a path was painstakingly fashioned through the
compacted melee of objects, a searcher came across the body of
Homer Collyer, sixty-six, a former engineer, and one of two
brothers who owned the home. It took seventeen days to remove

enough trash and objects — including toys, tools, guns, dress-making dummies, animal bones, and an X-ray machine — to find the body of the older second brother, Langley, a Columbia University–educated lawyer. Langley had suffocated under bundles of newspapers that had toppled over on him as he crawled through one of the narrow junk tunnels used to bring food to Homer, who had gone blind. Ultimately, more than 130 tons of junk were excavated from the home, all of which raised less than $2,000 at auction.

The tale of the Collyer brothers is an odd one, but not quite as odd as you might think. In December 2003 alone, New York City firefighters twice had to rescue residents nearly killed by the spectacular clutter in their homes — one trapped for days under a massive heap of magazines and books, the other almost unreachable behind a thick crop of ceiling-high piles of paper and other materials that had somehow ignited. (The rescuing firefighter in the latter case may be one of the few people ever to be officially commended for heroism in the face of life-threatening home clutter.) A dozen major U.S. cities have set up teams specifically tasked with helping people whose homes have become dangerously overfilled. It's far from unheard of for people to close off entire sections of their homes with im-passable junk. Among the several stories of extreme clutter re-ported in the survey conducted for this book was one about a couple who snuck into a parent's home when he was away in order to clear out the ceiling-high piles upstairs, only to have the ceil-ing in one room collapse partway through the job — it turned out the piles had been supporting the ceiling, which was strain-ing under the weight of the massive store of clutter in the attic.

The tendency to irrationally amass and hang on to extraor-dinarily large and dense collections of mostly useless items is sometimes known as *compulsive hoarding* or even *Collyer brothers syndrome*, but is usually simply called *hoarding*. Though hoarding hasn't yet earned its own official diagnostic criteria in *DSM-IV*, the manual that serves as a guide for categorizing mental illness, it is mentioned there as a common symptom of obsessive-compulsive disorder (OCD). Psychologists Tamara Hartl of Stanford University and Randy Frost of Smith College have long specialized in studying hoarding and together came up with these widely accepted diagnostic criteria:

1. The acquisition of, and failure to discard, a large number of possessions that appear to be useless or of limited value
2. Living spaces sufficiently cluttered so as to preclude activities for which those spaces were designed
3. Significant distress or impairment in functioning caused by the hoarding

These criteria may be a bit broad. Does suffering shame over having lost a dining room table to old magazines or a shower to organizing gizmos qualify? But the important issue is clear: at some point one has to distinguish between the sort of ordinary, mostly harmless messiness that might even be a side effect of useful prioritizing, and an extreme, highly dysfunctional messiness that can severely impinge on daily life and may be associated with mental illness or at least a general failure to cope with the routine demands of the world.

There are several different flavors of hoarding. Its typical classification as an offshoot of OCD suggests that sufferers are compelled to collect and retain odd items in much the same way they might experience an irresistible urge to wash their hands hundreds of times a day or count all the tiles in a floor. Sanjaya Saxena, director of UCLA's OCD research program, estimates that there are in the range of one million people in the United States who are OCD-driven hoarders. But OCD may not account for the majority of hoarders. Senior citizens afflicted with so-called Diogenes syndrome lose the motivation to care for themselves and lack interest in removing items that accumulate in their homes; the resulting clutter often consists largely of mounds of trash, a subdisorder called *syllogomania*. One reason the elderly are particularly vulnerable is that the tendency to self-neglect and hoard can be amplified by physical illness, loss of vision or hearing, and bereavement, notes Carlos Reyes-Ortiz, a geriatrician with the University of Texas Medical Branch who has studied the problem. Though there aren't good figures to indicate how frequently a particular mental illness leads to hoarding, a study by researchers at King's College in London of eighty-one people who "live in squalor" found that 49 percent of the people were over age sixty-five and 70 percent were diagnosed with a mental disorder. In a study of 233 people in Dublin who refused to let volunteers or the government provide some needed service, 54 percent were identified as hoarders and 47 percent as sufferers of Diogenes.

Smith College's Frost is among those who argue that hoarding should be diagnosable as a unique mental illness on its own, along with what are often accompanying symptoms, including paranoia. Some hoarders appear to develop a turbocharged version of the common attachment to things professional organizers often observe in their clients, so that they actually become fearful of tossing out items. Yet another subdisorder, this fear is sometimes informally called *disposophobia*. Hoarding can also be focused on specific types of items, a frequent and especially problematic one being animals, as with the beleaguered "cat ladies" who occasionally pop up in local news. In other words, the diagnosis and thus the treatment of hoarding is itself a bit of a nasty mess and one that may leave millions of Americans metaphorically, and in some cases almost literally, drowning in their clutter.

Hopefully it's clear by now that messiness and disorder are not always good things. Far from it. There are many situations in which mess simply gets out of control, hoarding being an obvious and striking instance. Let's look at some other, more subtle examples, including a few where the troublesomeness of a mess depends on one's point of view.

Mess and the Quirky Mind

Judith Kolberg, the Atlanta-based professional organizer whose "body doubling" strategies were mentioned in chapter 6, noticed soon after she began taking on clients in the late 1980s that a small portion of them seemed to face deeper difficulties. "Five to ten percent of them just weren't getting it," she says. "They'd try all the traditional organizational and time-management techniques over and over again, and they just kept failing." One client had to endure a police investigation when a new housecleaner showed up and fled, believing the client's home had been invaded and ransacked. Another filled the kitchen with empty margarine tubs and plastic bags, leaving her husband concerned for her mental health. Yet another, an otherwise successful manager, seemed incapable of gathering data into progress reports for his bosses and risked losing his job over it. One faced eviction over her clutter. These people weren't merely anxious, guilty, or ashamed about messiness; their lives were taking sharp turns for the worse because of it.

When Kolberg attended the National Association of Professional Organizers conference in 1990, she mentioned her observation to some of her peers and was surprised to hear that most of them were similarly aware of a uniquely organizationally challenged minority among their clients. Other organizers tended to throw up their hands at these sorts of clients, but Kolberg was convinced they could be helped — just not through conventional organizing techniques. Some of these clients were probably suffering to some extent from attention deficit hyperactivity disorder or other diagnosable conditions, but that didn't seem to be the point when it came to helping them get minimally organized. The broader issue, Kolberg decided, was that these people didn't seem to relate to conventional notions of organization.

So Kolberg attempted to come at organization from new angles. Instead of foisting standard techniques on these clients, Kolberg tried to determine what they were good at and then create individualized organizational styles to match their strengths. Called in by a high-powered scientific researcher whose inability to file had led to desk piles tall enough to block his view of the doorway and had left him unable to find even the most important papers, Kolberg noticed that he seemed to think of documents in highly idiosyncratic, personal terms; a tax document, for example, reminded him of a cat veterinary bill he had taken as a deduction. So Kolberg devised an "emotional filing system" consisting of three categories: "Keeping Me Out of Jail" (alimony, traffic violations, IRS and other documents critically requiring response), "Keeping People Off My Back" (bills and reports), and "Me" (awards, newspaper clips, and other items of personal interest). She suggested a system based on anatomy to sort out the disarray in a doctor's office, including a "stomach" to digest information, a "brain" to make decisions about it, and a "liver" to remove waste. The manager who couldn't put together reports turned out to be an aspiring actor, so she helped him devise "scenes" with his subordinates in which he played the role of various characters performing acts of information-gathering, such as a lawyer taking testimony from a witness. While such clients rarely became paragons of organization, Kolberg found her techniques could keep them just ordered enough to avoid the sorts of small disasters they had been facing.

Kolberg went on to write the book *Conquering Chronic Disorganization* and founded the National Study Group on Chronic Disorganization, which sponsors research and disseminates information to professionals and the public. One publication from the organization available on its Web site defines five levels of clutter; if you feel anxiety over your messiness, it will almost certainly help put your problems into perspective. Level III, for example, includes light structural damage to the home, a television stored outside, audible evidence of rodents, the presence of hazardous chemicals and broken glass, and "obvious and irritating" odors. Bear in mind there are two full levels worse than this one, but they're not for the faint of heart. On the other hand, some professional organizers' promotional literature lists far more routine levels of mess, such as a cluttered dining room table, as sure signs of chronic disorganization, apparently in the hopes of literally scaring up business. Take it from the real experts: messy dining room tables and unmade beds aren't the problem. It's when you can't get through the doorways of your home or can't find room enough on your bed to lie down that it's time to seek help.

There are several mental disorders listed in the *DSM-IV* whose symptoms can include various types of mess. These include the OCD-related hoarding already noted, as well as difficulties in "planning, organizing, [and] sequencing" associated with Alzheimer's and other types of dementia. But if you're looking for a diagnosable mental disorder whose symptoms read much like a red-flag checklist ripped from a professional organizer's leather binder, then you've got to go with attention deficit hyperactivity disorder. ADHD, sometimes referred to as ADD, for attention deficit disorder — the hyperactivity isn't always part of the package — includes as possible diagnostic criteria the following, as excerpted from the manual:

   often fails to give close attention to details
   often has difficulty sustaining attention
   often has difficulty organizing tasks and details
   often loses things
   is often easily distracted
   often runs about or climbs excessively

Thus encompassing time sprawl, distraction, improvisation, blur, and bounce, ADHD appears to comprise a wide-ranging portfolio of mess. These forms of mess can be highly useful, of course. But it's not hard to see how a child — or an adult, given that up to two-thirds of children with ADHD are now believed to carry the disorder into their grown-up years — might well be considered a victim of pathological mess. After all, it's not as if someone with ADHD can pick and choose when, how, and in what modest measure they will apply which type of mess. Professional organizer and "coach" Denslow Brown, who specializes in working with people with ADHD, explains that for many of her clients, simply getting dressed in the morning in a reasonable amount of time is a daunting challenge. To help them, Brown breaks down the task into a set sequence of small steps, such as selecting a pair of socks, sitting down on the side of the bed, placing a sock on the left foot, and so forth. Without this sort of prepared sequence in the morning, and sometimes throughout the day, her clients can end up jumping around between partially completed tasks, many of which they lose track of. "They have trouble handling interruptions," she says. "The family, the mail, the TV, the phone — it's an onslaught to them, and whatever makes the loudest noise gets their attention."

But is the mess associated with ADHD necessarily all that bad? Edward Hallowell, for example, has done pretty well with ADHD, which he has never outgrown. Now in his late fifties, Hallowell struggled with the disorder as a child, as well as with dyslexia — there's a large overlap between the two — but eventually became a strong student and went to Harvard. It's a story much like Louis Strymish's, and in fact, like Strymish, Hallowell found himself pulled into the book business. But not right away. He first took a small detour getting his medical degree and becoming a Harvard Medical School professor. When he did finally throw himself into books, it wasn't as a bookseller, but as a bestselling writer of books on ADHD. His most recent, published in December 2005, is *Delivered from Distraction*, coauthored with John Ratey, a Harvard Medical School psychiatrist who also has ADHD.

Early in 2005, Hallowell and Ratey gave a talk at the public library in the small, prim bedroom community of Wellesley, Massachusetts. A standing-room-only crowd of about 150 people — apparently mostly the parents of children with ADHD — listened with what seemed a sort of desperate gratitude as the two men took turns describing how the disorder's disorder, in spite of the heavy challenges it can present, can also be a real gift. "I wouldn't trade my ADD for anything," said Hallowell. "As far as I'm concerned, you all have attention surplus disorder." He went on to describe the ADHD mind as "a Ferrari with Chevrolet brakes," by which he meant that people with ADHD often seem to think more intensely and about more things than the rest of us, but with less control. "It shouldn't be called a 'deficit' of attention," he said. "It's a *wandering* of attention."

Until recently, and going back to antiquity, this messy form of thought was given what Hallowell calls a "moral diagnosis" of bad behavior and laziness, with a treatment plan that typically consisted of humiliation and beatings. But with tolerance and encouragement, he said, those with ADHD often turn out to be more creative and productive than others. (He himself lucked onto an unusually nurturing first-grade teacher.) As an example, he offered up David Neeleman, the CEO of JetBlue Airways, and an ADHD diagnosee with whom Hallowell has worked. Hallowell said Neeleman told him how his distraction had caused him to keep forgetting to bring in a tree surgeon to take care of a tree growing up against his house — until finally he sold the house, saying it was easier to arrange. That unpredictable and somewhat boldly erratic thinking style also led Neeleman to invent ticketless travel and a novel reservation system that allows agents to handle customer calls from their homes.

Part of the reason ADHD's mental messiness isn't always pathological is that there's a less-appreciated flip side to ADHD, namely a tendency to have that wandering focus sometimes latch on to a particular task or idea. This "hyperfocus" sets up a sort of scan-and-lock mode of thinking, in that someone with ADHD sometimes furiously samples various aspects of the world around her, suddenly zooming in on whatever seems most engaging. That can be a highly productive approach to solving a problem — though it is not without its own problems. Denslow Brown says some of her ADHD clients sometimes grab on to a single task at work with such tenaciousness that they'll miss meetings, leading her to recommend that they set loud-ringing timers in front of them. Hallowell related the story of one patient of his, a poet who was making ends meet by driving a school bus. The man once drove his entire route without remembering to stop and let any of the small children off the bus — but he was able to make considerable progress on a poem he had been thinking about all the while.

Sometimes the mess associated with a psychiatric disorder, while not necessarily helpful, can at least be considerably less pathological in its impact than one might expect. One fellow who suffers from Tourette's syndrome, complete with its bouts of irrepressible tics, relates that the affliction is a complete non-issue in his job as a trader on the frenzied floor of a major exchange, where hundreds of other traders are constantly barking and twitching in the normal courses of their jobs. He doesn't even feel the need to suppress the occasional random urge to shout Tourette's-fueled obscenities at his colleagues; when he curses someone out, he explains, the colleague will blithely swear back at him, and that's that, with no hard feelings.

Autism, in some of its incarnations, is an interesting example of how mess can be both problematic and helpful in the context of a psychiatric disorder. For some autistic children, the troublesome mess isn't in their head, it's in the world around them — they often crave order, consistency, and predictability, and if they don't get it they can become highly agitated. One therapist tells of an autistic preschooler who enjoys going to the gym in his school — as long as he always goes with the same group, at the same time, and gets to stand on the same side of the gym; otherwise, he becomes inconsolably distraught. And yet according to a leading school of thought in the treatment of autistic children, one pioneered by George Washington University Medical School psychiatrist Stanley Greenspan, *increasing* the disorder in autistic children's environments can be a key to helping them. The approach centers on a technique called *floor time*, in which a parent, teacher, or other caregiver insists on joining the child's normally solitary play, making a point of gently disrupting whatever order the child tries to establish — flipping over a toy car that's part of a neat line of identically arranged cars, pulling the child's chair away from the table, changing a tape the child plays repeatedly, removing a piece of a puzzle. The intention is both to provoke an interaction between the child and the caregiver, building social and communication skills, and to create a problem that the child wants to solve, sharpening his cognitive abilities.

In the previous chapter we learned of some researchers who hope noise might somehow be inserted into the human brain as a form of treatment. Actually, one could say that crude forms of induced brain mess have been employed for decades, often highly effectively. The most prominent example is electroconvulsive therapy, popularly called electroshock therapy, in which an electric shock applied to the skull essentially forces a seizure and, speaking very roughly, scrambles the patient's thought patterns. Though presumed by much of the public to be a violent, almost barbaric treatment, ECT today is widely used — about one hundred thousand patients receive it every year — and is considered by most experts to be fairly benign, though there is still some debate over possible memory loss and mild cognitive impairment. While it is generally a last line of treatment, it is more effective than any other approach against chronic, severe depression, and is also often helpful with some types of schizophrenia and with bipolar disorder. A Mayo Clinic study found that 91 percent of patients who received ECT said they were glad to have had it — an unusually high rate of satisfaction for a mental health treatment, and all the more extraordinary for coming from a group that is by definition difficult to treat, not to mention normally downbeat.

The Relativity of Mess

While scientists can sometimes measure disorder according to objective, technical criteria, our everyday assessment of what makes for an unpleasant mess and what doesn't must be attributed to a vaguer and more subjective process. In many cases, our perception of disruptive mess is an entirely psychological construct. Consider, for example, that the consumer who returns a stereo to an electronics store because its musical output is marred by a deeply irritating background hiss might use his store credit to purchase a "sleep machine" that generates much the same hiss for the purpose of soothing the way to peaceful slumber. Simply put, pathological mess often turns out to be in the mind of the beholder.

An interesting example of the relativity of mess can be found in France in La Hague, a popular resort area on the western tip of Normandy's Cotentin Peninsula. La Hague is a pleasantly breezy region of stone-walled fields grazed by goats and cows, and of grassy dunes lining the ocean. In summer, tourist buses and pop-up tent trailers crowd the winding, hilly roads that lead to La Hague's beaches. There's plenty in the area other than the ocean to keep visitors busy, including restaurants that, along with many Parisian eateries, serve butter and cheese made from the milk of those goats and cows, and oysters plucked from the sands near those dunes. Visitors can also explore parks, chateaus, and botanical gardens. And if there's time left over, they can take the popular tour of the world's largest nuclear-waste-processing plant, located just up the hill and affording some of the loveliest views of the area.

Nuclear power has always been at least vaguely creepy to Americans, and worse than that since 1979. That's when the popular film *The China Syndrome* hit a nerve with its dramatic, fictional account of a near-meltdown at a nuclear power plant, thanks in large part to the fact that, about a week after the movie's opening, reactor 2 at the Three Mile Island nuclear plant obliged the film's publicity machine by overheating and releasing radioactive steam over the Pennsylvania towns and farmland along the Susquehanna River. (No one was directly injured, though there are claims that the incident bumped up cancer rates in the area.) *Syndrome* star Jane Fonda was out stumping about the threat of nuclear power before the reactor had cooled, and though Fonda had some history of taking positions that would in retrospect seem embarrassing to everyone involved, the country by and large went along with this one and has hardly looked back. All orders for new nuclear plants were immediately canceled, and there hasn't been another plant ordered in the United States since. Today, the face of the U.S. nuclear power industry is Homer Simpson's, and nuclear waste is just about the scariest, most repulsive form of mess that Americans can conjure — even when it's to be buried beneath a cubic mile of volcanic rock and soil in the middle of the desert, judging by the widespread opposition to the plans to store radioactive waste below Yucca Mountain in Nevada.

Not so in most of the rest of the world, and especially in China, Japan, and France. In France, where 75 percent of the electricity comes from nuclear power, schoolchildren in some parts of the country are more likely to have had a pleasant tour of the inside of a nuclear plant than to have visited the Eiffel Tower. Homes and farms lap right up to the edges of the plants, and warm water from the plants' cooling systems is circulated through local greenhouses. At the pristine, bucolically situated La Hague facility, which sprawls over more than a square mile and lies close to a bustling village (Yucca Mountain's nearest commercial neighbor is a brothel fifteen miles away), tourists can ogle the processes by which spent fuel from French plants, as well as that of five other countries, is separated into uranium and plutonium, both of which can be reused in plants as fuel, with about 3 percent of the original fuel stored on site as sealed waste in the form of a glasslike substance.

The French may have this one right. Not only do nuclear power plants produce energy more cheaply than do gas- and coal-burning plants, they also have better safety records (excluding grossly inadequate, old-line Soviet designs like that of the Chernobyl plant, which were known to be disasters waiting to happen). Furthermore, they have none of the conventional plants' vast emissions of globally warming greenhouse gases, and they even release *less radioactivity* into the environment than coal-burning plants. (That's right; coal is one of those slightly radioactive ordinary substances mentioned earlier.) So what's the scarier mess? The thirty tons of highly shielded, recyclable or buriable waste generated by a nuclear power plant in a year? Or the eight million tons of ozone-eating carbon dioxide and fifty thousand tons of toxic sulfur dioxide spewed into the air each year by a conventional power plant? For once, it may be Americans who are clinging to the superfluous *interdit*.

Advertising presents another example of the relativity of undesirable mess. Talk to almost anyone in the advertising business and it probably won't be long before she mentions the "clutter" problem — the idea that the public is so awash in advertising pitches that it has mostly tuned them all out. But this is a simplistic interpretation. According to Eric Webber, a vice president at advertising agency GSD&M, the problem isn't necessarily that there's too much advertising. It's that advertising has been largely confined to traditional formats — TV ads, print ads, billboards, banners on Web pages — that are especially easy to tune out or to avoid altogether. Says Webber: "Advertising was built around 'the Cleaver model'" — he's referring to the fictional family in the late 1950s to early 1960s television show *Leave It to Beaver* — "which is based on the idea that dad is home at 5:30, dinner is at 6:00, you settle in to watch television that has a couple of channels to choose from, and you listen to whatever messages marketers wanted you to hear." But the brain is masterful at ignoring repeated, predictable signals that aren't of special interest, which is why the wailing and whooping of someone else's 130-decibel car alarm just down the street rarely holds attention for more than a minute. Now advertisers are recognizing that to avoid being filtered out in the same way, they need to scatter around a broader variety of more attention-grabbing ads. For the advertising industry, the problem isn't advertising clutter; it's a *lack* of clutter.

Does the idea that advertisers want to work more advertising into your daily life strike you as a scary one? It should. Two-thirds of people surveyed in a Yankelovich study said they already feel "constantly bombarded" by ads, and 59 percent said the ads they see have little or no relevance to them. But this second figure is worth focusing on. Is it possible many of us might come to *like* advertising clutter if advertisements were customized to our interests? We're all about to find out.

For example, a company called Massive has developed a technique for changing the ads embedded in the scenery of video games to match an individual player's moves and preferences. In four Massachusetts Stop & Shop supermarkets, an electronic tablet attached to the shopping cart asks for a swipe of the shopper's loyalty card and in return provides a shopping list that the store's computers have prepared based on the shopper's past purchases — as well as popping up targeted electronic coupons when the shopper turns down the aisle with the featured product, pumping impulse buys. And a company called

Mall Radio Network pipes music into malls, sticking in now-on-sale-at-RadioShack-on-level-two sorts of ads that can be tailored to where a listener is standing and to what's selling or not selling in the stores. Soon toaster ovens and orange-juice cartons may be flashing ads at you as you walk by them in stores, thanks to new, cheap, ultrathin electronic displays recently brought out by Siemens. Taxi-top electronic messaging signs from a firm called Vert are tied to GPS location sensors, so that wherever a cab roams, it can pitch a nearby store or restaurant. General Motors has been experimenting with location-aware sponsored messages tied to its OnStar communications system. Smart Sign Media operates digital highway billboards that detect the radio stations playing in passing cars, and flash up client ads that best match the profiles of those stations' listeners. Mobiltrak places car-radio-station-identifying sensors in the parking lots of retail clients. And Reactrix Systems makes a high-tech projector that can turn a sidewalk or restaurant floor into a crowd-raising interactive video-game-cum-advertisement. According to Reactrix CEO Michael Ribero, studies have shown that as many as 80 percent of the people who line up to interact with the Reactrix image can recall the sponsor days later, compared to 5 percent for prime-time television advertising.

Answer your cell phone — the future of advertising is calling. McDonald's and Dunkin' Donuts are among the companies that have beamed coupons to the cell phones of Americans who have expressed interest in them, eliciting coupon-redemption rates as high as 17 percent, where a 3 percent rate is a blockbuster by ordinary standards. Mike Baker, president of Boston-based mobile-marketing firm Enpocket, which ran the Dunkin' Donuts campaign, notes there are already more mobile phones in use worldwide than televisions and computers combined. Throw in location tracking, a capability U.S. mobile phones are getting right now, and you've got a device that can prompt you with a coupon for a discount oil change just as you're driving by the lube shop. Enpocket has already run such a "location-aware" mobile-phone campaign in Singapore on behalf of Intel.

Who knows where people will be most receptive to an ad? According to a 2004 AOL survey, 4 percent of Internet users have checked their e-mail on a portable device while in the bathroom. Perhaps some day, ads will be targeted accordingly. It might be an appropriate time, for example, to pitch a weekend at the nuclear waste resort.

CHAPTER THIRTEEN

The Aesthetics of Mess

To find a form that accommodates the mess,
that is the task of the artist now.
— SAMUEL BECKETT

Of all the jazz artists and jam-banders who might spring to mind when it comes to improvisation, the superstar musician who may be the greatest improvisationalist of all time is well known to the public for everything *except* his improvisation. Yet so intense was this performer's dedication to jumping beyond the music as written that otherwise adoring audiences and backup musicians sometimes became annoyed at the length and off-the-wall intricacy of his extemporaneous musical wanderings, and he lost gigs over it. Even when sitting in with other musicians, he couldn't resist changing their compositions on the fly.

The irrepressible improviser was Johann Sebastian Bach. If you're wondering how Bach managed to reconcile improvisation with the highly ordered, intricate, precise domain of baroque music, consider that in the eighteenth century improvisation was regarded as an integral component of serious music. It would have been a second-rate performer indeed who thought to limit recitals to prescribed notes. The opportunity — the imperative, really — for improvisation was explicitly written into baroque compositions and in more than one way. Bach and other composers of the time rarely spelled out parts for cello, bassoon, harpsichord, and organ note-for-note, instead providing the players of these and other low-range instruments suggested chords on which they were expected to riff. Concertos contained cadenzas that challenged the soloist to cut loose from the confines of the sheet music, and the resulting long, furious improvisations were often the highlights of performances. Even when notes were specified on the sheet, musicians routinely threw in improvised flourishes, like chefs sprinkling an extra dash of this and sprig of that, and the ability to spontaneously insert such ornamentation was considered a basic element of musicianship.

Bach was thus hardly a renegade in his time for being fond of improvisation, but he was infamous for the extent and boldness of it. He would embellish at length on the organ, even in the middle of church services, apparently sometimes dismaying the officiators, choirs, congregations, and others who were simply trying to get through the liturgy. In other performances, he would take musical themes tossed at him from the audience and immediately improvise around them, much in the style of a contemporary nightclub comedian. Bach also enjoyed the then-popular practice of challenging other composers to musical duels of improvisation, as he did with the renowned French organist and composer Louis Marchand. So prodigious was Bach's improvisational bent that today experts believe we only have a portion of his compositional oeuvre, much of it having been whipped up in performance and left untranscribed.

Bach and his colleagues could not have predicted that by the middle of the twentieth century the improvisational elements of their compositions, and of all classical music, would have been gradually and thoroughly excised. Composers had later filled in the bass lines and cadenzas with note-for-note versions, so that today musicians play only what's on the page, and every performance is melodically identical to every other. Taking it on oneself to add off-the-cuff flourishes to the music in the middle of a performance would be seen not as an exhibition of musicianship and creativity, but as a career-ending stunt that violated the music — even though to do so would be far more in keeping with the composer's intentions than the frozen-in-place versions we hear today. It has been a centuries-long organizing project that almost certainly would have appalled some of the very composers we most ardently lionize.

Throughout this book we've seen some of the ways in which mess and disorder, in their various forms, can be a great deal less harmful than they are usually made out to be. We've even seen how useful, and even necessary, they can be in many situations. Now, in this final chapter, let's add one more claim: mess and disorder can be beautiful.

The Art of Mess

The presumed aesthetic failings of mess and disorder are prime — and sometimes the sole — motivators for straightening up and organizing. That is, much of what is objectionable to people about certain types of mess is simply that the mess seems ugly. But it's often easy enough and perfectly sensible to add a cosmetically acceptable veneer to a mess — throwing clutter into a closet; stacking papers in piles; resurfacing narrow, winding roads instead of building new ones; hiding a convoluted order-entry process behind a stylish retail Web site; housing a fractious local government in a handsome town hall. The U.S. Marines are peerless warriors in large part for their freewheeling, independent, and improvisational style of operation, but the public gets the more comforting image of an immaculately squared away, ultradisciplined, strictly hierarchical corps.

In the realm of the arts, though, mess isn't always best tucked away behind an ordered facade. Instead, mess can be an integral element of the creative vision; sometimes the disorder of a work of art is its most affecting element. As a conspicuous example, consider James Joyce's *Ulysses*, widely held to be one of the greatest works of literature in the English language. *Ulysses* is a mess in almost every way that a book can be a mess, short of having the pages fall out when you pick it up. The plot is nearly impenetrably convoluted, the language dense and obscure. A fairly typical example:

> You were going to do wonders, what? Missionary to Europe after fiery Columbanus. Fiacre and Scotus on their creepystools in heaven spilt from their pintpots, loudlatinlaughing: *Euge! Euge!* Pretending to speak broken English as you dragged your valise, porter threepence, across the slimy pier at Newhaven. *Comment?* Rich booty you brought back: *Le Tutu*, five tattered number of *Pantalon Blanc et Culotte Rouge*, a blue French telegram, curiosity to show:
> — Mother dying come home father.

It's hard to imagine *Ulysses* inspiring the sort of reverence that it has if its story had been laid out in neater, clearer fashion, something more along the lines of the CliffsNotes version. Today it's more the rule than the exception for the narrative of novels to jump around in time and space and between different points of view, to lay out a character's confused thoughts in a form that is itself confusing, and to generally sprinkle in a measure of randomness and convolution. The disorder in a work of literature can even have the paradoxical effect of clarifying. Neal Stephenson maintains that his 2004 book *The Confusion* is in fact an intertwining of two separate novels. The author (or a character standing in for him) explains up front in a note to the reader that he has "interleaved sections of one with sections of the other so that the two stories move forward in synchrony," in the hopes that "being thus confused shall render them the less confusing to the Reader."

Filmmakers, too, sometimes inject a measure of mess into their works with satisfying results. In films such as *M*A*S*H*, *Nashville*, *Short Cuts*, *Gosford Park*, and the more recent *A Prairie Home Companion*, the director Robert Altman doesn't so much weave a story as heap it on the viewer in pieces that often have a disjointed, spontaneous, rambling feel. Some of the films directed by the provocative director Gus Van Sant, most notably *Elephant* and *Last Days*, leave the notion of a conventional narrative thread almost entirely behind, instead presenting snatches of images, events, and dialogue that gradually acquire force in sum. Woody Allen is famous for relying on improvisation in his filming and is said to restrict his actors' access to scripts to ensure it. Even Steven Spielberg, whose films tend to hew to more conventional exposition, managed to slip a substantial helping of mess into one of his megahits. *Close Encounters of the Third Kind* lurches and bounces its way through multiple, confusing plot lines built around frenetic scenes in which parallel lines of dialogue often clash, and where the important action sometimes takes place in the background, pushing the viewer to experience some of the main character's bewilderment and anxiety.

Mess in classical music gets its due elsewhere in this chapter, but it's worth mentioning that popular music has evidenced its share of disorder as well, ranging from the distortion, or "fuzz," lovingly added by generations of rock musicians to their guitars — in 1975 Lou Reed put out a double album consisting entirely of guitar feedback — to the street and other background noises mixed into recordings by everyone from the Beatles to Nelly Furtado. (Some might also be quick to point out that more-contemporary classical compositions, with their frequent dissonances and staggered rhythms, are also showcases for explicit disorder and noise in music. But actually, the structure and flow of these pieces tend to be highly calculated, sometimes emerging from mathematical progressions, even if the underlying order isn't always obvious. A good example would be the more challenging works of the early-twentieth-century Austrian-American composer Arnold Schoenberg, whose unconventional melodic constructions were carefully wrought, though they at first struck some audiences as so distressingly and unmusically noiselike that performances were occasionally marred by angry shouting and even brawls.)

The interdependence of art and mess is even stronger, or at least more explicit, in painting and sculpture. In Japan, this is to some extent old hat; the tradition of *wabi sabi*, or the beauty of imperfection, is said to date back at least five hundred years. The West was a bit slower to catch on. When the visual arts blossomed in Europe in the seventeenth and eighteenth centuries, a widely embraced guiding principle was to hold up order, in its various forms, as an ideal. In balanced, standardized, uncluttered composition, in the heroic stances or graceful curves of subjects, and in virtuous and biblical themes, artists often strived to reveal order as a form of beauty and vice versa. There were certainly exceptions, especially among Dutch painters such as Vermeer and Rembrandt, who by the mid-seventeenth century were already experimenting with crowded, random-looking placements of figures and objects. But it was during the Romantic movement of the early nineteenth century that artists began to pick in earnest at the ordered conventions of painting, by literally blurring images, employing thicker and even lurid brushstrokes, and dropping the Sunday-schoolish lessons in codes of behavior. There is little of the neat and orderly in Delacroix's dreamlike depictions of lions tearing into horses.

Impressionism widened art's rift from the orderly, often taking the stuff of everyday peasant life and visually refracting it into bursts of color. Van Gogh took this messy process so far that even today many experts tend to regard his genius as the flip side of his mental disintegration. But madness wasn't a prerequisite for pushing art into the realm of the disordered. While romanticism and impressionism were assaults on the orderly, expressionism and cubism, which followed in the beginning of the twentieth century, demolished it. After centuries of trying to nudge reality in the direction of perfection, the task of the artist had become in part to mess reality up.

Indeed, one of the greatest challenges to contemporary artists has been to come up with novel, provocative ways of being messy. Dadaism got this endeavor off to a rollicking start around 1915 by self-consciously breaking away from the established order of art in all ways — even by pointedly refusing to be a clearly definable movement of art. That is, to the extent that it was about anything, Dadaism was a disorganized embracing of disorder. That's not easy to top, mess-wise. But many have tried. The formless blotches of abstract expressionism, the bizarre pairing of images employed by surrealists like René Magritte and Salvador Dalí, the riotous dribblings of Jasper

Johns, the scrap collages of Robert Rauschenberg — all are at least in part attempts to employ some form of disorder, be it clutter, mixture, blur, noise, or convolution, among others. Today there are hundreds of established painters and sculptors who prominently incorporate elements of mess and disorder into their works. Among the messaphilic artists who have been the subject of major shows in recent years: Richard Tuttle, who wrangles bits of wire, plywood, rope, and other found objects into small, abstract works; Jon Kessler, who assembles video monitors, moving contraptions, and blotchy paintings into sprawling kinetic sculptures; Chris Jordan, who photographs industrial refuse such as sawdust piles, bales of recycled metal, and discarded cell phones; and Elizabeth Murray, who paints on a jumble of screwed-together minicanvases.

The German philosopher Martin Heidegger suggested that art resists categorization. That's certainly right, but if one were forced to try, a category of "messy" would probably be at least as handy as any other.

Messy Tastes

In 1990, at age seventeen, Edward Zaki moved to Montreal from his native Egypt. By the time he was twenty-three, he owned two convenience stores. Returning to Alexandria, Egypt, in 1996, he reflected on the fact that he didn't miss the stores so much as the food counters he operated in them, so he decided to open a restaurant. But what kind? He was torn between his exposure to the informal cuisine of North America, the classic French dishes worshipped in Montreal, the more ascetic influences of his childhood roots, and the coastal influences of Alexandria. Choosing not to choose, Zaki opened a Danny Meyer–like chain comprising an American bistro, a classic French restaurant, an alcohol-free restaurant, and a seafood restaurant. All were successful, but Zaki wasn't done bouncing. He still had a brother in Montreal, and in late 2000 moved back. Higher costs there precluded immediately opening more than one restaurant, so he was again faced with choosing a theme. Or was he?

Walking into Zaki's restaurant today is almost as disorienting as entering Harvey's Hardware or Strymish's emporia. It's nestled in the heart of Montreal's student-dominated Latin Quarter on Rue St. Denis, lined with restaurants that are uniformly informal, each focused on one of an array of ethnic cuisines. Zaki's eatery, on the other hand, is clearly more upscale than its neighbors — this isn't a souvlaki or bagel joint — but figuring out what sort of food it might serve, and even whether it's a club or a bistro or a café or a gourmet restaurant, is a challenge. There is blue lighting in the front, and red toward the back; some of the lights have flowers inside them. White tablecloths are in force in the center, but a bit to the side people are dining at long, bare, counterlike affairs that are internally illuminated as if intended for browsing X-rays. What's more, some of the diners are sitting not in chairs, but in playground swings hung from the ceiling. Toward the back, the tables are unadorned metal. A staircase by the entrance provides a glimpse upstairs of butcher-block tables glowing by firelight. The mystery only deepens with the long menu. Grilled octopus tentacles, foie gras, snapper encased in burned whole wheat, cheese-stuffed grapes in ham, raw vegetables, flaming cheese — no cuisine, approach, or even sensibility suggests itself. What's more, the dishes are served in the Spanish style of tapas, small portions normally intended for snacking, though here they're intended to be jointly amassed by a party of diners as full meals. It's in this disordered themelessness, of course, that Zaki found his theme. And he provides fair warning in the name of the restaurant: Confusion.

Zaki explains with amiable intensity that his restaurant and menu both reflect and resolve his inner convolution. "I don't have a sense of belonging to a certain place," he says. "Instead of an inspiration, I had multiple inspirations." Certainly, he had noted the popularity of "fusion" cuisine, dishes based on a careful, calculated blend of two styles, usually Asian and Western, as with Danny Meyer's Tabla. But Zaki was looking for something more disordered, even unsettling. "I wanted to provoke," he says. "I didn't want someone to say, 'Oh yeah, I had this in Paris once.' I wanted to serve food that customers would either love because it's different or hate because it's different. What I didn't want to hear was someone saying, 'That was very good.'" Though an odd juxtaposition of dishes on the menu might set customers to scratching their heads, he wanted the clash to reach their palates — hence the tapas servings, ensuring that diners would combine them. In addition, the small portions make ordering more of a shared group experience, with all the sticky issues that might entail. "If you're just ordering duck for yourself, you don't have to have a discussion about it with your friends," he says. "But if two or three people are sharing six or seven dishes, then they're choosing together and talking about it." Even the choice of the Latin Quarter's mismatched ambience was part of the effort to thwart diners' expectations.

The notion of mixing disparate decors and pushing customers to combine multiple cuisines into a meal is a bit off the wall. But when you think about it, given the hundreds of thousands of restaurants in North America, the oddest thing about the idea is that it hasn't been tried more often. Perhaps with good reason, or so it seemed when Confusion opened. Even adventurous Montreal diners were initially nonplussed at Confusion's fare, and dining parties debated long and hard among themselves and with their waiters over how to cobble together an appropriate meal before finally ordering. Zaki had been hoping for a certain amount of dialogue, but the debates were proving interminable enough to hurt the business — as was the fact that when the orders were finally put in, they tended to be on the skimpy side, simply because customers, wary of mix-and-match dining, were erring on the conservative side by trying fewer things. Zaki reluctantly put in a quick fix, in the form of a series of suggested seven-dish meals. Diners jumped at them, apparently finding them a satisfying compromise between the utter disorder of an undifferentiated, long list of strange, small dishes, and the ordinary, highly ordered experience of ordering a single dish. This way, they got some mess, but not a paralyzing dose of it. Not only do customers who order the preset meals tend to end up with more dishes, but they're more likely to gravitate toward some of the more intimidating dishes. For example, few people ordered the foie gras at US$18 for a small serving, which had first led Zaki to consider taking it off the menu. But the preset meals that include foie gras have proved the most popular, and as a result, he is adding more versions of foie gras to the menu and is even considering making it a mini-specialty of the restaurant.

Zaki concedes that there are certain inefficiencies that go along with a messy menu. Higher-end restaurants typically rotate a new dish onto a menu of perhaps six entrées every week or so, but at Confusion trying to rotate one-sixth of the forty or so nondessert dishes every week would be exhausting. Instead, he aims to rotate a little over half the menu once every three months, in part based on what people seem to be gravitating to and in part just to shake things up. One planned change, for example, is to introduce several kosher-style dishes, which no one has been asking for.

Zaki intends to build an empire of disordered eateries. Needless to say, it will not be accomplished by cloning Confusion. Instead, he has embraced vertigo, or more precisely *"Vertige"*; French for "giddiness," this is the name of the new Montreal restaurant he opened at the end of 2005. Vertige takes a different approach to pulling diners out of their comfort zone and confounding their expectations. It appears at first glance to be a purveyor of classic French haute cuisine, and is located smack in the middle of a small beltway of mostly conventional chic eateries, but in this way Vertige is subversive. The menu at first suggests the French standards, but a closer look reveals some pointed oddities. In fact, every item on the menu features some sort of play on order. One multicourse meal, for example, is prepared as per classical tradition, but the courses are served in reverse order. In another, the sweet ingredients are swapped for salty ones and vice versa. The restaurant made an immediate impact, at least to read the Montreal newspaper *Le Devoir*, which pronounced barely a month after Vertige's opening that it "already belongs on the list of Montreal's finer restaurants."

Riding high on this momentum, Zaki is considering a third restaurant. After all, he hasn't yet begun to experiment with noise, clutter, and time sprawl.

Name That Tuning

Nick Keelan, a professor at the Lawrence University Conservatory of Music, describes a trombone part in the fourth movement of Beethoven's Fifth Symphony that tends to make professional trombonists sweat. It's not that the part is jammed with technically challenging runs of notes; it isn't. True, the part is "exposed" — that is, it stands out prominently against a relatively muted background — but that's not it either. Nor is it the fact that the part demands a clear, round, majestic blast of sound, with sure and crisp transitions between notes. These are all routine demands for pros. The challenge, says Keelan, is to come in on tune.

Those of us who aren't musicians, or at least trained in music theory, might think playing on key is the simplest, most basic demand on a musician — that sour notes, whether sharp or flat, are the sort of thing that good musicians leave behind in junior high school. What excuse could there be for playing out of tune? After all, orchestral musicians conspicuously take pains to tune their instruments in the noisy preperformance ritual initiated by a clear, workmanlike note from the oboe — a hard-to-tune instrument saved by tradition from having to adjust. And that should be that for tuning.

Or perhaps you know enough to realize it's not quite that simple. Temperature is a factor, for example, in that instruments tend to heat up over the course of a performance, which changes their tuning. The change depends on the surrounding temperature, how much and how loudly the instrument has been playing, and whether the instrument is in sunshine or close to stage lights, among other factors. Correcting for it in the case of the trombone can involve adjusting the instrument's tuning slide, changing how far out the main slide is pulled, or even just altering the precise position of the musician's lips. Temperature can indeed be a factor in the case of the Beethoven part, because it's the first time the trombonists play in the symphony. After having sat through the first three and a half movements without getting to hear what their instruments sound like, the musicians must guess at how their own instruments' temperatures have changed. But experienced musicians learn how to estimate temperature-related tuning changes with surprising accuracy, and thus correcting for it isn't the main source of tuning worries for trombonists playing the Fifth Symphony.

The real problem is inherent to tuning itself. Tuning to the oboe, far from settling the question, is really just a tentative beginning to what turns out to be a wild ride in tuning that can twist and turn from note to note and from instrument to instrument. At the heart of the matter is the fact that there's really no absolute, universal meaning to "being in tune" — it's a variable, inconsistent, dynamic judgment. In this sense, even the most disciplined, orderly performance of a familiar piece by a superb ensemble is really built on a slippery platform. And it's exactly this sort of inescapable messiness that helps imbue performances with the sort of variation and unpredictability that can leave audiences mesmerized one day and bored the next.

To start to appreciate the vagaries of tuning, consider the piano. Until the eighteenth century, keyboard instruments were tuned like other instruments, which is to say via "just tuning." Very simply put, just tuning involves tuning the keys so that when a scale is played one note at a time, the scale will sound pleasing as it climbs up the keyboard. That's an intuitive scheme, and it's how most people assume keyboard instruments are tuned today. But they aren't, because it turns out there's a thorny problem with just tuning relating to chords, or combinations of notes played simultaneously. Owing to an odd glitch in the relationships between the different sorts of notes that seem perfect to our ears, chords that sound lovely when played on one part of the keyboard of a just-tuned instrument can produce wobbling and other clashy effects when played on another part. The disharmony creeps in because the progression of notes in a just-tuned scale is somewhat irregular — a jump from one note to the note that is one full tone higher, as for example from a "do" to a "re" in the "do re mi" progression, typically ends up being slightly larger or smaller than a one-tone jump between two notes located elsewhere on the scale, such as "re" to "mi." As a result, when the same scale is played in a different key — that is, when the scale starts on a different note — it can sound a tiny bit different. These small differences don't much affect the integrity of the scales, but they end up hobbling some chords as they are moved from key to key. Through the seventeenth century, composers simply avoided these troubled chords. That works fine, as long as the piece isn't transposed into a different key — that is, shifted up or down wholesale to a higher or lower pitch, as is often done when, for example, a piece is to be played with instruments other than the ones it was initially written for or even when a composer wishes to move a musical theme to a different key within a single piece.

By the eighteenth century, a number of composers, most notably the keyboard-centric Bach, had come to find the restrictions imposed by just tuning on chords and transposition burdensome and started to embrace another approach to tuning keyboard instruments. In this alternate technique, called *tempered tuning*, a keyboard instrument is essentially purposely mistuned. To oversimplify a bit, the tuner smooths out the variations in note-to-note jumps by rendering some notes very slightly flat and others very slightly sharp as compared to just tuning. The result is that scales no longer sound quite right when played note by note — that the notes are slightly off can be audible even to a musical layman with a moderately keen sense of pitch.

But because the note-to-note jumps are more consistent than they are with just tuning, a chord that sounds good in one key will sound pretty good in any other key.

Bach advocated strongly for this useful mistuning, and publicly embraced one form of it, called "well-tempered tuning," via one of his best-known compositions, "The Well-Tempered Clavier," written specifically to demonstrate how the quality of a composition played on a tempered-tuned harpsichord is reasonably, if not perfectly, well preserved as it is transposed through different keys. (The *key* of a musical composition specifies the seven notes that make up the main scale around which the composition, or part of the composition, is based.)

Just tuning and various versions of tempered tuning competed for keyboard musicians' allegiance throughout the first half of the eighteenth century. To make things worse, there was no widespread agreement on *concert pitch* — that is, on the pitch of A above middle C, the note to which the process of tuning is calibrated. As a result, the tuning of keyboard instruments and to some extent of entire orchestras varied in Europe from town to town, and might vary in one town from week to week. In fact, today's international standard for concert pitch wasn't accepted until 1939 — and some well-known orchestras, including the Berlin Philharmonic, still insist on tuning to a different pitch. A slightly tweaked version of well-tempered tuning called *even-tempered tuning*, in which all the jumps between notes are made perfectly consistent, finally became more or less standard for keyboard instruments in the 1850s, and today keyboard instruments are tuned by this technique. (Bear in mind, therefore, that when you hear a performance of music written before the second half of the eighteenth century, you're probably not hearing exactly what the composer intended, unless the musicians have taken the trouble to ensure they are adhering to the tuning scheme in effect in the composer's day and town.)

Unlike pianos and other keyboard instruments, virtually all the standard instruments in an orchestra enlist just tuning to get those pleasing progressions of single notes. But the problem of aberrant harmonies between multiple notes played simultaneously doesn't go away; with many instruments playing many different notes, there's plenty of opportunity for the notes to clash. A piano player doesn't have to worry about it, simply because she is stuck with whatever the piano tuner has wrought. But a trombonist or trumpet player or violinist has no such excuse — he has to shoulder a share of the responsibility for avoiding interpreting notes in a way that unpleasantly combines with those of other instruments and has to do it *by adjusting tuning on the fly* throughout the performance. How big an alteration is called for depends on the instrument (all instruments produce unique overtones that affect harmonies), the note, the key in which the note is being played, and the specific qualities of sound that the musician and conductor hope to achieve. The required adjustments aren't always the sort of small touches that only a perfectionist conductor would appreciate. Nick Keelan points out that it's not at all uncommon for an orchestra musician to have to alter a single, extended note by nearly a quarter tone — that is, half the distance from a C-sharp to a D — right in the middle of the note, because of other instruments coming in. Were the musician to simply hold the note as written, without retuning on the fly, it might be enough to evoke a wince from a sizable percentage of the audience. And almost everyone in the orchestra is constantly making these adjustments and readjustments in response to the music and to each other.

And so back to the trombonists' challenge in Beethoven's

Fifth. Over the course of the more than half an hour of music that flies by before the trombonists' conspicuous entrance, there is no way for a musician without perfect pitch — an ability nine out of ten students at the Juilliard School of Music do not possess — to know exactly where all the other instruments have gotten to in their own tuning, and even if there were, there's really no precise specification of what unique tuning adjustment would be perfectly suited to it. There are so many variables that, in the end, the trombonists have to make their own technical and aesthetic judgments as to what tonal shade of the written note to play. And while this instance is a particularly challenging one, the same basic task faces every musician in an orchestra in a smaller way throughout every piece, note to note, and often even in the middle of an individual note. That even the pros can occasionally be more inspired than usual in this endeavor is all part of the magic of a performance.

In fact, the only time when tuning is a neat, straightforward task is before the start of the performance, when the oboe sounds that ethereal note, and the musicians commence their individual tuning rituals. Here, during that sudden cacophony of clashing scales, is the one occasion where there's no ambiguity or variation in the meaning of notes. Then the orchestra becomes quiet, the conductor taps his baton, and the real mess begins.

Last and Misguidedly Least: Smell

Hans Rindisbacher, the Pomona College German studies professor who, in chapter 9, offered observations on German attitudes toward disordered behavior, has an interesting and fairly unique academic sideline. He studies smelliness. It's a surprisingly rich field, encompassing brain science, culture, industry, and history, among other areas, and it's one that is largely neglected. And that's exactly what most fascinates Rindisbacher about the topic; our attitudes about odor make it, literally, the most unspeakable of messes.

Part of the cause of our inattention to smell may simply be that we don't have much of an idiom of smell. The lack of an odor-related vocabulary impairs our ability to think meaningfully about smells, says Rindisbacher, and even to be fully aware of them. "Odor isn't well grounded in language," he notes. "You can't describe a smell the way you can say something you see is square, blue, or angled. You have to rely on borrowed terms, and that's where you run into trouble." What he means is that aside from a few primitive, vague terms such as *smelly*, or *awful*, or *sweet*, we tend to categorize smells in terms of a relatively small number of odorously familiar entities: fish, flowers, wet fur, new cars, feces, vanilla, and so forth. Our reliance on doing so prevents us from being able to describe a novel smell on its own terms and leads us to overlook an odor's subtleties and complexities.

How did we come to lack a richer language of odor? It's because somewhere along the line, says Rindisbacher, we *wanted* to stop talking about smell. Odors rarely come up in conversation because bringing up the smelly is often regarded as impolite, crude, and discomforting. The disconnect is especially striking in literature, he contends, where writers who take great pains to precisely and creatively transmit the visual appearance of scenes, people, and objects routinely fail to offer more than a cursory suggestion, if any at all, of how they smell. Those authors who do make a point of occasionally bringing smells front and center, including Marcel Proust, Vladimir Nabokov, and Charles Dickens, stand out as exceptions for having done so.

That may be because writers, if unconsciously, regard smell as a risky business. "You can't control what an olfactory description will invoke in readers," says Rindisbacher. "You have to refer to the odor of other objects to do it, and you don't know what associations go with it." Both reflecting and compounding the problem is that Western society — and especially the United States — has largely eradicated its smells. "Even supermarkets, with acres of food, are utterly unodorous," he points out. The result is an average background smell level so low that anything that *does* smell strikes us as unusual, and more often than not unpleasantly invasive. In other words, smell for most of us has become a sort of cartoon sense, providing exaggerated feedback on a tiny portion of the world around us.

That's strange, really, because smell may be the most exquisitely discriminating of our senses. With their noses, dogs can detect cancerous tumors in humans; squirrels can recognize each other by the smells emanating from any one of five different glands. Studies suggest that we humans actually smell far more than we're consciously aware of. Though our senses of smell are hundreds of times less sensitive than those of dogs, who can smell a few molecules' worth of a substance, we're capable of distinguishing some ten thousand distinct odors, sometimes in surprisingly small quantities. For example, we can pick out mere billionths of an ounce of E-3-methyl-2-hexenoic acid, a key component of human body odor. And while we may marvel at the ability of mice to pick out their kin by smell, the fact is we might be able to do much the same. Infants can distinguish parents from strangers by smell, and in experiments many people turn out even to be perfectly capable of not only distinguishing other people by smell but also mice. If we didn't go through so much trouble stripping ourselves of our smells and trying to dodge what smells remain, we might well open up whole new lines of communication.

Smell provides the only direct link between our brains and the environment. We smell something only when we've inhaled a piece of it into our nostrils, where it comes into physical contact with the tips of long, strandlike brain cells. The detection signals race from our nose along the brain cell to the olfactory bulb at the base of our brain. From there the signals move to the limbic system, the part of the brain responsible for moods, sexual urges, and fear, and then travel to the hippocampus, which controls memories. The signals then spread to the neocortex, which is thought to give rise to consciousness. Thus, smells have a unique pipeline to our emotions, recollections, and thoughts. As Nabokov put it, "Nothing revives the past so completely as a smell that was once associated with it." Dickens made Scrooge "conscious of a thousand odors floating in the air, each one connected with a thousand thoughts, and hopes, and joys, and cares long, long forgotten."

Truly appreciating smell may require losing it, as have approximately two million Americans. Anosmia, as the condition is called, can result from a gene defect, aging, viral infections, allergies, and prescription drugs, or from a head trauma, when a jarring of the brain shears off the delicate brain cells that snake to the nose through a bony plate in the skull. Without smell, people lose their primary defense from fires, gases, and spoiled food, as well as most of their ability to taste food. Specific anosmia, the inability to smell particular odors, is less devastating — which is fortunate, since studies suggest more than half of all people suffer from it. For that reason, any two people are likely to register different odors in many situations, making smell the only sense that gives us a window on the world that relatively few others share.

Rindisbacher contends our shunning of most things smelly got its start two centuries ago, with the general trend toward neatness and organization. "Now we think of smelly places as backward and inferior," he says. Not surprisingly, few people advocate for the return of smelliness. And so we remain mostly oblivious to smell in everyday life, which means we don't care to talk about it, which means we don't acquire a language for it, which means we lose our ability to talk about it, which makes smell all the more distant from us, which leads us to work harder to suppress it.

But who knows? Perhaps the process could work in reverse. Were we to start talking more about smells, perhaps we'd come to better appreciate them, leading us to ease up on our squelching of odors. And if we gave a closer look to other kinds of mess — well, it just might help relieve our increasing obsession with neatness and order.

Most people, no doubt, would be quicker to predict that society will inexorably push toward ever-higher standards of neatness and order, leaving us to keep striving for tighter schedules, more focused goals, better organized companies, tidier homes, longer-range planning, and more consistent behavior. But must it be so? Perhaps right now, somewhere in the world, a beaker has been overturned, or a corporate brainstorm has been sparked by a random word, or two papers have ended up next to each other on a messy desk, or an impulsive politician is changing her position — and the results are going to lead us down a surprising new path.

After all, you know how much stock to put in predictions.

SOURCE NOTES

The following is a list of articles, books, and other written sources from which bits of information in this book were cribbed. The intention is not to provide a formal, comprehensive trail of research, for this is not a scholarly work, but to give credit where credit is due. Most everything else in the book either came from a source named or clearly implied in the text (via firsthand interviews, typically), is readily verifiable from multiple obvious and easily accessible sources, or is a matter of opinion. Inevitably, some sources that are due credit will have been unintentionally omitted here, for which apologies are offered.

1. THE COST OF NEATNESS

17 Shooting of boy: "Jail Ordered for Man Who Accidentally Shot His Son," *Marinette (Wisconsin) Eagle Herald*, July 21, 2005.

18 Stabbing of mother: Kieran Crowley, "Dirty Room Led Girl, 12, to Slay Mom," *New York Post*, June 1, 2005.

20 Sutton comment: Robert Sutton, "Turning Knowledge into Action," *Chief Executive*, August–September 2002.

2. A MESS SAMPLER

26 DuBrin quote: Stacey Hirsh, "Order versus Chaos," *Baltimore Sun*, February 23, 2005.

26 GM and UPS clean-desk policies: Motoko Rich, "Controlling Clutter Creep — With Office Space Shrinking, Bosses Try Clean-Desk Policies, New Furniture to Keep Peace," *Wall Street Journal*, May 29, 2002.

27 Howell Raines and book stacking: Timothy Noah, "'Hard News': Troubled Times," *New York Times*, December 26, 2004.

27 Firing of Bradford chief: Harold T. Beck, "The Publisher's Page," *Mountain Laurel Review*, May 14, 1999.

27 Fining of postal employee: Peter Munro, "Pin-up Protest Spreads at Call Centre," *Sydney Morning Herald*, July 16, 2002.

28 Messy Chicago professors: Mary Ruth Yoe, "Kings of Chaos," *University of Chicago Magazine*, June 2001.

32 Heppel's story: Maxine Singer, "Leon Heppel and the Early Days of RNA Biochemistry," *Journal of Biological Chemistry*, November 28, 2003.

35 Lawn costs and pesticide usage: Jim Motavalli, "The Chemical Meadow," *Environmental Defense*, April 1, 2000, http://www.environmentaldefense.org/article.cfm?contentid=984.

43 Strategic planning–related data: William H. Starbuck, "Strategizing in the Real World," in "Technological Foundations of Strategic Management," special issue, *International Journal of Technology Management* 8, no. 1/2 (1992).

3. The History of Mess

58 Medieval neatness: Norbert Elias, *The Civilizing Process: Sociogenetic and Psychogenetic Investigations*, ed. Eric Dunning, Johan Goudsblom, and Stephen Mennell and trans. Edmund Jephcott (Oxford: Blackwell Publishers, 2000).

64 The efficiency movement: Samuel Haber, *Efficiency and Uplift: Scientific Management in the Progressive Era 1890–1920* (Chicago: University of Chicago Press, 1964).

68 Einstein time line: Sidebar to Dennis Overbye, "The Next Einstein," *New York Times*, March 1, 2005.

68 Citations of Brownian motion paper: Matthew Chalmers, "Five Papers That Shook the World," *Physics World*, January 2005.

4. The Benefits of Mess

75 Schwarzenegger not keeping a calendar: Charlie Leduff and John M. Broder, "Schwarzenegger, Confident and Ready for Prime Time," *New York Times*, June 24, 2004.

83 Edison's filaments: Frank Lewis Dyer, *Edison, His Life and Inventions* (New York: Harper & Brothers Publishers, 1910). (In the public domain and available online from multiple sources.)

86 Fleming quote: Andre Bernard and Clifton Fadiman, eds., *Bartlett's Book of Anecdotes* (New York: Little, Brown, 2000).

86 Danger of electric cars: Gary Richards, "Quiet Hybrids Pose an 'Invisible' Risk," *San Jose Mercury News*, February 3, 2006.

87 Frank Gehry: Based primarily on a study conducted and kindly shared by Richard J. Boland Jr., Kalle Lyytinen, and Youngjin Yoo at Case Western Reserve University.

91 Ronfeldt quote: David Ronfeldt, "Al Qaeda and Its Affiliates," *First Monday*, March 7, 2005, http://www.firstmonday.org/issues/issue10_3/ronfeldt/index.html.

92 Future Combat Systems spending figure: David Talbot, "How Technology Failed in Iraq," *Technology Review*, November 2004.

93 Focusing on midlevel terrorists: Kathleen M. Carley, "Estimating Vulnerabilities in Large Covert Networks," *Proceedings of the 9th International Command and Control Research and Technology Symposium*, Washington, DC, June 2004.

93 Schneier comment: Charles C. Mann, "Homeland Insecurity," *Atlantic Monthly*, September 2002.

5. MESSY PEOPLE

110 Iraq marriages: John Tierney, "The Struggle for Iraq: Traditions; Iraqi Family Ties Complicate American Efforts for Change," *New York Times*, September 28, 2003.

112 Self-storage availability: "Investment Landscape for Self-Storage," *The Institutional Real Estate Letter*, 2005.

116 Poll of parents with children ages six to twelve: Conducted on behalf of Capture Carpet Cleaning System, reported in a press release, July 27, 2005.

6. MESSY HOMES

133 Ilse Crawford quotes: Rick Marin, "Guy Décor: There's a Method to the Mess," *New York Times*, August 4, 2005.

136 Memory stamping: Judith R. Birsh, *Multisensory Teaching of Basic Language Skills* (Baltimore: Brookes Publishing, 2005).

7. MESS AND ORGANIZATIONS

146 A few bits of Strymish family history: Doreen Iudica Vigue, "A Landmark Built of Books," *Boston Globe*, July 9, 1995; Sheryl Julian, "Cook's Domain," *Boston Globe*, February 19, 1997.

164 Extra text in digital files: Tom Zeller Jr., "Beware Your Trail of Digital Fingerprints," *New York Times*, November 7, 2005.

165 Amtrak maintenance manual: Matthew L. Wald, "Amtrak Official Outlines Roots of Acela Problem," *New York Times*, May 12, 2005.

9. THE POLITICS OF MESS

201 Paris and Haussmann: Map Library, the British Library, "An Imperial Capital: Baron Haussmann's Transformation of Paris," http://www.mapforum.com/15/blmap.htm.

209 Farmers' hearing loss: New York Center for Agricultural Medicine and Health.

214 Chirac comment on immigrants: Elaine Sciolino, "Chirac, Lover of Spotlight, Avoids Glare of France's Fires," *New York Times*, November 10, 2005.

217 Japan trash-sorting: Norimitsu Onishi, "How Do Japanese Dump Trash?" *New York Times*, May 12, 2005.

218 Japan train: "Train Crash Kills 71, Injures 441," *Japan Times*, April 26, 2005.

225 Speed bumps and humps: Kathleen Calongne, "Politics of Traffic Calming Projects," http://home.cfl.rr.com/gidusko/texts/politics.htm.

226 Big Dig: Seth Stern, "$14.6 Billion Later, Boston's Big Dig Wraps Up," *Christian Science Monitor*, December 19, 2003.

10. Optimizing Mess

239 IBM/NFL deal: IBM press release, October 20, 2005.

244 World Series of Poker winners: http://en.wikipedia.org/wiki/World_Series_of_Poker.

11. Messy Thinking

253 Roulette system: John Grochowski, "The House Edge Trumps All Roulette Systems," *Detroit News*, August 18, 2005.

12. Pathological Mess

273 Saxena and Frost comments: Sanjaya Saxena, "The Neurobiology and Medication Treatment of Compulsive Hoarding," *OCD Newsletter*, Winter 2004.

274 Reyes-Ortiz comment: Denise Nelesen, "Self-neglect, Hoarding Often Linked," *San Diego Union-Tribune*, April 27, 2002.

282 Number of ECT patients: Marianne Szegedy-Maszak, "Magnetism and the Brain," *U.S. News & World Report*, February 16, 2004.

13. The Aesthetics of Mess

289 Bach and improvisation: William Bell, "Bach Improvising at the Organ," *Music and Letters* 32, no. 2 (1951).

290 Classical embellishment: Ronald Roseman, "Baroque Ornamentation," *Journal of the International Double Reed Society*, Number 3, 1975, http://idrs.colorado.edu/Publications/Journal/JNL3/baroque.html.

302 Tuning history: Edward E. Swenson, "The History of Musical Pitch in Tuning the Pianoforte," http://www.mozartpiano.com/pitch.html.

304 Tuning theory: "Math and Musical Scales" (a discussion), http://mathforum.org/library/drmath/view/52470.html.

Acknowledgments

There's hardly a friend, relative, or colleague who didn't provide me with some helpful observation, anecdote, or suggestion for this book, but let me single out just a few: Fred Guterl and Karl Weber, for enthusiastic readings of the proposal; Charles Mann, for insightful commentary on some early chapters; and David Abrahamson, for advice on mess in different countries. Larry Kanter and the gang at *Inc.* magazine were gracious in adjusting assignments and deadlines in support of the book. Alex Kerr was briefly, but outstandingly, my research assistant. Laszlo Kish of Texas A&M and Robert Levy of Lawrence University were among those who provided me with long and interesting interviews that didn't make it into the book for structural reasons. On behalf of both Eric and myself, thanks to Sheena Iyengar for the lead on the magazine stores.

What luck to get Liz Nagle as an editor; she has from the first been hugely supportive, wise, and attentive. Marie Salter added a great many nice touches. Any surviving mistakes or awkwardnesses are my fault alone. Rick Balkin is nominally my agent, but that doesn't begin to get at the breadth of his contribution. My children, Rachel, Alex, and Jason, refused to let me get bogged down, plus they contributed tangibly to one section of a chapter each. And in addition to all the normal lines of support one would hope to get from a significant other, my wife, Laurie, was good for a stream of invaluable ideas, information, contacts, and criticism. She's messy, too. (Where else could I say that as a compliment?)

— DHF

INDEX